SQL and NoSQL Databases

Michael Kaufmann • Andreas Meier

SQL and NoSQL Databases

Modeling, Languages, Security and Architectures for Big Data Management

Second Edition

 Springer

Michael Kaufmann
Informatik
Hochschule Luzern
Rotkreuz, Switzerland

Andreas Meier
Institute of Informatics
Universität Fribourg
Fribourg, Switzerland

ISBN 978-3-031-27907-2   ISBN 978-3-031-27908-9   (eBook)
https://doi.org/10.1007/978-3-031-27908-9

This Springer imprint is published by the registered company Springer Nature Switzerland AG
The registered company address is: Gewerbestrasse 11, 6330 Cham, Switzerland

Foreword

The term database has long since become part of people's everyday vocabulary, for managers and clerks as well as students of most subjects. They use it to describe a logically organized collection of electronically stored data that can be directly searched and viewed. However, they are generally more than happy to leave the whys and hows of its inner workings to the experts.

Users of databases are rarely aware of the immaterial and concrete business values contained in any individual database. This applies as much to a car importer's spare parts inventory as the IT solution containing all customer depots at a bank or the patient information system of a hospital. Yet failure of these systems, or even cumulative errors, can threaten the very existence of the respective company or institution. For that reason, it is important for a much larger audience than just the "database specialists" to be well-informed about what is going on. Anyone involved with databases should understand what these tools are effectively able to do and which conditions must be created and maintained for them to do so.

Probably the most important aspect concerning databases involves (a) the distinction between their administration and the data stored in them (user data) and (b) the economic magnitude of these two areas. Database administration consists of various technical and administrative factors, from computers, database systems, and additional storage to the experts setting up and maintaining all these components—the aforementioned database specialists. It is crucial to keep in mind that the administration is by far the smaller part of standard database operation, constituting only about a quarter of the entire efforts.

Most of the work and expenses concerning databases lie in gathering, maintaining, and utilizing the user data. This includes the labor costs for all employees who enter data into the database, revise it, retrieve information from the database, or create files using this information. In the above examples, this means warehouse employees, bank tellers, or hospital personnel in a wide variety of fields—usually for several years.

In order to be able to properly evaluate the importance of the tasks connected with data maintenance and utilization on the one hand and database administration on the other hand, it is vital to understand and internalize this difference in the effort required for each of them. Database administration starts with the design of the database, which already touches on many specialized topics such as determining the

vi   Foreword

consistency checks for data manipulation or regulating data redundancies, which are as undesirable on the logical level as they are essential on the storage level. The development of database solutions is always targeted on their later use, so ill-considered decisions in the development process may have a permanent impact on everyday operations. Finding ideal solutions, such as the golden mean between too strict and too flexible when determining consistency conditions, may require some experience. Unduly strict conditions will interfere with regular operations, while excessively lax rules will entail a need for repeated expensive data repairs.

To avoid such issues, it is invaluable for anyone concerned with database development and operation, whether in management or as a database specialist, to gain systematic insight into this field of computer sciences. The table of contents gives an overview of the wide variety of topics covered in this book. The title already shows that, in addition to an in-depth explanation of the field of conventional databases (relational model, SQL), the book also provides highly educational information about current advancements and related fields, the keywords being NoSQL and Big Data. I am confident that the newest edition of this book will once again be well-received by both students and professionals—its authors are quite familiar with both groups.

Professor Emeritus for Databases   Carl August Zehnder
ETH Zürich
Zürich, Switzerland

Preface

It is remarkable how stable some concepts are in the field of databases. Information technology is generally known to be subject to rapid development, bringing forth new technologies at an unbelievable pace. However, this is only superficially the case. Many aspects of computer science do not essentially change. This includes not only the basics, such as the functional principles of universal computing machines, processors, compilers, operating systems, databases and information systems, and distributed systems, but also computer language technologies such as C, TCP/IP, or HTML that are decades old but in many ways provide a stable fundament of the global, earth-spanning information system known as the World Wide Web. Likewise, the SQL language (Structured Query Language) has been in use for almost five decades and will remain so in the foreseeable future. The theory of relational database systems was initiated in the 1970s by Codd (relation model) and Chamberlin and Boyce (SEQUEL). However, these technologies have a major impact on the practice of data management today. Especially, with the Big Data revolution and the widespread use of data science methods for decision support, relational databases and the use of SQL for data analysis are actually becoming more important. Even though sophisticated statistics and machine learning are enhancing the possibilities for knowledge extraction from data, many if not most data analyses for decision support rely on descriptive statistics using SQL for grouped aggregation. SQL is also used in the field of Big Data with MapReduce technology. In this sense, although SQL database technology is quite mature, it is more relevant today than ever.

Nevertheless, the developments in the Big Data ecosystem brought new technologies into the world of databases, to which we pay enough attention too. Non-relational database technologies, which find more and more fields of application under the generic term NoSQL, differ not only superficially from the classical relational databases but also in the underlying principles. Relational databases were developed in the twentieth century with the purpose of tightly organized, operational forms of data management, which provided stability but limited flexibility. In contrast, the NoSQL database movement emerged in the beginning of the new century, focusing on horizontal partitioning, schema flexibility, and index-free neighborhood with the goal of solving the Big Data problems of volume, variety, and velocity, especially in Web-scale data systems. This has far-reaching consequences and leads to a new approach in data management, which deviate significantly from the previous theories on the basic concept of databases: the way data is modeled, how data is queried and manipulated, how data consistency is handled, and how data is stored and made accessible. That is why in all chapters we compare these two worlds, SQL and NoSQL databases.

In the first five chapters, we analyze in detail the management, modeling, languages, security, and architecture of SQL databases, graph databases, and, in the second English edition, new document databases. In Chaps. 6 and 7, we provide an overview of other SQL- and NoSQL-based database approaches.

In addition to classic concepts such as the entity and relationship model and its mapping in SQL or NoSQL database schemas, query languages, or transaction management, we explain aspects for NoSQL databases such as the MapReduce procedure, distribution options (fragments, replication), or the CAP theorem (consistency, availability, partition tolerance).

In the second English edition, we offer a new in-depth introduction to document databases with a method for modeling document structures, an overview of the database language MQL, as well as security and architecture aspects. The new edition also takes into account new developments in the Cypher language. The topic of database security is newly introduced as a separate chapter and analyzed in detail with regard to data protection, integrity, and transactions. Texts on data management, database programming, and data warehousing and data lakes have been updated. In addition, the second English edition explains the concepts of JSON, JSON Schema, BSON, index-free neighborhood, cloud databases, search engines, and time series databases.

We have launched a Website called sql-nosql.org, where we share teaching and tutoring materials such as slides, tutorials for SQL and Cypher, case studies, and a workbench for MySQL and Neo4j, so that language training can be done either with SQL or with Cypher, the graph-oriented query language of the NoSQL database Neo4j.

We thank Alexander Denzler and Marcel Wehrle for the development of the workbench for relational and graph-oriented databases. For the redesign of the graphics, we were able to work with Thomas Riediker. We thank him for his tireless efforts. He has succeeded in giving the pictures a modern style and an individual touch. In the ninth edition, we have tried to keep his style in our new graphics. For the further development of the tutorials and case studies, which are available on the website sql-nosql.org, we thank the computer science students Andreas Waldis, Bettina Willi, Markus Ineichen, and Simon Studer for their contributions to the tutorial in Cypher, respectively, to the case study Travelblitz with OpenOffice Base and with Neo4J. For the feedback on the manuscript, we thank Alexander Denzler, Daniel Fasel, Konrad Marfurt, Thomas Olnhoff, and Stefan Edlich for their willingness to contribute to the quality of our work with reading our manuscript and with providing valuable feedback. A heartfelt thank you goes out to Michael Kaufmann's wife Melody Reymond for proofreading our manuscript. Special thanks to Andy

Oppel of the University of California, Berkeley, for grammatical and technological review of the English text. A big thank goes to Leonardo Milla of Springer, who has supported us with patience and expertise.

Rotkreuz, Switzerland   Michael Kaufmann
Fribourg, Switzerland   Andreas Meier
October 2022

Contents

Database Management

1

1.1 Information Systems and Databases

The evolution from the industrial society via the service society to the information and knowledge society is represented by the assessment of information as a factor in production. The following characteristics distinguish *information* from material goods:

- **Representation**: Information is specified by data (signs, signals, messages, or language elements).
- **Processing**: Information can be transmitted, stored, categorized, found, or converted into other representation formats using algorithms and data structures (calculation rules).
- **Combination**: Information can be freely combined. The origin of individual parts cannot be traced. Manipulation is possible at any point.
- **Age**: Information is not subject to physical aging processes.
- **Original**: Information can be copied without limit and does not distinguish between original and copy.
- **Vagueness**: Information can be imprecise and of differing validity (quality).
- **Medium**: Information does not require a fixed medium and is therefore independent of location.

These properties clearly show that digital goods (information, software, multimedia, etc.), i.e., data, are vastly different from material goods in both handling and economic or legal evaluation. A good example is the loss in value that physical products often experience when they are used—the shared use of information, on the other hand, may increase its value. Another difference lies in the potentially high production costs for material goods, while information can be multiplied easily and at significantly lower costs (only computing power and storage medium). This causes difficulties in determining property rights and ownership, even though digital watermarks and other privacy and security measures are available.

© The Author(s), under exclusive license to Springer Nature Switzerland AG 2023
M. Kaufmann, A. Meier, *SQL and NoSQL Databases*,
https://doi.org/10.1007/978-3-031-27908-9_1

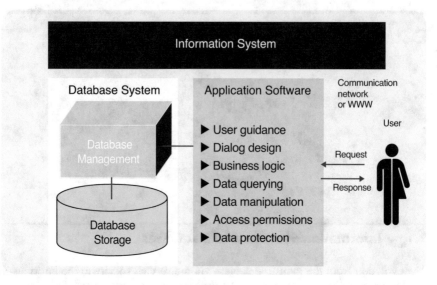

Fig. 1.1 Architecture and components of information systems

Considering *data as the basis of information as a production factor* in a company has significant consequences:

- **Basis for decision-making**: Data allows well-informed decisions, making it vital for all organizational functions.
- **Quality level**: Data can be available from different sources; information quality depends on the availability, correctness, and completeness of the data.
- **Need for investments**: Data gathering, storage, and processing cause work and expenses.
- **Degree of integration**: Fields and holders of duties within any organization are connected by informational relations, meaning that the fulfillment of the said duties largely depends on the degree of data integration.

Once data is viewed as a factor in production, it must be planned, governed, monitored, and controlled. This makes it necessary to see data management as a task for the executive level, inducing a major change within the company. In addition to the technical function of operating the information and communication infrastructure (production), planning and design of data flows (application portfolio) is crucial.

As shown in Fig. 1.1, an *information system* enables users to store and connect information interactively, to ask questions, and to get answers. Depending on the type of information system, the acceptable questions may be limited. There are, however, open information systems and online platforms in the World Wide Web that use search engines to process arbitrary queries.

The computer-based information system in Fig. 1.1 is connected to a communication network such as the World Wide Web in order to allow for online interaction and global information exchange in addition to company-specific analyses. Any information system of a certain size uses database systems to avoid the necessity to redevelop database management, querying, and analysis every time it is used.

Database systems are software for application-independently describing, storing, and querying data. All database systems contain a storage and a management component. The storage component called the database includes all data stored in organized form plus their description. The management component called the database management system (DBMS) contains a query and data manipulation language for evaluating and editing the data and information. This component not only does serve the user interface but also manages all access and editing permissions for users and applications.

SQL databases (SQL = Structured Query Language, cf. Sect. 1.2) are the most common in practical use. However, providing real-time Web-based services referencing heterogeneous data sets is especially challenging (cf. Sect. 1.3 on Big Data) and has called for new solutions such as NoSQL approaches (cf. Sect. 1.4).

When deciding whether to use relational or non-relational technologies, pros and cons have to be considered carefully—in some use cases, it may even be ideal to combine different technologies (cf. operating a Web shop in Sect. 5.6). Modern hybrid DBMS approaches combine SQL with non-relational aspects, either by providing NoSQL features in relational databases or by exposing an SQL querying interface to non-relational databases. Depending on the database architecture of choice, data management within the company must be established and developed with the support of qualified experts (Sect. 1.5). Further reading is listed in Sect. 1.6.

1.2   SQL Databases

1.2.1   Relational Model

One of the simplest and most intuitive ways to collect and present data is in a table. Most tabular data sets can be read and understood without additional explanations.

To collect information about employees, a table structure as shown in Fig. 1.2 can be used. The all-capitalized table name EMPLOYEE refers to the entire table, while the individual columns are given the desired attribute names as headers, for example, the employee number "*E#*," the employee's name "Name," and their city of residence "City."

An *attribute* assigns a specific data value from a predefined value range called *domain* as a property to each entry in the table. In the EMPLOYEE table, the attribute *E#* allows to uniquely identify individual employees, making it the *key* of the table. To mark key attributes more clearly, they will be written in italics in the table headers throughout this book.[1] The attribute City is used to label the respective

---

[1] Some major works of database literature mark key attributes by underlining.

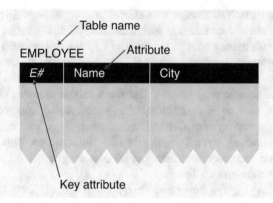

Fig. 1.2 Table structure for an EMPLOYEE table

EMPLOYEE

E#	Name	City
E19	Stewart	Stow
E4	Bell	Kent
E1	Murphy	Kent
E7	Howard	Cleveland

Fig. 1.3 EMPLOYEE table with manifestations

places of residence and the attribute Name for the names of the respective employees (Fig. 1.3).

The required information of the employees can now easily be entered row by row. In the columns, values may appear more than once. In our example, Kent is listed as the place of residence of two employees. This is an important fact, telling us that both employee Murphy and employee Bell are living in Kent. In our EMPLOYEE table, not only cities but also employee names may exist multiple times. For that reason, the aforementioned key attribute *E#* is required to uniquely identify each employee in the table.

Identification Key

An *identification key* or just *key* of a table is one attribute or a minimal combination of attributes whose values uniquely identify the records (called *rows* or *tuples*) within the table. If there are multiple keys, one of them can be chosen as the *primary key*. This short definition lets us infer two important *properties* of keys:

- **Uniqueness**: Each key value uniquely identifies one record within the table, i.e., different tuples must not have identical keys.
- **Minimality**: If the key is a combination of attributes, this combination must be minimal, i.e., no attribute can be removed from the combination without eliminating the unique identification.

The requirements of uniqueness and minimality fully characterize an identification key. However, keys are also commonly used to reference tables among themselves.

Instead of a natural attribute or a combination of natural attributes, an artificial attribute can be introduced into the table as key. The employee number *E#* in our example is an artificial attribute, as it is not a natural characteristic of the employees.

While we are hesitant to include artificial keys or numbers as identifying attributes, especially when the information in question is personal, natural keys often result in issues with uniqueness and/or privacy. For example, if a key is constructed from parts of the name and the date of birth, it may not necessarily be unique. Moreover, natural or intelligent keys divulge information about the respective person, potentially infringing on their privacy.

Due to these considerations, artificial keys should be defined *application-independent and without semantics* (meaning, informational value). As soon as any information can be deduced from the data values of a key, there is room for interpretation. Additionally, it is quite possible that the originally well-defined principle behind the key values changes or is lost over time.

Table Definition

To summarize, a *table* is a set of rows presented in tabular form. The data records stored in the table rows, also called tuples, establish a *relation* between singular data values. According to this definition, the *relational model* considers each table as a set of unordered tuples. Tables in this sense meet the following requirements:

- **Table name**: A table has a unique table name.
- **Attribute name**: All attribute names are unique within a table and label one specific column with the required property.
- **No column order**: The number of attributes is not set, and the order of the columns within the table does not matter.
- **No row order**: The number of tuples is not set, and the order of the rows within the table does not matter.

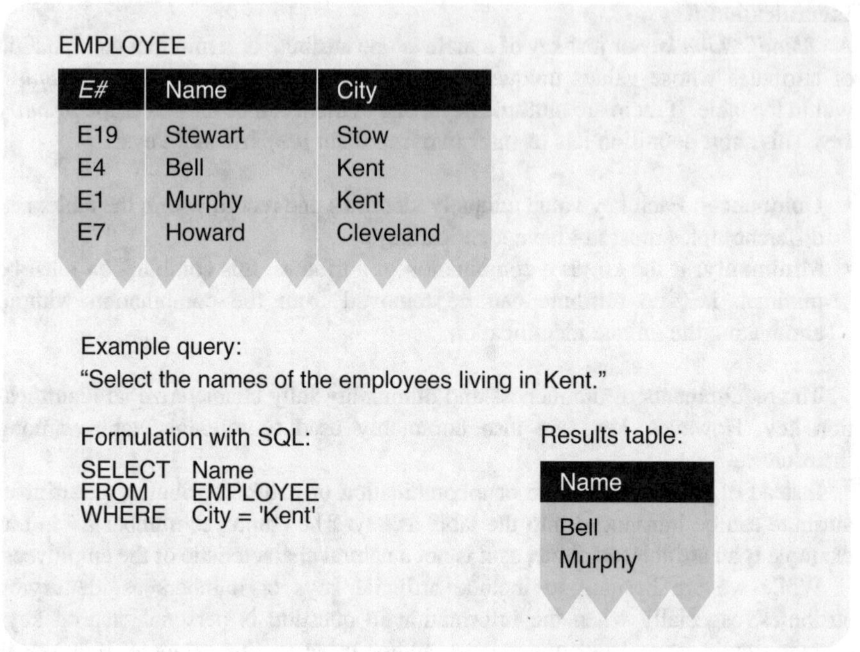

EMPLOYEE

E#	Name	City
E19	Stewart	Stow
E4	Bell	Kent
E1	Murphy	Kent
E7	Howard	Cleveland

Example query:
"Select the names of the employees living in Kent."

Formulation with SQL:

```
SELECT   Name
FROM     EMPLOYEE
WHERE    City = 'Kent'
```

Results table:

Name
Bell
Murphy

Fig. 1.4 Formulating a query in SQL

- **Identification key**: Strictly speaking, tables represent relations in the mathematical sense only if there are no duplicate rows. Therefore, one attribute or a combination of attributes can uniquely identify the tuples within the table and is declared the identification key.

1.2.2   Structured Query Language SQL

As explained, the relational model presents information in tabular form, where each table is a set of tuples (or records) of the same type. Seeing all the data as sets makes it possible to offer *query and manipulation options based on sets*.

The result of a selective operation, for example, is a set, i.e., each search result is returned by the database management system as a table. If no tuples of the scanned table show the respective properties, the user gets a blank result table. Manipulation operations similarly target sets and affect an entire table or individual table sections.

The primary query and data manipulation language for tables is called *Structured Query Language*, usually shortened to SQL (see Fig. 1.4). It was standardized by

ANSI (American National Standards Institute) and ISO (International Organization for Standardization).[2]

SQL is a descriptive language, as the statements describe the desired result instead of the necessary computing steps. SQL queries follow a basic pattern as illustrated by the query from Fig. 1.4:

"SELECT the attribute Name FROM the EMPLOYEE table WHERE the city is Kent."

A SELECT-FROM-WHERE query can apply to one or several tables and always generates a table as a result. In our example, the query would yield a results table with the names Bell and Murphy, as desired.

The set-based method offers users a major advantage, since a single SQL query can trigger multiple actions within the database management system. *Relational query and data manipulation languages are descriptive.* Users get the desired results by merely setting the requested properties in the SELECT expression. They do not have to provide the procedure for computing the required records. The database management system takes on this task, processes the query or manipulation with its own search and access methods, and generates the results table.

With procedural database languages on the other hand, the methods for retrieving the requested information must be programmed by the user. In that case, each query yields only one record, not a set of tuples.

With its descriptive query formula, SQL requires only the specification of the desired selection conditions in the WHERE clause, while procedural languages require the user to specify an algorithm for finding the individual records. As an example, let us take a look at a query language for hierarchical databases (see Fig. 1.5): For our initial operation, we use GET_FIRST to search for the first record that meets our search criteria. Next, we access all other corresponding records individually with the command GET_NEXT until we reach the end of the file or a new hierarchy level within the database.

Overall, we can conclude that procedural database management languages use record-based or navigating commands to manipulate collections of data, requiring some experience and knowledge of the database's inner structure from the users. Occasional users basically cannot independently access and use the contents of a database. Unlike procedural languages, relational query and manipulation languages do not require the specification of access paths, processing procedures, or navigational routes, which significantly reduces the development effort for database utilization.

If database queries and analyses are to be done by end users instead of IT professionals, the descriptive approach is extremely useful. Research on descriptive database interfaces has shown that *even occasional users have a high probability of successfully executing* the desired analyses using descriptive language elements. Figure 1.5 also illustrates the similarities between SQL and natural language. In

---

[2]ANSI is the national standards organization of the USA. The national standardization organizations are part of ISO.

Natural language:

"Select the names of the employees living in Kent."

Descriptive language:

```
SELECT  Name
FROM    EMPLOYEE
WHERE   City = 'Kent'
```

Procedural language:

```
get first EMPLOYEE

while status = 0 do
begin
   if City = 'Kent' then print(Name)
   get next EMPLOYEE

end
```

Fig. 1.5 The difference between descriptive and procedural languages

fact, there are modern relational database management systems that can be accessed with natural language.

1.2.3   Relational Database Management System

Databases are used in the development and operation of information systems in order to store data centrally, permanently, and in a structured manner.

As shown in Fig. 1.6, relational database management systems are integrated systems for the consistent management of tables. They offer service functionalities and the descriptive language SQL for data description, selection, and manipulation.

Every relational database management system consists of a storage and a management component. The storage component stores both data and the relationships between pieces of information in tables. In addition to tables with user data from various applications, it contains predefined system tables necessary for database operation. These contain descriptive information and can be queried, but not manipulated, by users.

The management component's most important part is the language SQL for relational data definition, selection, and manipulation. This component also contains service functions for data restoration after errors, for data protection, and for backup. *Relational database management systems* (RDBMS) have the following properties:

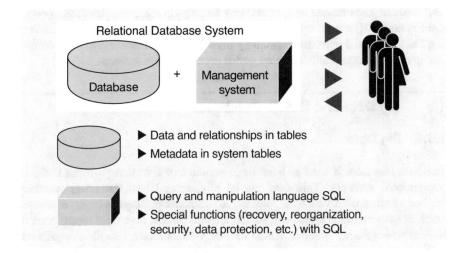

Fig. 1.6   Basic structure of a relational database management system

- **Model**: The database model follows the relational model, i.e., all data and data relations are represented in tables. Dependencies between attribute values of tuples or multiple instances of data can be discovered (cf. normal forms in Sect. 2.3.1).
- **Schema**: The definitions of tables and attributes are stored in the relational database schema. The schema further contains the definition of the identification keys and rules for integrity assurance.
- **Language**: The database system includes SQL for data definition, selection, and manipulation. The language component is descriptive and facilitates analyses and programming tasks for users.
- **Architecture**: The system ensures extensive *data independence*, i.e., data and applications are mostly segregated. This independence is reached by separating the actual storage component from the user side using the management component. Ideally, physical changes to relational databases are possible without having to adjust related applications.
- **Multi-user operation**: The system supports multi-user operation (cf. Sect. 4.1), i.e., several users can query or manipulate the same database at the same time. The RDBMS ensures that parallel transactions in one database do not interfere with each other or worse, with the correctness of data (Sect. 4.2).
- **Consistency assurance**: The database management system provides tools for ensuring data integrity, i.e., the correct and uncompromised storage of data.
- **Data security and data protection**: The database management system provides mechanisms to protect data from destruction, loss, or unauthorized access.

NoSQL database management systems meet these criteria only partially (see Chaps. 4 and 7). For that reason, most corporations, organizations, and especially

SMEs (small and medium enterprises) rely heavily on relational database management systems. However, for spread-out Web applications or applications handling Big Data, relational database technology must be augmented with NoSQL technology in order to ensure uninterrupted global access to these services.

1.3   Big Data and NoSQL Databases

1.3.1   Big Data

The term Big Data is used to label large volumes of data that push the limits of conventional software. This data can be unstructured (see Sect. 5.1) and may originate from a wide variety of sources: social media postings; e-mails; electronic archives with multimedia content; search engine queries; document repositories of content management systems; sensor data of various kinds; rate developments at stock exchanges; traffic flow data and satellite images; smart meters in household appliances; order, purchase, and payment processes in online stores; e-health applications; monitoring systems; etc.

There is no binding definition for Big Data yet, but most data specialists will agree on three Vs: *volume* (extensive amounts of data), *variety* (multiple formats: structured, semi-structured, and unstructured data; see Fig. 1.7), and *velocity* (high-speed and real-time processing). Gartner Group's IT glossary offers the following definition:

Big Data
"Big data is high-volume, high-velocity and high-variety information assets that demand cost-effective, innovative forms of information processing for enhanced insight and decision making."

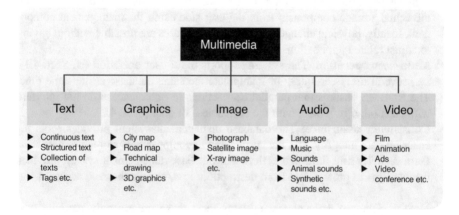

Fig. 1.7 Variety of sources for Big Data

With this definition, Big Data are *information assets* for companies. It is indeed vital for companies and organizations to generate decision-relevant knowledge in order to survive. In addition to internal information systems, they increasingly utilize the numerous resources available online to better anticipate economic, ecologic, and social developments on the markets.

Big Data is a challenge faced by not only for-profit-oriented companies in digital markets but also governments, public authorities, NGOs (non-governmental organizations), and NPOs (nonprofit organizations).

A good example are programs to create smart or ubiquitous cities, i.e., by using Big Data technologies in cities and urban agglomerations for sustainable development of social and ecologic aspects of human living spaces. They include projects facilitating mobility, the use of intelligent systems for water and energy supply, the promotion of social networks, expansion of political participation, encouragement of entrepreneurship, protection of the environment, and an increase of security and quality of life.

All use of Big Data applications requires successful management of the three Vs mentioned above:

- **Volume**: There are massive amounts of data involved, ranging from giga- to zettabytes (megabyte, 10^6 bytes; gigabyte, 10^9 bytes; terabyte, 10^{12} bytes; petabyte, 10^{15} bytes; exabyte, 10^{18} bytes; zettabyte, 10^{21} bytes).
- **Variety**: Big Data involves storing structured, semi-structured, and unstructured multimedia data (text, graphics, images, audio, and video; cf. Fig. 1.7).
- **Velocity**: Applications must be able to process and analyze data streams in real time as the data is gathered.

Big Data can be considered an information asset, which is why sometimes another V is added:

- **Value**: Big Data applications are meant to increase the enterprise value, so investments in personnel and technical infrastructure are made where they will bring leverage or added value can be generated.

To complete our discussion of the concept of Big Data, we will look at another V:

- **Veracity**: Since much data is vague or inaccurate, specific algorithms evaluating the validity and assessing result quality are needed. Large amounts of data do not automatically mean better analyses.

Veracity is an important factor in Big Data, where the available data is of variable quality, which must be taken into consideration in analyses. Aside from statistical methods, there are fuzzy methods of soft computing which assign a truth value between 0 (false) and 1 (true) to any result or statement.

1.3.2   NoSQL Database Management System

Before Ted Codd's introduction of the relational model, non-relational databases such as hierarchical or network-like databases existed. After the development of relational database management systems, non-relational models were still used in technical or scientific applications. For instance, running CAD (computer-aided design) systems for structural or machine components on relational technology is rather difficult. Splitting technical objects across a multitude of tables proved problematic, as geometric, topological, and graphical manipulations all had to be executed in real time.

The omnipresence of the Internet and numerous Web-based and mobile applications has provided quite a boost to the relevance of non-relational data concepts vs. relational ones, as managing Big Data applications with relational database technology is hard to impossible.

While "non-relational" would be a better description than NoSQL, the latter has become established with database researchers and providers on the market over the last few years.

NoSQL
The term NoSQL is used for any *non-relational database management approach* meeting at least one of two criteria:

- The data is not stored in tables.
- The database language is not SQL.

NoSQL technologies are in demand, especially where the applications in the framework for Big Data (speed, volume, variety) are in the foreground, because non-relational structures are often better suited for this. Sometimes, the term NoSQL is translated to "Not only SQL." This is to express that non-relational storage and language functions are used in addition to SQL in an application. For example, there are SQL language interfaces for non-relational systems, either native or as middleware; and relational databases today also offer NoSQL functions, e.g., document data types or graph analyses.

The basic structure of a NoSQL database system is outlined in Fig. 1.8. Mostly, a NoSQL database system is subject to a massively distributed data storage architecture. Data is stored in alternative non-tabular structures depending on the type of NoSQL database. As an example, Fig. 1.9 shows key/value stores, document databases, and graph databases. To ensure high availability and to protect the NoSQL database system against failures, different replication concepts are supported. With a massively distributed and replicated computer architecture, parallel evaluation procedures can be used. The analysis of extensive data volumes or the search for specific facts can be accelerated with distributed computation procedures. In the MapReduce procedure, subtasks are distributed to various computer nodes, and simple key-value pairs are extracted (Map) before the partial results are combined and output (Reduce).

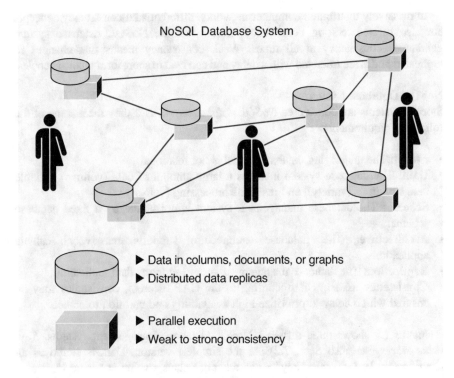

Fig. 1.8 Basic structure of a NoSQL database management system

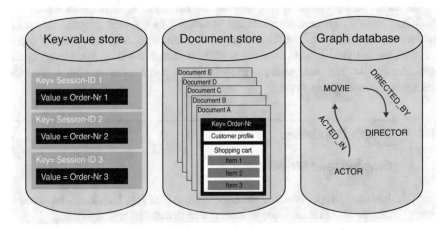

Fig. 1.9 Three different NoSQL databases

In massively distributed computer networks, differentiated consistency concepts are also offered. Strong consistency means that the NoSQL database system guarantees consistency at all times. Weak consistency means that changes to replicated nodes are tolerated with a delay and can lead to short-term inconsistencies.

NoSQL Database System
Storage systems are considered *NoSQL database systems* if they meet some of the following requirements:

- **Model**: The underlying database model is not relational.
- **Data**: The database system includes a large amount of data (volume), flexible data structures (variety), and real-time processing (velocity).
- **Schema**: The database management system is not bound by a fixed database schema.
- **Architecture**: The database architecture supports massively scalable applications.
- **Replication**: The database management system supports data replication.
- **Consistency assurance**: According to the CAP theorem, consistency may be ensured with a delay to prioritize high availability and partition tolerance.

Figure 1.9 shows three different NoSQL database management systems. *Key-value stores* (see also Sect. 7.2) are the simplest version. Data is stored as an identification key <key = "key"> and a list of values <value = "value 1", "value 2", ...>. A good example is an online store with session management and shopping basket. The session ID is the identification key; the order number is the value stored in the cache. In *document stores*, records are managed as documents within the NoSQL database. These documents are structured files which describe an entire subject matter in a self-contained manner. For instance, together with an order number, the individual items from the basket are stored as values in addition to the customer profile. The third example shows a *graph database* on movies and actors discussed in the next section.

1.4 Graph Databases

1.4.1 Graph-Based Model

NoSQL databases support various database models (see Fig. 1.9). Here, we discuss graph databases as a first example to look at and discuss its characteristics.

Property Graph
Property graphs consist of *nodes* (concepts, objects) and *directed edges* (relationships) connecting the nodes. Both nodes and edges are given a *label* and can have *properties*. Properties are given as attribute-value pairs with the names of attributes and the respective values.

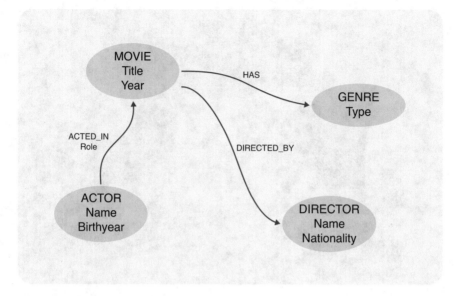

Fig. 1.10 Section of a property graph on movies

A graph abstractly presents the nodes and edges with their properties. Figure 1.10 shows part of a movie collection as an example. It contains the nodes MOVIE with attributes *Title* and *Year* (of release), GENRE with the respective *Type* (e.g., crime, mystery, comedy, drama, thriller, western, science fiction, documentary, etc.), ACTOR with *Name* and *Year of Birth*, and DIRECTOR with *Name* and *Nationality*.

The example uses three directed edges: The edge ACTED_IN shows which artist from the ACTOR node starred in which film from the MOVIE node. This edge also has a property, the *Role* of the actor in the movie. The other two edges, HAS and DIRECTED_BY, go from the MOVIE node to the GENRE and DIRECTOR node, respectively.

In the manifestation level, i.e., the graph database, the property graph contains the concrete values (Fig. 1.11). For each node and for each edge, a separate record is stored. Thus, in contrast to relational databases, the connections between the data are not stored and indexed as key references, but as separate records. This leads to efficient processing of network analyses.

1.4.2 Graph Query Language Cypher

Cypher is a declarative query language for extracting patterns from graph databases. ISO plans to extend Cypher to become the international standard for graph-based database languages as Graph Query Language (GQL) by 2023.

Users define their query by specifying nodes and edges. The database management system then calculates all patterns meeting the criteria by analyzing the

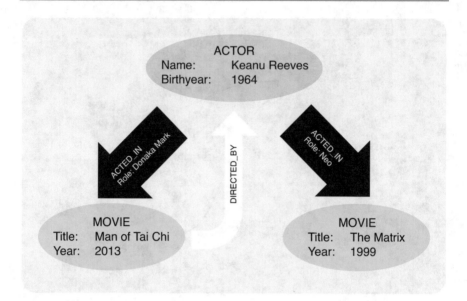

Fig. 1.11 Section of a graph database on movies

possible paths (connections between nodes via edges). The user declares the structure of the desired pattern, and the database management system's algorithms traverse all necessary connections (paths) and assemble the results.

As described in Sect. 1.4.1, the data model of a graph database consists of *nodes* (concepts, objects) and *directed edges* (relationships between nodes). In addition to their name, both nodes and edges can have a set of properties (see Property Graph in Sect. 1.4.1). These properties are represented by attribute-value pairs.

Figure 1.11 shows a segment of a graph database on movies and actors. To keep things simple, only two types of nodes are shown: ACTOR and MOVIE. ACTOR nodes contain two attribute-value pairs, specifically (*Name*: FirstName LastName) and (*YearOfBirth*: Year).

The segment in Fig. 1.11 includes different types of edges: The ACTED_IN relationship represents which actors starred in which movies. Edges can also have properties if attribute-value pairs are added to them. For the ACTED_IN relationship, the respective roles of the actors in the movies are listed. For example, Keanu Reeves is the hacker Neo in "The Matrix."

Nodes can be connected by multiple relationship edges. The movie "Man of Tai Chi" and actor Keanu Reeves are linked not only by the actor's role (ACTED_IN) but also by the director position (DIRECTED_BY). The diagram therefore shows that Keanu Reeves both directed the movie "Man of Tai Chi" and starred in it as Donaka Mark.

If we want to analyze this graph database on movies, we can use Cypher. It uses the following basic query elements:

- MATCH: Specification of nodes and edges, as well as declaration of search patterns
- WHERE: Conditions for filtering results
- RETURN: Specification of the desired search result, aggregated if necessary

For instance, the Cypher query for the year the movie "The Matrix" was released would be:

```
MATCH (m: Movie {Title: "The Matrix"})
RETURN m.Year
```

The query sends out the variable m for the movie "The Matrix" to return the movie's year of release by m.Year. In Cypher, parentheses always indicate nodes, i.e., (m: Movie) declares the control variable m for the MOVIE node. In addition to control variables, individual attribute-value pairs can be included in curly brackets. Since we are specifically interested in the movie "The Matrix," we can add {Title: "The Matrix"} to the node (m: Movie).

Queries regarding the relationships within the graph database are a bit more complicated. Relationships between two arbitrary nodes (a) and (b) are expressed in Cypher by the arrow symbol "->," i.e., the path from (a) to (b) is declared as "(a) -> (b)." If the specific relationship between (a) and (b) is of importance, the edge [r] can be inserted in the middle of the arrow. The square brackets represent edges, and r is our variable for relationships.

Now, if we want to find out who played Neo in "The Matrix," we use the following query to analyze the ACTED_IN path between ACTOR and MOVIE:

```
MATCH (a: Actor) -[: Acted_In {Role: "Neo"}] ->
(: Movie {Title: "The Matrix"}])
RETURN a.Name
```

Cypher will return the result Keanu Reeves. For a list of movie titles (m), actor names (a), and respective roles (r), the query would have to be:

```
MATCH  (a: Actor) -[r: Acted_In] -> (m: Movie)
RETURN m.Title, a.Name, r.Role
```

Since our example graph database only contains one actor and two movies, the result would be the movie "Man of Tai Chi" with actor Keanu Reeves in the role of Donaka Mark and the movie "The Matrix" with Keanu Reeves as Neo.

In real life, however, such a graph database of actors, movies, and roles has countless entries. A manageable query would therefore have to remain limited, e.g., to actor Keanu Reeves, and would then look like this:

```
MATCH   (a: Actor) -[r: Acted_In] -> (m: Movie)
WHERE   (a.Name = "Keanu Reeves")
RETURN m.Title, a.Name, r.Role
```

Similar to SQL, Cypher uses declarative queries where the user specifies the desired properties of the result pattern (Cypher) or results table (SQL) and the respective database management system then calculates the results. However, analyzing relationship networks, using recursive search strategies, or analyzing graph properties is hardly possible with SQL.

Graph databases are even more relationship-oriented than relational databases. Both nodes and edges of the graph are independent data sets. This allows efficient traversal of the graph for network-like information. However, there are applications that focus on structured objects as a unit. Document databases are suitable for this purpose, which will be described in the next section.

1.5   Document Databases

1.5.1   Document Model

As a second example of NoSQL databases, we introduce document databases here. A document is a written record that describes a specific subject matter for which it contains all relevant information. As an example of a document, an invoice (see Fig. 1.12 to the left) describes information about customers, suppliers, dates, articles, and prices.

A document database describes the entire facts of an invoice in a self-contained data set that contains all information relevant to the facts. Such a complete data set is called a document, analogous to a written record.

Digital Document
A digital document is a set of information that describes a subject matter as a closed unit and is stored as a file in a computer system.

In contrast, as shown in the previous section, a graph database would use different node and edge types. A separate data set would be stored for each node and for each edge. The data would be divided in a network-like manner (cf. Fig. 1.12 to the right).

Data records in document databases have a structuring that divides the content into recognizable subunits. Lists of field values can be nested in a tree-like manner. For example, the invoice document in Fig. 1.12 contains an "Item" field. This contains a list of items, each of which again has fields such as "Name" and

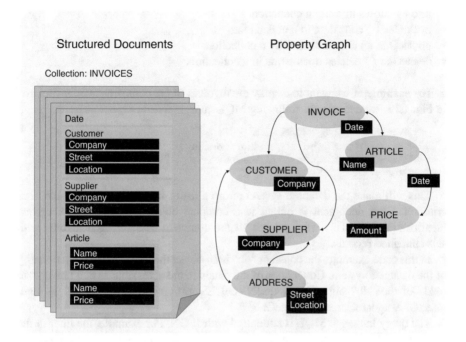

Fig. 1.12 Invoice data is stored in a self-contained manner in the document model

"Price" with corresponding values. More often than lists or arrays, the complex object structure is used to organize documents. The JSON (JavaScript Object Notation) format is a syntax for describing complex objects that is particularly suitable for Web development in JavaScript (see Sect. 2.5.1).

1.5.2   Document-Oriented Database Language MQL

MongoDB Query Language (MQL) is an object-oriented language for interacting with document databases to create, read, update, delete, and transform data. The JavaScript-based language was originally developed for server-side Web programming.

The database model of an MQL document database consists of collections of structured digital documents. For example, in Fig. 1.12, there are five invoice documents in the INVOICES collection. Because they are schema-free, the documents in a collection can have any number of fields. Thus, new fields and objects can be created very flexibly at any time. For example, for private persons, the fields "First name" and "Last name" can be stored instead of the field "Company." As a rule, however, documents with predominantly identical fields are collected in collections. Collections provide the following basic elements as methods in MQL:

- find ( ) allows filtering a collection.
- insertOne ( ) adds data to a collection.
- updateOne ( ) allows to modify a collection.
- deleteOne ( ) deletes documents in a collection.

For example, if we want to display the invoices of the company "Miller Elektro" in Fig. 1.12, we can use the following MQL query:

```
db.INVOICES.find ( {"Vendor.Company": "Miller Elektro"} )
```

This will make the database system return a list of invoices that match the filter criterion. Each document is output in a complex object structure with a unique identification key. This way, we get all the complete data for each invoice with self-contained records.

In this code example, the constant "db" is an object that provides the functionality of the database system. Collections of the database are accessible as child objects in fields of the "db" object, e.g., db.INVOICES, providing methods such as find, insertOne, updateOne, and deleteOne.

The query language MQL is structured with JSON. For example, the filter in the find() method is passed as a parameter in JSON notation, which lists the filter criteria as a field-value pair.

If we want to output a list of customers to whom the company "Miller Elektro" has written an invoice, this is accomplished with a second argument:

```
db.INVOICES. find(
{"Vendor.Company": "Miller Elektro"},
{"customer.company": 1, _id: 0} )
```

The second list defines the projection with fields that are either included (value 1) or excluded (value 0). Here, the field "Company" of the subobject "Customer" is included in the result as an inclusion projection; the field _id is excluded. Thus, we get a list of JSON documents containing only the values of the included fields:

```
{ customer: { company: "Mega IT" } }
{ customer: { company: "Bakery Becker" } }
{ customer: { company: "Sewing Studio Needle" } }
...
```

Unlike SQL, MQL evolved in practice and is based on the JSON format, whose creator says he did not invent it but "discovered" it because it already "existed in nature." Because of this organic development, many concepts of MQL appear somewhat different from those of SQL, which have been theorized based on mathematical principles.

1.6   Organization of Data Management

Many companies and organizations view their data as a vital resource, increasingly joining in public information gathering (open data) in addition to maintaining their own data. The continuous global increase of data volume and the growth of information providers and their 24/7 services reinforce the importance of Web-based data pools.

The necessity for current information based in the real world has a direct impact on the conception of the field of IT. In many places, specific positions for data management have been created for a more targeted approach to data-related tasks and obligations. Proactive data management deals both strategically with information gathering and utilization and operatively with the efficient provision and analysis of current and consistent data.

Development and operation of data management incur high costs, while the return is initially hard to measure. Flexible data architecture, non-contradictory and easy-to-understand data description, clean and consistent databases, effective security concepts, current information readiness, and other factors involved are hard to assess and include in profitability considerations. Only the realization of the data's importance and longevity makes the necessary investments worthwhile for the company.

For better comprehension of the term data management, we will look at the four subfields: data architecture, data governance, data technology, and data utilization. Figure 1.13 illustrates the objectives and tools of these four fields within data management.

Data utilization enables the actual, profitable application of business data. A specialized team of data scientists conducts business analytics, providing and reporting on data analyses to management. They also support individual departments, e.g., marketing, sales, customer service, etc., in generating specific relevant insights from Big Data. Questions that arise in connection with data use are the following:

- What purpose does the database serve?
- Which decisions are supported by which data, and how?
- Where does the data come from, and for what reason?
- What results are provided based on the data, and how are they presented?
- How can users interact with the data?

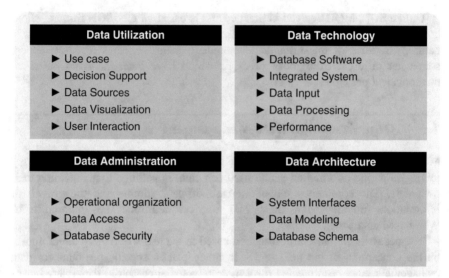

Fig. 1.13 The four cornerstones of data management

Employees in *data architecture* analyze, categorize, and structure the relevant data, system components, and interfaces by a sophisticated methodology. In addition to the assessment of data and information requirements, the major data classes and their relationships with each other must be documented in data models of varying specificity. These models, created from the abstraction of reality and matched to each other, form the foundation of the database schemas. Data architecture answers the following questions:

- What are the components, interfaces, and data flows of the database and information systems?
- Which entities, relationships, and attributes are mapped for the use case?
- Which data structures and data types are used by the DBMS to organize the data?

Data administration aims for a unified coverage of the responsibilities in order to ensure a cross-application use of the long-lived data. Today's tendency toward increased data security leads to a growing responsibility of data administrators for security concepts and assigning permissions. For this purpose, the following points are addressed from the data administration point of view:

- Who plans, develops, and operates the database and information systems using what methods?
- Who has what access to the data?
- How are security, confidentiality, integrity, and availability requirements met?

Data technology specialists install, monitor, and reorganize databases and are in charge of their multilayer security. Their field further includes technology management and the need for the integration of new extensions and constant updates and improvements of existing tools and methods. The data flows from and to the database systems, and the user interfaces are also provided technologically. For Big Data, it is of central importance that the speed of data processing is also optimized for large data volumes. Thus, data engineering deals with the following questions:

- Which SQL or NoSQL database software is used and for what reasons?
- How is the database system implemented and integrated?
- How is the data entered or migrated into the database?
- How is the data queried, manipulated, and transformed?
- How can the database system and queries be optimized in terms of volume and speed?

Based on the characterization of data-related tasks and obligations, data management can be defined as:

Data Management
Data management includes all *operational*, *organizational*, and *technical aspects* of data usage, data architecture, data administration, and data technology that optimize the deployment of data as a resource.

Data Management Plan
A planning document that outlines solutions for the use, architecture, technology, and administration of data, and addresses corresponding issues, is called a data management plan.

Such a plan is often prepared prior to implementing a database system. If all of the questions listed above are answered, a data management system is anchored in a comprehensive breadth of context and planned accordingly. Locally, however, some questions are only answered iteratively during operation.

Bibliography

Celko, J.: Joe Celko's Complete Guide to NoSQL – What every SQL professional needs to know about nonrelational databases. Morgan Kaufmann (2014)

Connolly, T., Begg, C.: Database Systems – A Practical Approach to Design, Implementation, and Management. Pearson (2015)

Coronel, C., Morris, S.: Database Systems – Design, Implementation, & Management. Cengage Learning (2018)

Edlich, S., Friedland, A., Hampe, J., Brauer, B., Brückner, M.: NoSQL – Einstieg in die Welt nichtrelationaler Web 2.0 Datenbanken. Carl Hanser Verlag (2011)

Elmasri, R., Navathe, S.: Fundamentals of Database Systems. Addison-Wesley (2022)

Fasel, D., Meier, A. (eds.): Big Data – Grundlagen, Systeme und Nutzungspotenziale. Edition HMD, Springer (2016)

Hoffer, J., Venkataraman, R.: Modern Database Management. Pearson (2019)

Kemper, A., Eikler, A.: Datenbanksysteme – Eine Einführung. DeGruyter (2015)

MongoDB, Inc.: MongoDB Documentation (2022)

Perkins, L., Redmond, E., Wilson, J.R.: Seven Databases in Seven Weeks: A Guide to Modern Databases and the Nosql Movement, 2nd edn. O'Reilly UK Ltd., Raleigh, NC (2018)

Ploetz, A., Kandhare, D., Kadambi, S., Wu, X.: Seven NoSQL Database in a Week – Get Up and Running with the Fundamentals and Functionalities of Seven of the Most Popular NoSQL Databases. Packt Publishing (2018)

Saake, G., Sattler, K.-U., Heuer, A.: Datenbanken – Konzepte und Sprachen. mitp (2018)

Silberschatz, A., Korth, H., Sudarshan, S.: Database Systems Concepts. McGraw Hill (2019)

Steiner, R.: Grundkurs Relationale Datenbanken – Einführung in die Praxis der Datenbankentwicklung für Ausbildung, Studium und IT-Beruf. Springer Vieweg (2021)

Ullman, J., Garcia-Molina, H., Widom, H.: Database Systems – The Complete Book. Pearson (2013)

Database Modeling

2

2.1 From Requirements Analysis to Database

Data models provide a structured and formal description of the data and data relationships required for an information system. Based on this, a database model or schema defines the corresponding structuring of the database. When data is needed for IT projects, such as the information about employees, departments, and projects in Fig. 2.1, the necessary data categories and their relationships with each other can be defined. The definition of those data categories, called entity sets, and the determination of relationship sets are at this point done without considering the kind of database management system (SQL or NoSQL) to be used for entering, storing, and maintaining the data later. This is to ensure that the data and data relationships will remain *stable from the users' perspective* throughout the development and expansion of information systems.

It takes three steps to set up a database structure: requirement analysis, conceptual data modeling, and implementing database schemas by mapping the entity relationship model to SQL or NoSQL databases.

The goal of requirement analysis (see point 1 in Fig. 2.1) is to find, in cooperation with the user, the data required for the information system and their relationships to each other including the quantity structure. This is vital for an early determination of the system boundaries. The *requirements catalog* is prepared in an iterative process, based on interviews, demand analyses, questionnaires, form compilations, etc. It contains at least a verbal task description with clearly formulated objectives and a *list of relevant pieces of information* (see the example in Fig. 2.1). The written description of data connections can be complemented by graphical illustrations or a summarizing example. It is imperative that the requirement analysis puts the facts necessary for the later development of a database in the language of the users.

Step 2 in Fig. 2.1 shows the conception of the *entity-relationship model*, which contains both the required entity sets and the relevant relationship sets. Our model depicts the entity sets as rectangles and the relationship sets as rhombi. Based on the requirement catalog from step 1, the main entity sets are DEPARTMENT,

© The Author(s), under exclusive license to Springer Nature Switzerland AG 2023   25
M. Kaufmann, A. Meier, *SQL and NoSQL Databases*,
https://doi.org/10.1007/978-3-031-27908-9_2

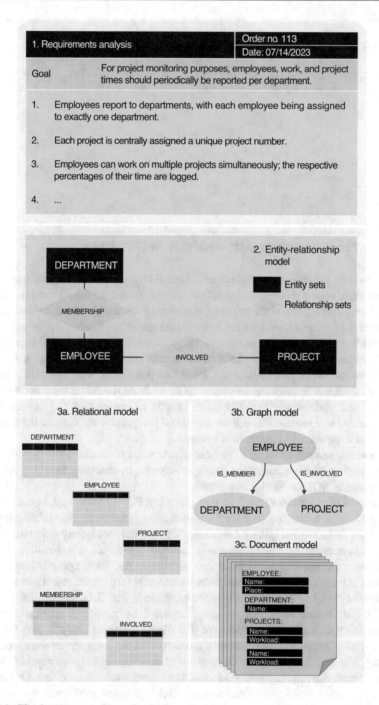

Fig. 2.1 The three steps necessary for database modeling

EMPLOYEE, and PROJECT.[1] To record which departments the employees are working in and which projects they are part of, the relationship sets MEMBERSHIP and INVOLVED are established and graphically connected to the respective entity sets. The entity-relationship model therefore allows for the structuring and graphic representation of the facts gathered during data analysis. However, it should be noted that the identification of entity and relationship sets, as well as the definition of the relevant attributes, is not always a simple, clear-cut process. Rather, this design step requires quite some experience and practice from the data architect.

Next, in step 3, the entity relationship model is mapped into a database schema, with different rules for SQL and NoSQL databases. This can be, e.g., a relational database schema (Fig. 2.1, 3a), a graph database schema (Fig. 2.1, 3b), or a document database schema (Fig. 2.1, 3c).

Since relational database management systems allow only tables as objects, the data records and their relationships *can only be expressed in terms of tables and columns.* For that reason, there is one entity set table each for the entity sets DEPARTMENT, EMPLOYEE, and PROJECT in Fig. 2.1, step 3a. In order to represent the relationships in tables as well, separate tables have to be defined for each relationship set. In our example, this results in the tables MEMBERSHIP and INVOLVED. Such relationship set tables always contain the keys of the entity sets affected by the relationship as foreign keys and potentially additional attributes of the relationship.

In step 3b of Fig. 2.1, we see the depiction of an equivalent graph database. Each entity set corresponds to a node in the graph, so we have the nodes DEPARTMENT, EMPLOYEE, and PROJECT. The relationship sets MEMBERSHIP and INVOLVED from the entity-relationship model are converted into edges in the graph-based model. The relationship set MEMBERSHIP becomes a directed edge type from the DEPARTMENT node to the EMPLOYEE node and is named IS_MEMBER. Similarly, a directed edge type with the name IS_INVOLVED is drawn from the EMPLOYEE to the PROJECT node types.

The mapping of the facts in document databases is shown in Fig. 2.1, 3c. Several related entities are serialized in a unified document structure. For this purpose, the entities are aggregated, i.e., nested. This implies an order of aggregation, which may vary depending on the use case. In the example in the figure, there is a field EMPLOYEE on the first level. This represents an employee object with fields name and location. On the second level, there is on the one hand a field DEPART-MENT, which embeds the corresponding department data per employee as a subobject. On the other hand, a list of project information is stored per employee in the PROJECTS field, including the workload, which is essential for reporting.

This is only a rough sketch of the process of data analysis, development of an entity-relationship model, and definition of a relational or graph-based database schema. The core insight is that a database design should be developed based on

---

[1] The names of entity and relationship sets are spelled in capital letters, analogous to table, node, and edge names.

Entity:	Employee Murphy, lives on Morris Road in Kent
Entity set:	Set of all employees with the attributes Name, Street, and City
Identification key:	Employee number as an artificial key

Representation in the entity-relationship model

Fig. 2.2 EMPLOYEE entity set

an entity-relationship model. This allows for the gathering and discussion of data modeling factors with the users, independent from any specific database system. Only in the next design step is the most suitable database schema determined and mapped out. For relational, graph-oriented, and document-oriented databases, there are clearly defined mapping rules.

2.2   The Entity-Relationship Model

2.2.1   Entities and Relationships

An *entity* is a specific object in the real world or our imagination that is distinct from all others. This can be an individual, an item, an abstract concept, or an event. Entities of the same type are combined into *entity sets* and further characterized by attributes. These attributes are property categories of the entity and/or the entity set, such as size, name, weight, etc.

For each entity set, an identification key, i.e., one attribute or a specific combination of attributes, is set as unique. In addition to uniqueness, it also has to meet the criterion of the minimal combination of attributes for identification keys as described in Sect. 1.2.1.

In Fig. 2.2, an individual employee is characterized as an entity by their concrete attributes. If, in the course of internal project monitoring, all employees are to be listed with their names and address data, an entity set EMPLOYEE is created. An artificial employee number in addition to the attributes Name, Street, and City allows

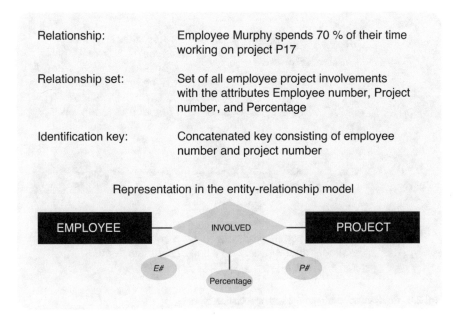

Relationship: Employee Murphy spends 70 % of their time
                                 working on project P17

Relationship set: Set of all employee project involvements
                                 with the attributes Employee number, Project
                                 number, and Percentage

Identification key: Concatenated key consisting of employee
                                 number and project number

Representation in the entity-relationship model

EMPLOYEE — INVOLVED — PROJECT

E# — Percentage — P#

Fig. 2.3 INVOLVED relationship between employees and projects

for the unique identification of the individual employees (entities) within the staff (entity set).

Besides the entity sets themselves, the *relationships* between them are of interest and can form sets of their own. Similar to entity sets, relationship sets can be characterized by attributes.

Figure 2.3 presents the statement "Employee Murphy does 70 % of their work on project P17" as a concrete example of an employee-project relationship. The respective relationship set INVOLVED is to list all project participations of the employees. It contains a concatenated key constructed from the foreign keys employee number and project number. This combination of attributes ensures the unique identification of each project participation by an employee. Along with the concatenated key, the relationship set receives its own attribute named "Percentage" specifying the percentage of working hours that employees allot to each project they are involved in.

In general, relationships can be understood as associations in two directions: The relationship set INVOLVED can be interpreted from the perspective of the EMPLOYEE entity set as "one employee can participate in multiple projects" and from the entity set PROJECT as "one project is handled by multiple employees."

2.2.2 Associations and Association Types

The *association* of an entity set ES_1 to another entity set ES_2, also called role, is the meaning of the relationship in that direction. As an example, the relationship

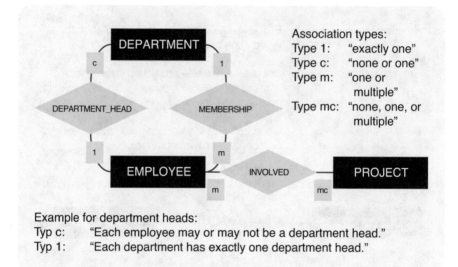

Association types:
Type 1:   "exactly one"
Type c: "none or one"
Type m: "one or multiple"
Type mc: "none, one, or multiple"

Example for department heads:
Typ c: "Each employee may or may not be a department head."
Typ 1:   "Each department has exactly one department head."

Fig. 2.4 Entity-relationship model with association types

DEPARTMENT_HEAD in Fig. 2.4 has two associations: On the one hand, each department has one employee in the role of department head; on the other hand, some employees could fill the role of department head for a specific department. Associations are sometimes also labeled. This is important when multiple relationships are possible between two identical entity sets.

Each association from an entity set ES_1 to an entity set ES_2 can be weighted by an association type. The association type from ES_1 to ES_2 indicates how many entities of the associated entity set ES_2 can be assigned to a specific entity from ES_1.[2] The main distinction is between single, conditional, multiple, and multiple-conditional association types.

Unique association (type 1)

In unique, or type 1, associations, each entity from the entity set ES_1 is assigned exactly one entity from the entity set ES_2. For example, our data analysis showed that each employee is a member of exactly one department, i.e., matrix management is not permitted. The MEMBERSHIP relationship from employees to departments in Fig. 2.4 therefore is a unique/type 1 association.

Conditional association (type c)

A type c association means that each entity from the entity set ES_1 is assigned zero or one, i.e., maximum one entity from the entity set ES_2. The relationship is

---

[2]It is common in database literature to note the association type from ES_1 to ES_2 next to the associated entity set, i.e., ES_2.

optional, so the association type is conditional. An example for a conditional association is the relationship DEPARTMENT_HEAD (see Fig. 2.4), since not every employee can have the role of a department head.

Multiple association (type m)
In multiple, or type m, associations, each entity from the entity set ES_1 is assigned *one or more* entities from the entity set ES_2. This association type is often called *complex*, since one entity from ES_1 can be related to an arbitrary number of entities from ES_2. An example for the multiple association type in Fig. 2.4 is the INVOLVED relationship from projects to employees: Each project can involve multiple employees, but must be handled by at least one.

Multiple-conditional association (type mc)
Each entity from the entity set ES_1 is assigned *zero, one, or multiple* entities from the entity set ES_2. Multiple-conditional associations differ from multiple associations in that not every entity from ES_1 must have a relationship to any entities in ES_2. In analogy to that type, they are also called conditional-complex. We will exemplify this with the INVOLVED relationship in Fig. 2.4 as well, but this time from the employees' perspective: While not every employee has to participate in projects, there are some employees involved in multiple projects.

The association types provide information about the cardinality of the relationship. As we have seen, each relationship contains two association types. The *cardinality of a relationship* between the entity sets ES_1 and ES_2 is therefore a *pair of association types* in the form:

Cardinality := (association type ES_1 to ES_2, association type ES_2 to ES_1).[3]

For example, the pair (mc,m) of association types between EMPLOYEE and PROJECT indicates that the INVOLVED relationship is (multiple-conditional, multiple).

Figure 2.5 shows all 16 possible combinations of association types. The first quadrant contains four options of unique-unique relationships (case B1 in Fig. 2.5). They are characterized by the cardinalities (1,1), (1,c), (c,1), and (c,c). For case B2, the unique-complex relationships, also called *hierarchical relationships*, there are eight possible combinations. The complex-complex or *network-like relationships* (case B3) comprise the four cases (m,m), (m,mc), (mc,m), and (mc,mc).

Instead of the association types, *minimum and maximum thresholds* can be set if deemed more practical. For instance, instead of the multiple association type from projects to employees, a range of (MIN,MAX) := (3,8) could be set. The lower threshold defines that at least three employees must be involved in a project, while the maximum threshold limits the number of participating employees to eight.

---

[3]The character combination ":=" stands for "is defined by."

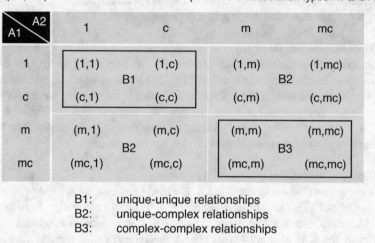

Bj := (A1, A2)   Cardinalities of relationships with the association types A1 and A2

B1:   unique-unique relationships
B2:   unique-complex relationships
B3:   complex-complex relationships

Fig. 2.5 Overview of the possible cardinalities of relationships

The entity relationship model is often abbreviated to ER model. It is very important for computer-based data modeling tools, as it is supported by many CASE (computer-aided software engineering) tools to some extent. Depending on the quality of these tools, both generalization and aggregation can be described in separate design steps, on top of entity and relationship sets. Only then can the *ER model be converted, in part automatically, into a database schema.* Since this is not always a one-on-one mapping, it is up to the data architect to make the appropriate decisions. Sections 2.3.2, 2.4.2, and 2.5.2 provide some simple mapping rules to help in converting an entity-relationship model into a relational, graph, or document database.

2.2.3 Generalization and Aggregation

Generalization is an abstraction process in which entities or entity sets are subsumed under a superordinate entity set. The dependent entity sets or subsets within a generalization hierarchy can vice versa be interpreted as *specializations*. The generalization of entity sets can result in various constellations:

- **Overlapping entity subsets**: The specialized entity set *overlap with each other*. As an example, if the entity set EMPLOYEE has two subsets PHOTO_CLUB and SPORTS_CLUB, the club members are consequently considered employees. However, employees can be active in both the company's photography and sports club, i.e., the entity subsets PHOTO_CLUB and SPORTS_CLUB overlap.
- **Overlapping complete entity subsets**: The specialization entity sets *overlap with each other and completely cover* the generalized entity set. If we add a

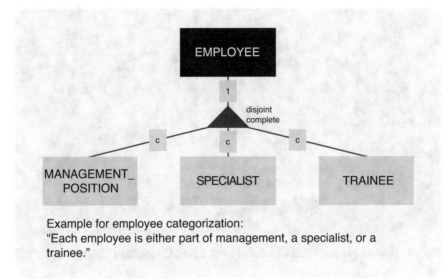

Example for employee categorization:
"Each employee is either part of management, a specialist, or a
trainee."

Fig. 2.6   Generalization, illustrated by EMPLOYEE

CHESS_CLUB entity subset to the PHOTO_CLUB and SPORTS_CLUB and
assume that every employee joins at least one of these clubs when starting work at
the company, we get an overlapping complete constellation. Every employee is a
member of at least one of the three clubs, but they can also be in two or all three
clubs.

- **Disjoint entity subsets**: The entity sets in the specialization are disjoint, i.e.,
  mutually exclusive. To illustrate this, we will once again use the EMPLOYEE
  entity set, but this time with the specializations MANAGEMENT_POSITION
  and SPECIALIST. Since employees cannot at the same time hold a leading
  position and pursue a specialization, the two entity subsets are disjoint.
- **Disjoint complete entity subsets**: The specialization entity sets are disjoint, but
  together completely cover the generalized entity set. As a result, there must be a
  sub-entity in the specialization for each entity in the superordinate entity set and
  vice versa. For example, take the entity set EMPLOYEE with a third specialization TRAINEE in addition to the MANAGEMENT_POSITION and SPECIAL-
  IST subsets, where every employee is either part of management, a technical
  specialist, or a trainee.

Generalization hierarchies are represented by specific forked connection symbols
marked "overlapping incomplete," "overlapping complete," "disjoint incomplete,"
or "disjoint complete."

Figure 2.6 shows the entity set EMPLOYEE as a disjoint and complete generalization of MANAGEMENT_POSITION, SPECIALIST, and TRAINEE. All dependent entities of the entity subsets, such as team lead or department head in
MANAGEMENT_POSITION, are also part of EMPLOYEE, since the respective

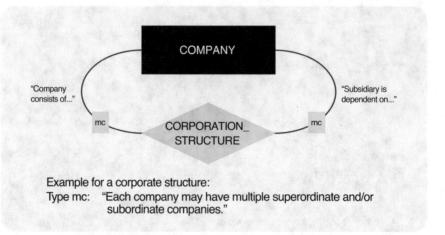

Fig. 2.7 Network-like aggregation, illustrated by CORPORATION_STRUCTURE

association type is 1. Generalization is therefore often called an *is-a relationship*: A team lead *is a(n)* employee, just as a department head *is a(n)* employee. In disjoint complete generalization hierarchies, the reverse association is also of type 1, i.e., every employee is part of exactly one entity subset.

Another important relationship structure beside generalization is *aggregation*, the combination of entities into a superordinate total by capturing their structural characteristics in a relationship set.

To model the holding structure of a corporation, as shown in Fig. 2.7, a relationship set CORPORATION_STRUCTURE is used. It describes the relationship network of the entity set COMPANY with itself. Each company ID from the COMPANY entity set is used in CORPORATION_STRUCTURE as a foreign key twice, once as ID for superordinate and once for subordinate company holdings. CORPORATION_STRUCTURE can also contain additional relationship attributes such as shares.

In general, aggregation describes the structured merging of entities in what is called a *part-of structure*. In CORPORATION_STRUCTURE, each company can be *part of* a corporate group. Since CORPORATION_STRUCTURE in our example is defined as a network, the association types of both super- and subordinate parts must be multiple-conditional.

The two abstraction processes of generalization and aggregation are major structuring elements in data modeling. In the entity-relationship model, they can be represented by specific graphic symbols or as special boxes. For instance, the aggregation from Fig. 2.7 could also be represented by a generalized entity set CORPORATION implicitly encompassing the entity set COMPANY and the relationship set CORPORATION_STRUCTURE.

PART-OF structures do not have to be networks, but can also be hierarchic. Let's assume an ITEM_LIST as illustration in Fig. 2.8: Each item can be composed of

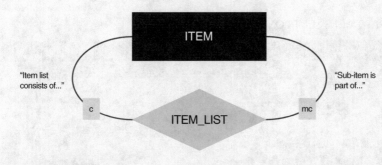

Example for an item list:
Type mc: "Each item may consist of multiple sub-items."
Type c: "Each sub-item is dependent on exactly one superordinate item."

Fig. 2.8 Hierarchical aggregation, illustrated by ITEM_LIST

multiple sub-items, while on the other hand, each sub-item points to exactly one superordinate item.

The entity-relationship model is very important for computer-based data modeling tools, as it is supported by many CASE (computer-aided software engineering) tools to some extent. Depending on the quality of these tools, both generalization and aggregation can be described in separate design steps, on top of entity and relationship sets. Only then can the *entity-relationship model be converted, in part automatically, into a database schema.* Since this is not always a one-to-one mapping, it is up to the data architect to make the appropriate decisions. The following sections provide some simple mapping rules to help in converting an entity-relationship model into a relational, graph, or document database.

2.3   Implementation in the Relational Model

2.3.1   Dependencies and Normal Forms

The study of the relational model has spawned a new database theory that precisely describes formal aspects.

Relational Model
The relational model represents both data and relationships between data as tables. Mathematically speaking, any relation R is simply a set of n-tuples. Such a relation is always a *subset of a Cartesian product of n attribute domains*, $R \subseteq D_1 \times D_2 \times \ldots \times D_n$, with D_i as the domain of the i-th attribute/property. A tuple is an ordered set of specific data values or manifestations, $r = (d_1, d_2, \ldots, d_n)$. Please note that this

DEPARTMENT_EMPLOYEE

E#	Name	Street	City	D#	DepartmentName
E19	Stewart	E Main Street	Stow	D6	Accounting
E1	Murphy	Morris Road	Kent	D3	IT
E7	Howard	Lorain Avenue	Cleveland	D5	HR
E4	Bell	S Water Street	Kent	D6	Accounting

Fig. 2.9 Redundant and anomalous table

definition means that any tuple may only exist once within any table, i.e., a relation R is a tuple set $R = \{r_1, r_2, \ldots, r_m\}$.

The relational model is based on the works of Edgar Frank Codd from the early 1970s. They were the foundation for the first *relational database systems*, created in research facilities and supporting SQL or similar database languages. Today, their sophisticated successors are firmly established in many practical uses.

One of the major fields within this theory are the *normal forms*, which are used to discover and study dependencies within tables in order to avoid redundant information and resulting anomalies.

Attribute Redundancy

An attribute in a table is redundant if individual values of this attribute can be omitted *without a loss of information*.

To give an example, the following table DEPARTMENT_EMPLOYEE contains employee number, name, street, and city for each employee, plus their department number and department name.

For every employee of department D6, the table in Fig. 2.9 lists the department name Accounting. If we assume that each department consists of multiple employees, similar repetitions would occur for all departments. We can say that the DepartmentName attribute is redundant, since the same value is listed in the table multiple times. It would be preferable to store the name going with each department number in a separate table for future reference instead of redundantly carrying it along for each employee.

Tables with redundant information can lead to *database anomalies*, which can take one of three forms: If, for organizational reasons, a new department D9, labeled marketing, is to be defined in the DEPARTMENT_EMPLOYEE table from Fig. 2.9, but there are not yet any employees assigned to that department, there is no way of

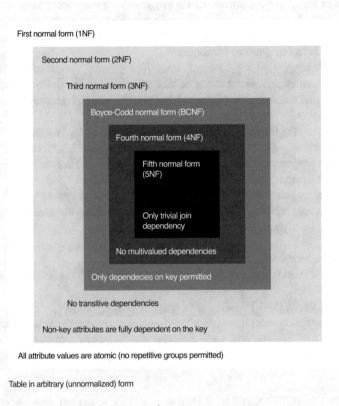

First normal form (1NF)

Second normal form (2NF)

Third normal form (3NF)

Boyce-Codd normal form (BCNF)

Fourth normal form (4NF)

Fifth normal form (5NF)

Only trivial join dependency

No multivalued dependencies

Only dependecies on key permitted

No transitive dependencies

Non-key attributes are fully dependent on the key

All attribute values are atomic (no repetitive groups permitted)

Table in arbitrary (unnormalized) form

Fig. 2.10 Overview of normal forms and their definitions

adding it. This is an *insertion anomaly*—no new table rows can be inserted without a unique employee number.

Deletion anomalies occur if the removal of some data results in the inadvertent loss of other data. For example, if we were to delete all employees from the DEPARTMENT_EMPLOYEE table, we would also lose the department numbers and names.

The last kind are *update anomalies* (or modification anomalies): If the name of department D3 were to be changed from IT to Data Processing, each of the department's employees would have to be edited individually, meaning that although only one detail is changed, the DEPARTMENT_EMPLOYEE table has to be adjusted in multiple places. This inconvenient situation is what we call an update anomaly.

The following paragraphs discuss normal forms, which help to avoid redundancies and anomalies. Figure 2.10 gives an overview over the various normal forms and their definition. Below, we will take a closer look at different kinds of dependencies and give some practical examples.

As seen in Fig. 2.10, the normal forms progressively limit acceptable tables. For instance, a table or entire database schema in the third normal form must meet all requirements of the first and second normal form, plus there must be no transitive dependencies between non-key attributes.

In the following, the first, second, and third normal forms are treated and discussed with examples. For reasons of lack of relevance for practice, even more restrictive normal forms are not discussed further. We refer to relevant literature for theoretical interest.[4]

Understanding the normal forms helps to make sense of the mapping rules from an entity-relationship model to a relational model (see Sect. 2.3.2). In fact, we will see that with a properly defined entity-relationship model and consistent application of the relevant mapping rules, the normal forms will always be met. Simply put, by creating an entity-relationship model and using mapping rules to map it onto a relational database schema, *we can mostly forget checking the normal forms for each individual design step.*

Functional Dependencies
The first normal form is the basis for all other normal forms and is defined as follows:

First Normal Form (1NF)
A table is in the first normal form when the *domains of the attributes* are atomic. The first normal form requires that each attribute get its values from an unstructured domain and there must be no sets, lists, or repetitive groups within the individual attributes.

The table PROJECT_PARTICIPANT in Fig. 2.11 is not yet normalized, since each employee tuple contains multiple numbers of projects the employee is involved in. The unnormalized table can be converted to the first normal form by simply creating a separate tuple for each project participation. This conversion of the PROJECT_PARTICIPANT table to 1NF requires the key of the table to be expanded, since we need both the employee and the project number to uniquely identify each tuple. It is common (but not required) with concatenated keys to put the key parts next to each other at the beginning of the table.

Paradoxically, using the first normal form leaves us with a table full of redundancies—in our example in Fig. 2.11, both the names and addresses of the employees are redundantly repeated for each project involvement. This is where the second normal form comes into play:

Second Normal Form (2NF)
A table is in the second normal form when, in addition to the requirements of the first normal form, each non-key attribute is *fully functionally dependent* on each key.

---

[4]For example, author Graeme C. Simsion presents a simplified hybrid of fourth and fifth normal forms he calls "Business Fifth Normal Form" in "Data Modeling Essentials," which is easy for newcomers to data modeling to understand.

PROJECT_EMPLOYEE (unnormalized)

E#	Name	City	P#
E7	Howard	Cleveland	[P1, P9]
E1	Murphy	Kent	[P7, P11, P9]

PROJECT EMPLOYEE (first normal form)

E#	P#	Name	City
E7	P1	Howard	Cleveland
E7	P9	Howard	Cleveland
E1	P7	Murphy	Kent
E1	P11	Murphy	Kent
E1	P9	Murphy	Kent

EMPLOYEE (2NF)

E#	Name	City
E7	Howard	Cleveland
E1	Murphy	Kent

INVOLVED (2NF)

E#	P#
E7	P1
E7	P9
E1	P7
E1	P11
E1	P9

Fig. 2.11 Tables in the first and second normal form

An attribute B is functionally dependent on an attribute A if for each value of A, there is exactly one value of B, written as A $\rightarrow$ B. A functional dependency of B on A therefore requires that each value of A uniquely identifies one value of B. As seen before, it is a property of identification keys that all non-key attributes are uniquely dependent on the key, so for an identification key K and an attribute B in one table, there is a functional dependency K $\rightarrow$ B.

Keys can consist of several columns in the relation model. This is typically the case for tables that establish relationships between two or more entities. For such concatenated keys, this functional dependency ($\rightarrow$) must become a full functional dependency ($\Rightarrow$). An attribute B is fully functionally dependent on a concatenated key consisting of K1 and K2 (written as (K1,K2) $\Rightarrow$ B) if B is functionally dependent on the entire key, but not its parts, i.e., full functional dependency means that only the entire concatenated key uniquely identifies the non-key attributes. While the functional dependency (K1,K2) $\Rightarrow$ B must apply, neither K1 $\rightarrow$ B nor K2 $\rightarrow$ B is allowed. *Full functional dependency* of an attribute from a composite key prohibits a functional dependency of the attribute from any part of the key.

The PROJECT_PARTICIPANT table in 1NF in Fig. 2.11 contains the concatenated key (*E#,P#*), i.e., it must be tested for full functional dependency. For the names and addresses of the project participants, the functional dependencies (*E#,P#*) $\rightarrow$ Name and (*E#,P#*) $\rightarrow$ City apply. However, while each combination of employee and project number uniquely identifies one name or place of residence, the project numbers have absolutely no bearing on this information, and it is already defined by the employee numbers alone. Both the Name and the City attribute are therefore functionally dependent on a part of the key, because *E#* $\rightarrow$ Name and *E#* $\rightarrow$ City. This violates the definition of full functional dependency, i.e., the PROJECT_PARTICIPANT table is not yet in the second normal form.

If a table with a concatenated key is not in 2NF, it has to be split into subtables. The attributes that are dependent on a part of the key are transferred to a separate table along with that key part, while the concatenated key and potential other relationship attributes remain in the original relationship table.

In our example from Fig. 2.11, this results in the tables EMPLOYEE and PROJECT_INVOLVEMENT, both of which fulfill both the first and the second normal form. The EMPLOYEE table does not have a concatenated key, and the requirements of the second normal form are obviously met. The PROJECT_INVOLVEMENT table has no non-key attributes, which saves us the need to check for 2NF here as well.

Transitive Dependencies

In Fig. 2.12, we return to the DEPARTMENT_EMPLOYEE table from earlier, which contains department information in addition to the employee details. We can immediately tell that the table is in both first and second normal form—since there is no concatenated key, we do not even have to check for full functional dependency. However, the DepartmentName attribute is still redundant. This can be fixed using the third normal form.

Third Normal Form (3NF)

A table is in the third normal form when, in addition to the requirements of the second form, *no non-key attribute is transitively dependent on any key attribute.*

Again, we use a dependency to define a normal form: In transitive dependency, formally symbolized by a double arrow $\Rightarrow$, an attribute is *indirectly functionally dependent* on another attribute. For instance, the attribute DepartmentName in our table is functionally dependent on the employee number via the department number. We can see functional dependency between the employee number and the department number, as well as between department number and department name. These

DEPARTMENT_EMPLOYEE (in second normal form)

E#	Name	Street	City	D#	DepartmentName
E19	Stewart	E Main Street	Stow	D6	Accounting
E1	Murphy	Morris Road	Kent	D3	IT
E7	Howard	Lorain Avenue	Cleveland	D5	HR
E4	Bell	S Water Street	Kent	D6	Accounting

Transitive dependency:

E# ⟶ D# ⟶ DepartmentName

D# is not functionally
dependent on E#

EMPLOYEE (in third normal form)   DEPARTMENT (3NF)

E#	Name	Street	City	D#_Sub
E19	Stewart	E Main Street	Stow	D6
E1	Murphy	Morris Road	Kent	D3
E7	Howard	Lorain Ave	Cleveland	D5
E4	Bell	S Water Street	Kent	D6

D#	DepartmentName
D3	IT
D5	HR
D6	Accounting

Fig. 2.12 Transitive dependency and third normal form

two functional dependencies $E\# \rightarrow D\#$ and $D\# \rightarrow$ DepartmentName can be merged to form a transitive dependency.

In general, given two functional dependencies A →B and B → C with a common attribute B, the merged dependency A → C will also be functional: if A uniquely identifies the values of B and B uniquely identifies the values of C, C inherits the dependency on A, i.e., the functional dependency A → C is definitely the case. In addition, the dependency is called transitive, if aside from the functional dependencies A → B and B → C, A is not also functionally dependent on B. This gives us the following definition for *transitive dependency*: An attribute C is transitively dependent on A if B is functionally dependent on A, C is functionally dependent on B, and A is not functionally dependent on B.

Since   the   DepartmentName   attribute   in   the   example DEPARTMENT_EMPLOYEE table in Fig. 2.12 is transitively dependent on the *E#* attribute, the table is by definition not in the third normal form. The transitive dependency can be removed by splitting off the redundant DepartmentName attribute and putting it in a separate DEPARTMENT table with the department numbers. The department number also stays in the remaining EMPLOYEE table as a foreign key (see attribute "*D#*_Sub"). The relationship between employees and departments is therefore still ensured.

The second and third normal forms succeed in eliminating redundancies in the non-key attributes. The detection of redundant information need not theoretically stop at the non-key attributes, since composite keys can also occur redundantly.

An extension of the third normal form that may be required is called the "Boyce-Codd normal form" or BCNF, based on the work of Boyce and Codd. Such a form comes into play when several key candidates occur in one and the same table.

In practice, however, the second and third normal forms are already more than sufficient. Often, even intentional denormalization, i.e., redundancy, is introduced to optimize the speed of processing for Big Data. This will be discussed in Sect. 2.5.

2.3.2   Mapping Rules for Relational Databases

This section discusses how to map the entity-relationship model onto a relational database schema, i.e., how *entity sets and relationship sets* can be represented in tables.

Database Schema
A *database schema* is the description of a database, i.e., the specification of the database structures and the associated integrity constraints. A relational database schema contains definitions of the tables, the attributes, and the primary keys. Integrity constraints set limits for the domains, the dependencies between tables, and the actual data.

There are two rules of major importance in mapping an entity-relationship model onto a relational database schema (see also Fig. 2.13):

Rule R1 (Entity Sets)
Each *entity set has to be defined as a separate table* with a unique primary key. The primary key can be either the key of the respective entity set or one selected candidate key. The entity set's remaining attributes are converted into corresponding attributes within the table.

By definition, a table requires a unique primary key (see Sect. 1.2.1). It is possible that there are multiple *candidate keys* in a table, all of which meet the requirement of uniqueness and minimality. In such cases, it is up to the data architects which candidate key they would like to use as the primary key.

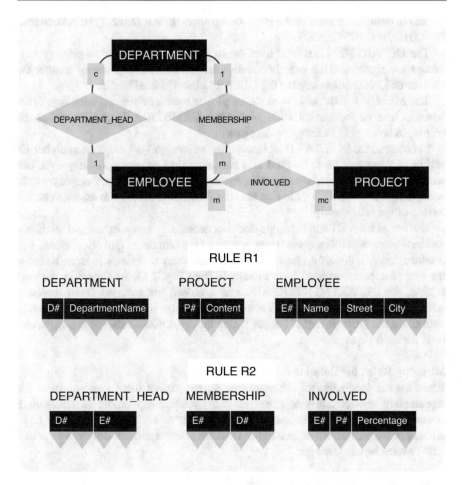

Fig. 2.13 Mapping entity and relationship sets onto tables

Rule R2 (Relationship Sets)
Each *relationship set can be defined as a separate table*; the identification keys of the corresponding entity sets must be included in this table as *foreign keys*. The primary key of the relationship set table can be a concatenated key made from the foreign keys or another candidate key, e.g., an artificial key. Other attributes of the relationship set are listed in the table as further attributes.

The term *foreign key* describes an attribute within a table that is used as an identification key in at least one other table (possibly also within this one). Identification keys can be reused in other tables to create the desired relationships between tables.

Figure 2.13 shows how rules R1 and R2 are applied to a concrete example: Each of the entity sets DEPARTMENT, EMPLOYEE, and PROJECT is mapped onto a corresponding table DEPARTMENT, EMPLOYEE, and PROJECT. Similarly,

tables are defined for each of the relationship sets DEPARTMENT_HEAD, MEM-
BERSHIP, and INVOLVED.

The DEPARTMENT_HEAD uses the department number $D\#$ as primary key.
Since each department has exactly one department head, the department number $D\#$
suffices as identification key for the DEPARTMENT_HEAD table.

The MEMBERSHIP table uses the employee number $E\#$ as primary key. Likewise, $E\#$ can be the identification key of the MEMBERSHIP table because each
employee belongs to exactly one department.

In contrast, the INVOLVED table requires the foreign keys employee number $E\#$
and project number $P\#$ to be used as a concatenated key, since one employee can
work on multiple projects and each project can involve multiple employees. In
addition, the INVOLVED table lists also the Percentage attribute as another characteristic of the relationship.

The use of rules R1 and R2 alone does not necessarily result in an ideal relational
database schema as this approach may lead to a high number of individual tables. For
instance, it seems doubtful whether it is really necessary to define a separate table for
the role of department head in our example from Fig. 2.13. As shown in the next
section, the DEPARTMENT_HEAD table is indeed not required under mapping
rule R5. The department head role would instead be integrated as an additional
attribute in the DEPARTMENT table, listing the employee number of the respective
head for each department.

Mapping Rules for Relationship Sets
Based on the cardinality of relationships, we can define three mapping rules for
representing relationship sets from the entity-relationship model as tables in a
corresponding relational database schema. In order to avoid an unnecessary large
number of tables, rule R3 expressly limits which relationship sets *always and in any
case require separate tables*:

Rule R3 (Network-Like Relationship Sets)
Every complex-complex relationship set must be defined as a separate table which
contains at least the identification keys of the associated entity sets as foreign
keys. The primary key of a relationship set table is either a concatenated key from
the foreign keys or another candidate key. Any further characteristics of the relationship set become attributes in the table.

This rule requires that the relationship set INVOLVED from Fig. 2.14 has to be a
separate table with a primary key, which in our case is the concatenated key
expressing the foreign key relationships to the tables EMPLOYEE and PROJECT.
The Percentage attribute describes the share of the project involvement in the
employee's workload.

Under rule R2, we could define a separate table for the MEMBERSHIP relationship set with the two foreign keys department number and employee number. This
would be useful if we were supporting matrix management and planning to get rid of
unique subordination with the association type 1, since this would result in a
complex-complex relationship between DEPARTMENT and EMPLOYEE.

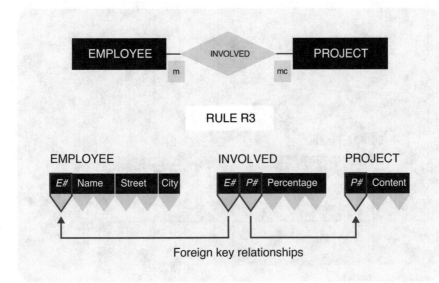

Fig. 2.14 Mapping rule for complex-complex relationship sets

However, if we are convinced that there will be no matrix management in the foreseeable future, we can apply rule R4 for the unique-complex relationship:

Rule R4 (Hierarchical Relationship Sets)
Unique-complex relationship sets can be represented without a separate relationship set table by the tables of the two associated entity sets. The unique association (i.e., association type 1 or c) allows for the primary key of the referenced table to simply be included in the referencing table as a foreign key with an appropriate *role name*.

Following rule R4, we forgo a separate MEMBERSHIP table in Fig. 2.15. Instead of the additional relationship set table, we add the foreign key D#_Sub to the EMPLOYEE table to list the appropriate department number for each employee. The foreign key relationship is defined by an attribute created from the carried-over identification key D# and the role name Subordination.

For unique-complex relationships, including the foreign key can uniquely identify the relationship. In Fig. 2.15, the department number is taken over into the EMPLOYEE table as a foreign key according to rule R4. If, reversely, the employee numbers were listed in the DEPARTMENT table, we would have to repeat the department name for each employee of a department. Such unnecessary and redundant information is unwanted and goes against the theory of the normal forms (in this case, conflict with the second normal form; see Sect. 2.3.1).

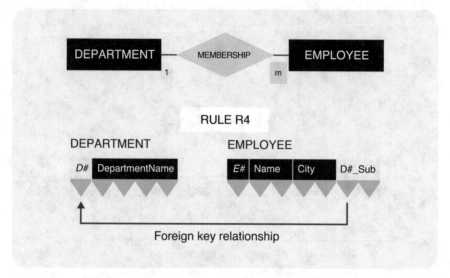

Fig. 2.15 Mapping rule for unique-complex relationship sets

Rule R5 (Unique-Unique Relationship Sets)

Unique-unique relationship sets can be represented without a separate table by the tables of the two associated entity sets. Again, an identification key from the referenced table can be included in the referencing table along with a role name.

Here, too, it is relevant which of the tables we take the foreign key from: Type 1 associations are preferable so the foreign key with its role name can be included in each tuple of the referencing table (avoidance of null values; see also Sect. 3.3.4).

In Fig. 2.16, the employee numbers of the department heads are added to the DEPARTMENT table, i.e., the DEPARTMENT_HEAD relationship set is represented by the *M#*_DepHead attribute. Each entry in this referencing attribute with the role "DepHead" shows who leads the respective department.

If we included the department numbers in the EMPLOYEE table instead, we would have to list null values for most employees and could only enter the respective department number for the few employees actually leading a department. Since null values often cause problems in practice, they should be avoided whenever possible, so it is better to have the "DepartmentHead" role in the DEPARTMENT table. For (1,c) and (c,1) relationships, we can therefore completely prevent null values in the foreign keys, while for (c,c) relationships, we should choose the option resulting in the fewest null values.

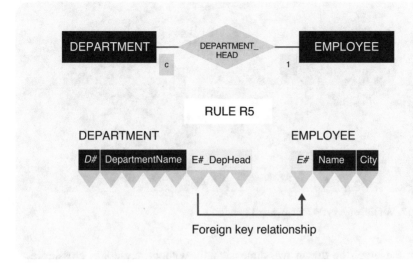

Fig. 2.16 Mapping rule for unique-unique relationship sets

2.4   Implementation in the Graph Model

2.4.1   Graph Properties

Graph theory is a complex subject matter vital to many fields of use where it is necessary to analyze or optimize network-like structures. Use cases range from computer networks, transport systems, work robots, power distribution grids, or electronic relays over social networks to economic areas such as corporation structures, workflows, customer management, logistics, process management, etc. In graph theory, a graph is defined by the sets of its nodes (or vertices) and edges plus assignments between these sets.

Undirected Graph
An undirected graph $G = (V,E)$ consists of a vertex set V and an edge set E, with each edge being assigned two (potentially identical) vertices.

Graph databases are often founded on the model of directed weighted graphs. However, we are not yet concerned with the type and characteristics of the vertices and edges, but rather the general abstract model of an undirected graph. This level of abstraction is sufficient to examine various properties of network structures, such as:

- How many edges have to be passed over to get from one node to another one?
- Is there a path between two nodes?
- Is it possible to traverse the edges of a graph visiting each vertex once?

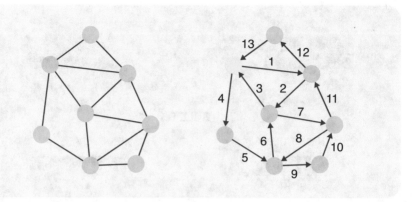

Fig. 2.17 An Eulerian cycle for crossing 13 bridges

- Can the graph be drawn two-dimensionally without any edges crossing each other?

These fundamental questions can be answered using graph theory and have practical applications in a wide variety of fields.

Connected Graph

A graph is connected if there are paths between any two vertices.

One of the oldest graph problems illustrates how powerful graph theory can be:

The Königsberg Bridge Decision Problem (Eulerian Cycles)

In 1736, mathematician Leonhard Euler discovered, based on the seven bridges in the town of Königsberg (now Kaliningrad), that a path traversing each edge of a graph exactly once can only exist if each vertex has an even degree.

Degree of a Vertex

The *degree* of a vertex is the number of edges *incident to it*, i.e., originating from it.

The decision problem for an Eulerian cycle is therefore easily answered: A graph G is Eulerian, if it is connected and each node has an even degree.

Figure 2.17 shows a street map with 13 bridges. The nodes represent districts, the edges connecting bridges between them. Every vertex in this example has an even degree, which means that there has to be an Eulerian cycle.

Dijkstra's Algorithm for Finding Shortest Paths

In 1959, Edsger W. Dijkstra published a three-page article describing an algorithm for calculating the shortest paths within a network. This algorithm, commonly called Dijkstra's algorithm, requires a weighted graph (edges weighted, e.g., as distances in meters or minutes) and an initial node from which the shortest path to any other vertex in the network is then determined.

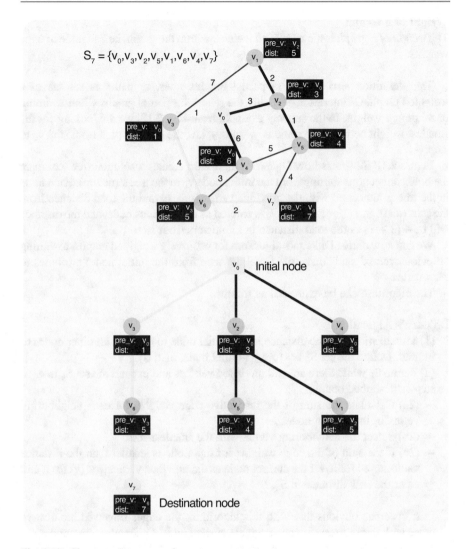

Fig. 2.18 Shortest subway route from stop v_0 to stop v_7

Weighted Graph

Weighted graphs are graphs whose vertices or edges have properties assigned to them.

As an example, Fig. 2.18 shows an edge-weighted graph representing a small subway network, with the stops as nodes and the connections between stops as edges. The weights of the edges are the distances between the stops, given in kilometers.

Weight of a Graph

The *weight of a graph* is the *sum of all weights* within the graph, i.e., all node or edge weights.

This definition also applies to partial graphs, trees, or paths as subsets of a weighted graph. Of interest is generally the search for partial graphs with maximum or minimum weight. In the subway example from Fig. 2.18, we are looking for the smallest weight between the stations v_0 and v_7, i.e., the shortest path from stop v_0 to stop v_7.

Figure 2.18 illustrates how Dijkstra's algorithm creates a solution tree (compare the bold connections starting from the initial node v_0 to the tree structure). Each node in the tree is annotated with the previous vertex (pre_v) and the total distance from the start (dist). In v_5, for instance, v_2 is entered as the previous node, and the distance will be 4 (3 + 1) as the total distance in kilometers from v_0 to v_5.

We can now derive Dijkstra's algorithm for positively weighted graphs, assigning "Previous vertex" and "distance" (total distance from the initial node) attributes to each vertex.

The algorithm can be expressed as follows:

Dijkstra's Algorithm

- (1) Initialization: Set the distance in the initial node to 0 and in all other nodes to infinite. Define the set $S_0 := \{$pre_v: initial node, dist: 0$\}$.
- (2) Iterate S_k while there are still unvisited vertices and expand the set S_k in each step as described below:
  - (2a) Calculate the sum of the respective edge weights for each neighboring vertex of the current node.
  - (2b) Select the neighboring vertex with the smallest sum.
  - (2c) If the sum of the edge weights for that node is smaller than the distance value stored for it, set the current node as the previous vertex (pre_v) for it and enter the new distance in S_k.

It becomes obvious that with this algorithm, the edges traversed are always those with the shortest distance from the current node. Other edges and nodes are considered only when all shorter paths have already been included. This method ensures that when a specific vertex is reached, there can be no shorter path (greedy algorithm[5]). The iterative procedure is repeated until either the distance from initial to destination node has been determined or all distances from the initial node to all other vertices have been calculated.

Property Graph

Graph databases have a structuring scheme, the property graph, which was introduced in Sect. 1.4.1. Formally, a property graph can be defined by a set of

---

[5]In each step, greedy algorithms select the locally optimal subsequent conditions according to the relevant metric.

edges E, a set of vertices V, a domain of properties P, an incidence mapping $i{:}V{\rightarrow}ExE$, and a property mapping p: $V \cup E {\rightarrow} 2^P$. Here, 2^P is the power set of the property domain, which contains all possible subsets of properties. Thus, the property function points from nodes or edges to the sets of properties belonging to them.

In a graph database, data is stored as nodes and edges, which contain as properties node and edge types and further data, e.g., in the form of attribute-value pairs. Unlike conventional graphs, property graphs are multigraphs, i.e., they allow multiple edges between two nodes. To do this, edges are given their own identity and are no longer defined by pairs of nodes, but by two indicators that define the beginning and end of the edge. This edge identity and the mapping of edges as their own data sets lead to the constant performance in graph analyses, independent of data volume (see Sect. 5. 2.7 on "Index-Free Adjacency").

2.4.2 Mapping Rules for Graph Databases

Parallel to the mapping rules R1 to R5 for deriving tables from an entity-relationship model, this section presents the rules G1 to G5 for graph databases. The objective is to convert entity and relationship sets into nodes and edges of a graph.

Figure 2.19 once again shows the previously used project management entity-relationship model (cf. Fig. 2.4). The first mapping rule, G1, concerns the conversion of entity sets into nodes:

Rule G1 (Entity Sets)
Each entity set has to be defined as an individual vertex in the graph database. The attributes of each entity set are made into properties of the respective vertex.

The center of Fig. 2.19 shows how the entity sets DEPARTMENT, EMPLOYEE, and PROJECT are mapped onto corresponding nodes of the graph database, with the attributes attached to the nodes (attributed vertices).

Rule G2 (Relationship Sets)
Each relationship set can be defined as an undirected edge within the graph database. The attributes of each relationship set are assigned to the respective edge (attributed edges).

Applying rule G2 to the relationship sets DEPARTMENT_HEAD, MEMBER-SHIP, and INVOLVED gives us the following constellation of edges: DEPARTMENT_HEAD and MEMBERSHIP between vertices D (for DEPART-MENT) and E (for EMPLOYEE) and INVOLVED between vertices E and P (PROJECT).

Relationship sets can also be represented as directed edges. In the next mapping rules, G3 (for network-like relationships), G4 (hierarchical relationships), and G5 (unique-unique relationships), we will focus on directed edge constellations. They are used to highlight one specific association of a relationship or the direction of the corresponding edge.

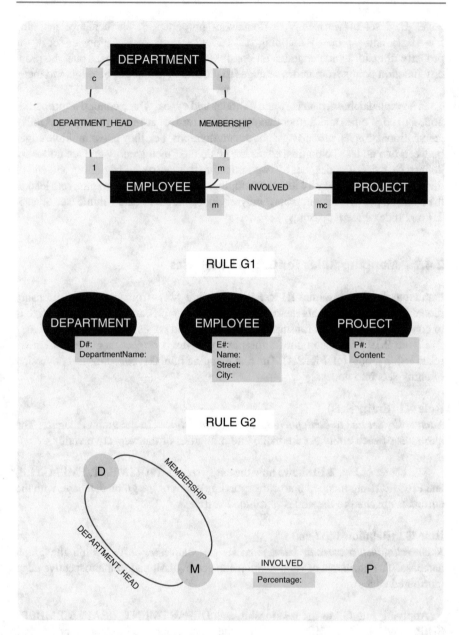

Fig. 2.19 Mapping entity and relationship sets onto graphs

Mapping Rules for Relationship Sets

First, we will look at complex-complex or network-like relationships. Figure 2.20 illustrates rule G3, which applies to these constellations.

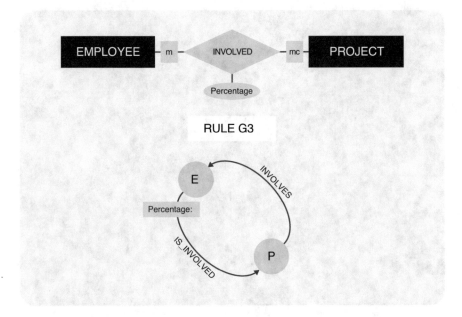

Fig. 2.20 Mapping rule for network-like relationship sets

Rule G3 (Network-Like Relationship Sets)
Any *complex-complex relationship set* can be represented by *two directed edges* where the associations of the relationship provide the names of the edges and the respective *association types are noted at the arrowheads*. One or both edges can have attributes of the corresponding relationship set attached.

In Fig. 2.20, rule G3 is applied to the project participation relationship set, resulting in the network-like relationship set INVOLVED being represented by the two edges IS_INVOLVED and INVOLVES. The former goes from the employees (E) to the projects (P) and has the attribute Percentage, i.e., the workload of the individual employees from their assigned projects. Since not necessarily all employees work on projects, the association type "mc" is noted at the arrowhead. The INVOLVES edge leads from the projects (P) to the employees (E) and has the association type "m."

It is also possible to define individual nodes for network-like relationship sets, if desired. Compared to the relational model, the graph model allows for a broader variety of options for representing entity and relationship sets: undirected graph, directed graph, relationship sets as edges, relationship sets as nodes, etc. Rules G3, G4, and G5, however, strongly suggest using directed edges for relationship sets. This serves to keep the definition of the graph database as simple and easy to understand as possible, so that infrequent users can intuitively use descriptive query languages for graphs. As a rule, directed edges point to unique nodes, i.e., to the entity sets which occur exactly once (association type 1) or, in the second priority, at most once (association type c) in a relation.

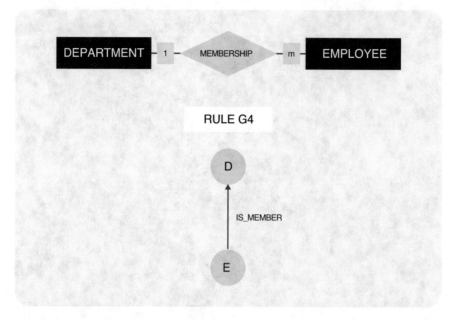

Fig. 2.21 Mapping rule for hierarchical relationship sets

Rule G4 (Hierarchical Relationship Sets)

Every unique-complex relationship set can be established as a directed edge between the corresponding vertices. The direction should be chosen so that the association type at the arrowhead is unique.

In Fig. 2.21, the hierarchical subordination of the employees of a department is shown. The directed edge IS_MEMBER leads from the leaf node E (for EMPLOYEES) to the root node D (DEPARTMENT). The association type 1 is associated with the end of the arrow, because all employees are member of exactly one department.

Rule G5 (Unique-Unique Relationship Sets)

Every *unique-unique relationship set* can be represented as a *directed edge* between the respective vertices. The direction of the edge should be chosen so that the *association type* at the arrowhead is *unique, if possible*.

For instance, Fig. 2.22 illustrates the definition of department heads: The relationship set DEPARTMENT_HEAD becomes the directed edge HAS_DEPARTMENT_HEAD leading from the DEPARTMENT node (D) to the EMPLOYEE node (E). The arrowhead is associated with "1," since each department has exactly one department head.

The graph-based model is highly flexible and offers lots of options, since it is not limited by normal forms. However, users can use this freedom too lavishly, which may result in overly complex, potentially redundant graph constellations. The

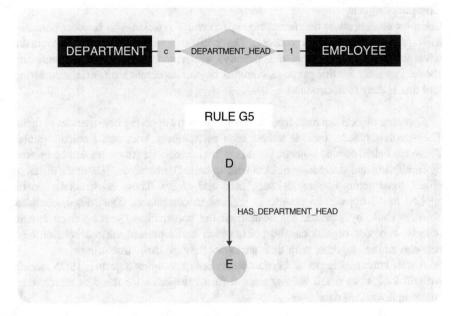

Fig. 2.22 Mapping rule for unique-unique relationship sets

presented mapping rules for entity sets (G1) and relationship sets (G2, G3, G4, and G5) are guidelines that may be ignored based on the individual use case.

2.5 Implementation in the Document Model

2.5.1 Document-Oriented Database Modeling

Document databases store structured data in records called documents. Common document databases have been designed designed to be used for Web and mobile applications. This makes them easy to integrate with Web technologies such as HTML, JavaScript, or HTTP. The structured document in this sense represents a complex object that describes a state of affairs in an app view completely (i.e., without references to other data records).

This requirement for completeness of a document makes foreign key relationships unnecessary. This makes it efficient to distribute documents in a computer cluster because there is no network latency as with foreign key resolution. This horizontal scaling combines different computers into one overall system. Large volumes of data (volume, the first V of Big Data) can thus be distributed across multiple computers. This mechanism is called sharding. Thus, in the case of document databases, the focus is on processing large volumes of heterogeneous data.

Complex Objects

Complex objects allow the *description of structural relationships* between semanti-
cally related data in their entirety. The holistic approach is intended to make
references and foreign keys unnecessary, which enables the scaling mentioned
above. Precisely for this purpose, complex objects represent a powerful structuring
tool that is easy to understand.

Complex objects are built from simpler objects by applying constructors to them.
The simplest objects include values such as numbers, text, and Boolean values.
These are called atomic objects. Based on this, composite structures can be created
by combining and structuring objects with so-called constructors. There are different
object constructors like tuples, sets, lists, and arrays. These constructors can be
applied to all objects: to atomic as well as to compound, constructed, complex
objects. Thus, by repeated application of the constructors, starting from atomic
objects, complex objects can be built, which can represent various relationships
between entities together with their attributes through their structuring.

A well-known example of a syntax for mapping complex objects is JSON, which
we will look at in detail below, since it forms the basis for the data structure of
common document databases.

JSON Data Format

JavaScript Object Notation (JSON) is a format for *describing complex objects*. It
originates from a subset of JavaScript but can be used independently in most
programming languages. The syntax is easy for both humans and machines to read
and write or parse and generate. These features have arguably contributed to JSON's
success.

JSON was originally specified in 1997 by Douglas Crockford as a private
initiative. Crockford said in a talk that he did not invent JSON, but discovered it
in JavaScript as a way to exchange data on the Web. He proposed the subset of the
notation for JavaScript objects as a data exchange format on his private website. The
format subsequently became widely used in Web development, much to his surprise.
Today, JSON is internationally standardized and used for Web APIs, client-server
data communication, mobile applications, and document databases. The JSON
syntax is built on five basic structures:

1. **Object**: Comma-separated set of fields enclosed by curly braces { }.
2. **Field**: A pair consisting of a property and a value, separated by a colon :.
3. **Property**: Name of the property as a string enclosed in quotation marks " ".
4. **Value**: Values are either another object (here the recursive nesting takes effect),
   simple strings in quotes, numbers, truth values (true, false, null), or lists.
5. **List**: Comma-separated lists of values enclosed by square brackets [ ].

The constructors OBJECT { } and LIST [ ] are orthogonal in the sense of complex
objects, because they can be applied to all values, i.e., to basic data types as well as to
more complex structures.

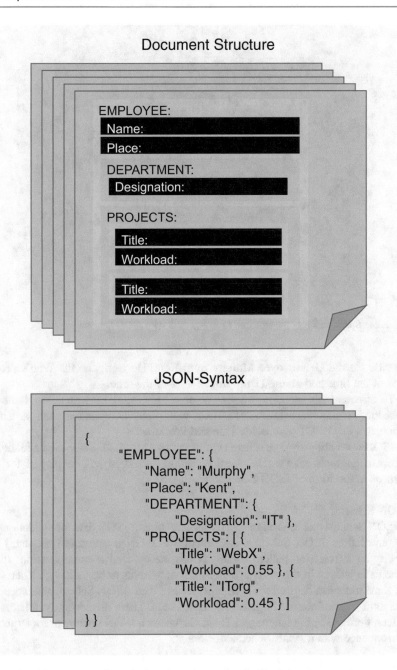

Fig. 2.23 JSON representation of a fact about the use case in Fig. 2.1

As an example, Fig. 2.23 shows a JSON structure that meets the requirements of the use case in Fig. 2.1. We see in a collection of JSON documents the description of

JSON-Schema

```
{
    "type": "object",
    "properties": {
        "EMPLOYEE": { "type": "object",
        "properties": {
            "Name": { "type": "string" },
            "Place": { "type": "string" },
            "DEPARTMENT": { "type": "object",
            "properties": {
                "Designation": { "type": "string" } } },
            "PROJECTS": { "type": "array",
            "items": [ { "type": "object",
            "properties": {
                "Title": { "type": "string" },
                "Workload": { "type": "integer" } } }
]}}}}}
```

Fig. 2.24 Specification of the structure from Fig. 2.23 with JSON Schema

the case for the IT employee Murphy from Kent. He works on the WebX project 55% of the time and on the ITorg project 45% of the time.

To represent this situation, we need an object EMPLOYEE with fields Name and Location, a subobject DEPARTMENT with field Designation, and a list of subobjects PROJECT with fields Title and Workload.

JSON does not provide a schema definition as a standard. Since the validation of data exchanges is relevant in practice, another standard has developed for this purpose in the form of JSON Schema (cf. Fig. 2.24).

JSON Schema
A JSON Schema can be used to specify the structure of JSON data for validation and documentation. JSON Schemas are descriptive JSON documents (metadata) that specify an intersection pattern for JSON data necessary for an application. JSON Schema is written in the same syntax as the documents to be validated. Therefore, the same tools can be used for both schemas and data. JSON Schema was specified in a draft by the Internet Engineering Task Force. There are several validators for different programming languages. These can check a JSON document for structural conformance with a JSON Schema document.

JSON Data Modeling with Prototypes
Because of the rich functionality of JSON Schema, the definition in Fig. 2.24 is rather complex, although the subject matter is very simple. In practice and for more

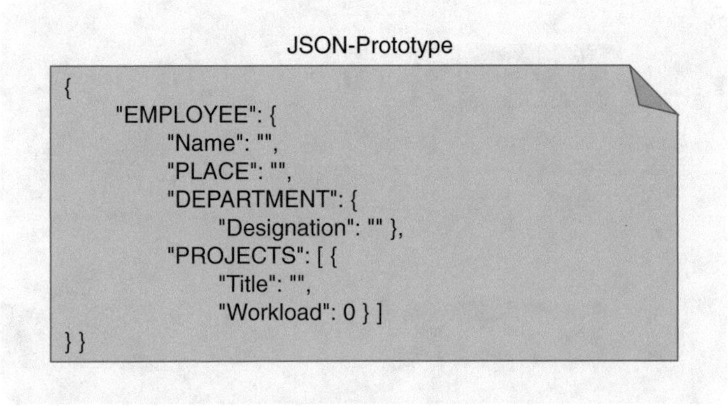

Fig. 2.25 Model of the structure in Fig. 2.23 as a JSON prototype

complex facts, JSON Schemas become unwieldy. They are well-suited for machine validation, but are not easy for humans to read.

Therefore, we propose the prototype method for conceptual JSON data modeling. A prototype (from Greek: πρωτότυπος, original image) is an exemplar that represents an entire category. Thus, a JSON prototype is a JSON document representing a class of JSON documents with the same structural elements (OBJECT, PROPERTY, LIST). A JSON prototype defines the structure not as a description by metadata, but by demonstration. For example, the document in Fig. 2.24 can be viewed as a blueprint for documents having the same objects, properties, and lists, where JSON data corresponding to this prototype can have arbitrary data values (FIELD, VALUE) of the same data type in the same fields.

However, to distinguish JSON prototypes from concrete data, we propose to represent the values with zero values instead of dummy values. These are the empty string ("") for text, zero (0) for numbers, and true for truth values. For lists, we assume that specified values represent repeatable patterns of the same structure.

In Fig. 2.25, we see a well-human-readable JSON prototype instead of the JSON Schema in Fig. 2.24 for modeling. For conceptual design, this human-oriented approach of the JSON prototype is recommended. Moreover, for machine validation, a JSON Schema can be generated from a prototype using appropriate tools.

For these reasons, we will use the JSON prototype method in the following for modeling JSON structures and for mapping entity-relationship models in JSON models.

2.5.2 Mapping Rules for Document Databases

Very similar to the mapping rules for the design of tables and the structuring of graphs, we now look at how we can map entity and relationship sets in JSON documents as objects, properties, and lists. As an illustrative example, Fig. 2.26

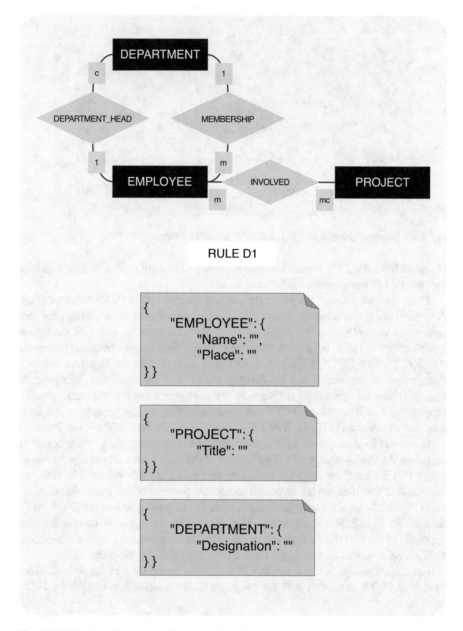

Fig. 2.26 Mapping of selected entity sets and attributes to objects and properties

gives the well-known entity-relationship model for project management (cf. Fig. 2.4).

The first mapping rule D1 is dedicated to the transformation of entity sets and attributes into objects and properties.

Rule D1 (Entity Sets and Attributes)
Selected entities are defined as objects in documents. The attributes are kept as its properties. A root element is suitable for information about the nature of the entity set: a parent object embeds the entity in a field whose only property is the entity set and whose value is the entity.

For example, in Fig. 2.26, the entity sets DEPARTMENT with attribute Designation, EMPLOYEE with attributes Name and Location, and PROJECT with attribute Title are mapped into corresponding objects with root element.

Now we consider the mapping of relationship sets to documents. Here we notice that a complete document mapping a set of facts with multiple entities and relationships implies an ordering of the entities and relationships. In the document model, the relationships are no longer symmetric, but aggregated.

Rule D2 (Aggregation)
For each symmetric set of relationships mapped in a document type, an asymmetric aggregation must be specified. It is decided which of the related entity sets will be superordinately associated in the present use case and which entity set will be subordinately associated.

These questions of aggregation need to be answered on a case-by-case basis. In the use case of the project report in Figs. 2.1 and 2.23, for the document type EMPLOYEES, it was decided to aggregate the DEPARTMENT information so that the employees can be stored as individual documents.

We propose to mark the root element, i.e. the entity set that is named first in the JSON structure of a document type, in the ER diagram with an additional frame. Furthermore, the aggregation directions for relationship sets can be marked by an additional wide frame on the child side of the relationship symbol.

As an example, we see in Fig. 2.27 that the entity set EMPLOYEE represents the root element of the document type. This is marked by the additional frame around the entity set symbol. The entity set DEPARTMENT is aggregated. This is marked on the relationship symbol with an additional wider frame on the side of the entity set that is aggregated in the JSON document.

In Fig. 2.27, the association of EMPLOYEE to DEPARTMENT is unique, so the child entity can be stored as a scalar value in an object field.

Rule D3 (Unique Child Association)
A child entity set whose association is unique (type 1 or c) is inserted as a child object in a field within the object of the parent associated entity set. The child entity set determines the name of the corresponding property.

Rule D4 (Multiple Child Association)
Any child entity set whose association is multiple (type m or mc) is inserted as a list of child objects in a field of the parent object. The child entity set determines the name of the property of this field.

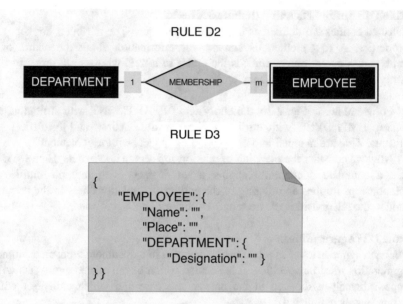

Fig. 2.27 Aggregation of a unique association as a field with a subobject

For multivalued associations, list fields are needed. As another example, we see in Fig. 2.28 that the association of EMPLOYEE to PROJECT is multiple (mc). Again, EMPLOYEE is marked root element with an extra rectangle. Also, in Fig. 2.28, INVOLVED is marked with a wider frame on the side of PROJECT to indicate that projects will be aggregated into the EMPLOYEE object in the document. However, this time, the association of EMPLOYEE to PROJECT is multiple. Employees can work on different projects with different workloads (Percentage). Therefore, in Fig. 2.28, the projects to employees are stored in a field with lists of subobjects of type PROJECTS.

The relationship attribute Percentage is stored as the property Workload in the subobject PROJECT in Fig. 2.28. Here we see that from the entity-relationship model, the attributes of relationships with composite keys (here, e.g., Percentage; cf. Fig. 2.3) can be mapped in JSON as fields of the subobjects (in this case, projects), since these take on the context of the parent objects (such as the employees in this case).

Rule D5 (Relationship Attributes)
Attributes of a relationship set whose associated entity set is aggregated can be embedded in the corresponding subobject because the subobject takes over the context of the parent object.

A document type stores a data structure with respect to a particular use case in an application. For example, this can be a view, a download, an editor, or a data interface. Different use cases may involve the same entity and relationship sets in

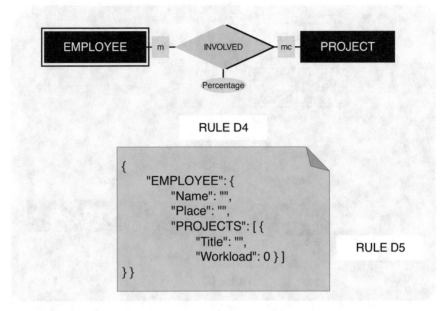

Fig. 2.28 Aggregation of an ambiguous association as a field with a list of subobjects, including relationship attributes

different perspectives. Because of the denormalized, application-oriented data storage in document databases, there is no one-to-one correspondence of entity and relationship sets to document types.

Rule D6 (Document Types)
For each document type, the selection of entity sets and attributes must be decided according to rule D1 and aggregation according to rule D2. Document types are determined by the application and are used for the performant storage and representation of a complete set of facts for a specific use case.

This means that one and the same entity can be subordinate at one time and superordinate at another time in different document types. For example, for project management data model in Fig. 2.1, there are two use cases:

First, the employee data is entered in an input mask according to the structure in Fig. 2.23 on the level of individual employees. For this write access, it is more efficient to store individual employee records as independent documents.

Second, all employees are reported per department with project workloads including calculated financial expenditure in one application view. For this read access, the transmission of a single document per department is more economical. Therefore, for the sake of performance, a deliberate redundancy can be inserted by serving both use cases with different document structures that use the same entity and relationship sets. Therefore, in Fig. 2.29, another document type has been

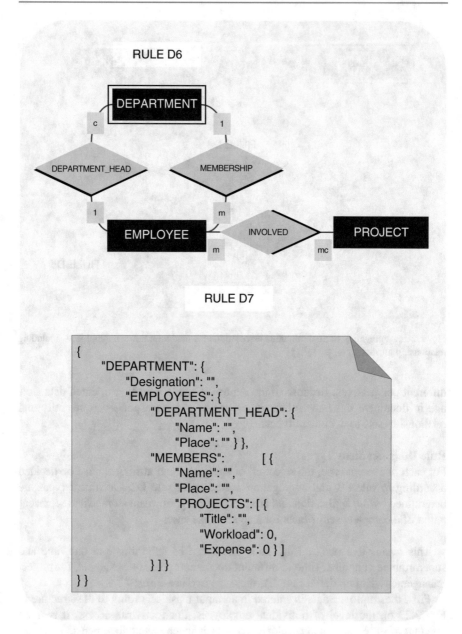

Fig. 2.29 Document type DEPARTMENT with aggregation of the same entity set EMPLOYEE in two different associations DEPARTMENT_HEAD and MEMBERS

defined for this purpose. This time, DEPARTMENT is the root entity, and employees are aggregated. Now, a second, unique association of department to employee has been added: the department head. Thus, a field named EMPLOYEE would not be unique. This has been solved here by adding another structural level under EMPLOYEES with two properties named after the DEPARTMENT_HEAD and MEMBERSHIP relationship sets.

Rule D7 (Relationship Sets)
If property names for aggregations according to rules D3–D4 are not unique because they concern the same entity set, they can each be disambiguated by another subordinate object field with the name of the corresponding relationship set.

Further, we see the new property Expense in subobjects of type PROJECTS. In the use case, this is a calculated field. Document databases often store application-oriented aggregated data rather than normalized granular data to optimize performance for Big Data.

2.6   Formula for Database Design

This section condenses our knowledge of data modeling into a formulaic action plan. The design steps can be characterized as follows: First, during the requirements analysis, the relevant information facts must be recorded in writing in a catalog. In the further design steps, this list can be supplemented and refined in consultation with the future users, since the design procedure is an iterative process. In the second step, the entity and relationship sets are determined as well as their identification keys and feature categories.

Then, generalization hierarchies and aggregation structures[6] can be examined in the third step. In the fourth step, the entity-relationship model is aligned with the existing application portfolio so that the further development of the information systems can be coordinated and driven forward in line with the longer-term corporate goals. In addition, this step serves to avoid legacy systems as far as possible and to preserve the enterprise value with regard to the data architecture.

The fifth step maps the entity-relationship model to an SQL and/or NoSQL database. In this process, the explained mapping rules for entity sets and relationship sets are used (cf. corresponding mapping rules for the relational, graph, and document models, respectively). In the sixth step, the integrity and privacy rules are defined. In the seventh step, the database design is checked for completeness by

---

[6]Two important abstraction principles in data modeling are aggregation and generalization. Under the title "Database Abstractions: Aggregation and Generalization," the two database specialists J.M. Smith and D.C.P Smith already pointed this out in 1977 in Transactions on Database Systems. Aggregation means the combination of entity sets to a whole; generalization means the generalization of entity sets to a superordinate entity set.

Steps in database design	Preliminary study	Rough concept	Detailed concept
1. Data analysis	✔	✔	✔
2. Entity and relationship sets	✔	✔	✔
3. Generalization and aggregation	✔	✔	✔
4. Alignment with the enterprise-wide data architecture	✔	✔	✔
5. Mapping of the entity-relationship model onto SQL and/or NoSQL databases		✔	✔
6. Definition of integrity constraints		✔	✔
7. Verification based on use cases		✔	✔
8. Determination of access paths			✔
9. Physical data structure			✔
10. Distribution and replication			✔

Fig. 2.30 From rough to detailed in ten design steps

developing important use cases (cf. Unified Modeling Language[7]) and prototyping them with descriptive query languages.

The determination of an actual quantity structure as well as the definition of the physical data structure takes place in the eighth step. This is followed by the physical distribution of the data sets and the selection of possible replication options in the ninth step. When using NoSQL databases, it must be weighed up here, among other things, whether or not availability and failure tolerance should be given preference over strict consistency (cf. CAP theorem in Sect. 4.5.1). Finally, performance testing and optimization of data and access structures must be performed in the tenth step to guarantee users from different stakeholder groups reasonable response times for their application processes or data searches.

The recipe shown in Fig. 2.30 is essentially limited to the data aspects. In addition to data, functions naturally play a major role in the design of information systems. Thus, CASE tools (CASE = computer-aided software engineering) have emerged in recent years to support not only database design but also function design.

---

[7]The Unified Modeling Language or UML is an ISO-standardized modeling language for the specification, construction, and documentation of software. An entity-relationship model can be easily transformed into a class diagram and vice versa.

Bibliography

Atkinson, M., Bancilhon, F., DeWitt, D., Dittrich, K., Maier, D., Zdonik, S.: The object-oriented database system manifesto. In: Deductive and Object-Oriented Databases. North-Holland, Amsterdam (1990)

Bray, T.: The JavaScript Object Notation (JSON) Data Interchange Format. Internet Engineering Task Force, Request for Comments RFC 8259 (2017)

Chen, P.P.-S.: The entity-relationship model – Towards a unified view of data. ACM Trans. Database Syst. 1(1), 9–36 (1976)

Codd, E.F.: A relational model of data for large shared data banks. Commun. ACM. 13(6), 377–387 (1970)

Dutka, A.F., Hanson, H.H.: Fundamentals of Data Normalization. Addison-Wesley (1989)

Kemper, A., Eikler, A.: Datenbanksysteme – Eine Einführung. DeGruyter (2015)

Knauer, U.: Algebraic Graph Theory – Morphisms, Monoids and Matrices. De Gruyter, Berlin (2019)

Marcus, D.A.: Graph Theory – A Problem Oriented Approach. The Mathematical Association of America (2008)

Pezoa, F., Reutter, J.L., Suarez, F., Ugarte, M., Vrgoč, D.: Foundations of JSON Schema. In: Proceedings of the 25th International Conference on World Wide Web, Republic and Canton of Geneva, pp. 263–273 (2016)

Smith, J.M., Smith, D.C.P.: Database abstractions: aggregation and generalization. ACM Trans. Database Syst. 2(2), 105–133 (1977)

Database Languages

3

3.1   Interacting with Databases

In the previous chapter, we have seen how to model databases. To operate the database, different stakeholders interact with it, as shown in Fig. 3.1.

Data architects define the database schema. They design an architecture to run the database system and embed it into the existing landscape with all necessary components. They also describe and document the data and structures. It makes sense for them to be supported by a data dictionary system (see "Glossary").

Database specialists, often called database administrators, install the database server. For schema-oriented database systems (e.g., relational), they create the database schema. For schema-free databases (e.g., document model), this step is not necessary, because the schema is created implicitly by inserting appropriate database objects. Based on this, large amounts of data can be imported into the database. To do this, there are extract-transform-load (ETL) tools or powerful import functionalities of the database software. To protect the data, administrators define users, roles, and access rights and ensure regular backup of the database. For large amounts of data, they ensure the performance and efficiency of the database system by, for example, creating indexes, optimizing queries syntactically, or distributing the database server across multiple computers.

Application programmers develop applications that allow users to insert, modify, and delete data in the database. They also implement interfaces through which data can be automatically exchanged with other databases.

Data analysts, who are also called data scientists if they are very highly specialized, analyze databases in order to support data-based decisions. To do this, they query data, evaluate it using statistical and/or soft computing-based methods (see, e.g., fuzzy databases in Chap. 6), and visualize the results.

To successfully operate a database, a database language is necessary that can cover the different requirements of the users. Query and manipulation languages for databases have the advantage that one and the same language can be used to create databases, assign user rights, or modify and evaluate data. In addition, a descriptive

M. Kaufmann, A. Meier, *SQL and NoSQL Databases*,
https://doi.org/10.1007/978-3-031-27908-9_3

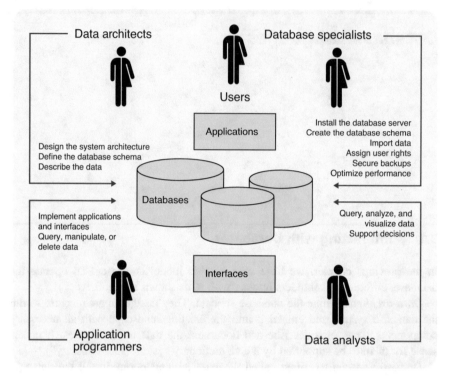

Fig. 3.1 Interaction with a database

language allows precise, reproducible interaction with the database without having to program routines and procedures. Therefore, we will look at different database languages in the following.

3.2   Relational Algebra

3.2.1   Overview of Operators

We start with a theoretical model for database languages. *The relational algebra* provides a *formal framework for database query languages*. It defines a number of algebraic operators that always apply to relations. Although most modern database languages do not use those operators directly, they provide analogous functionalities. However, they are only considered relationally complete languages in terms of the relational model if the original potential of relational algebra is retained.

Below, we will give an overview of the operators used in relational algebra, divided into set operators and relational operators, on two sample relations R and S. Operators work on either one or two tables and always output a new relation. This

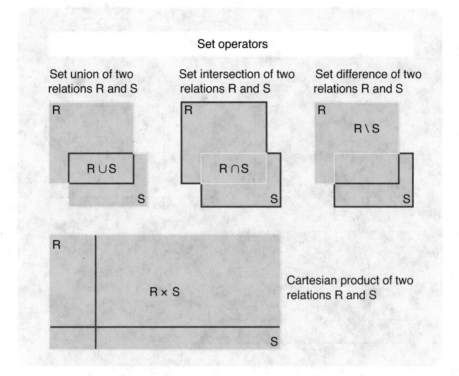

Fig. 3.2 Set union, set intersection, set difference, and Cartesian product of relations

consistency (algebraic property) allows for the combination of multiple operators and their effects on relations.

Set operators match the known set operations (see Fig. 3.2 and Sect. 3.2.2 below). This group consists of set union with the symbol ∪, set intersection ∩, set difference \, and Cartesian product ×. Two relations R and S that are union-compatible can be combined (R∪S), intersected (R∩S), or subtracted (R\S). The Cartesian product of two relations R and S (R×S) can be defined without conditions. These set operations result in a new set of tuples, i.e., a new relation.

The *relation operators* shown in Fig. 3.3 were defined by Ted Codd specifically for relations and are discussed in detail in Sect. 3.2.3. The project operator, represented by Greek letter π (pi), can be used to reduce relations to subsets. For instance, the expression $\pi_A(R)$ forms a subset of the relation R based on a set A of attributes. An expression $\sigma_F(R)$ with the select operator σ (Greek letter sigma) takes a range of tuples from the relation R based on a selection criterion or formula F. The join operator, symbol |×|, conjoins two relations into a new one. For instance, the two relations R and S can be combined by an operation $R|×|_P S$ with P specifying the applicable join condition or join predicate. Lastly, a divide operation R÷S, with the divide operator represented by the symbol ÷, calculates a new table by dividing the relation R by the relation S.

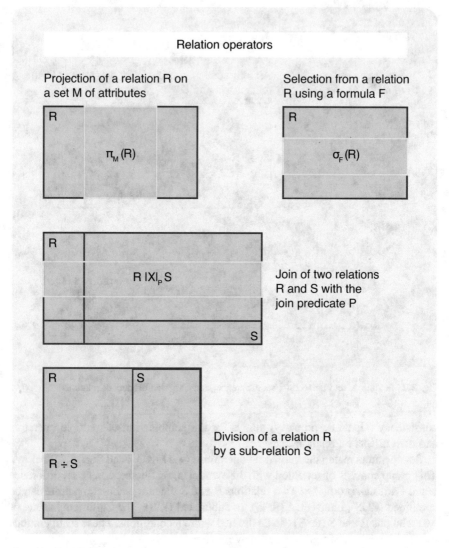

Fig. 3.3 Projection, selection, join, and division of relations

The following two sections provide a more detailed explanation of set and relation operators of relational algebra with illustrative examples.

3.2.2   Set Operators

Since every relation is a set of records (tuples), multiple relations can be correlated using set theory. However, it is only possible to form a set union, set intersection, or set difference of two relations if they are union-compatible.

Union Compatibility

Two relations are *union-compatible* if they meet both of the following criteria: Both relations have the same number of attributes and the data formats of the corresponding attribute categories are identical.

Figure 3.4 shows an example: For each of two company clubs, a table has been defined from an employee file, containing employee numbers, last names, and street names. The two tables SPORTS_CLUB and PHOTO_CLUB are union-compatible: They have the same number of attributes, with values from the same employee file and therefore defined from the same range.

In general, two union-compatible relations R and S are combined by a *set union* R∪S where *all entries from R and all entries from S are entered into the resulting table*. Identical records are automatically unified, since a distinction between tuples with identical attribute values in the resulting set R∪S is not possible.

The CLUB_MEMBERS table (Fig. 3.5) is a set union of the tables SPORTS_CLUB and PHOTO_CLUB. Each result tuple exists in the SPORTS_CLUB table, the PHOTO_CLUB table, or both of them. Club member Howard is only listed once in the result table, since duplicate results are not permitted in the unified set.

The other set operators are defined similarly: The *set intersection* R∩S of two union-compatible relations R and S holds only those entries found in both R and S. In our table excerpt, only employee Howard is an active member of both the SPORTS_CLUB and the PHOTO club.

The resulting set SPORTS_CLUB∩PHOTO_CLUB is a singleton, since exactly one person has both memberships.

SPORTS_CLUB

E#	Name	Street	City
E1	Murphy	Murray Road	Kent
E7	Howard	Lorain Ave.	Cleveland
E19	Stewart	E Main St.	Stow

PHOTO_CLUB

E#	Name	Street	City
E4	Bell	S Water St.	Kent
E7	Howard	Lorain Ave.	Cleveland

Fig. 3.4 Union-compatible tables SPORTS_CLUB and PHOTO_CLUB

CLUB_MEMBERS = SPORTS_CLUB ∪ PHOTO_CLUB

E#	Name	Street	City
E1	Murphy	Murray Road	Kent
E7	Howard	Lorain Ave.	Cleveland
E19	Stewart	E Main St.	Stow
E4	Bell	S Water St.	Kent

Fig. 3.5   Set union of the two tables SPORTS_CLUB and PHOTO_CLUB

Union-compatible relations can also be subtracted from each other: The *set difference* R\S is calculated by removing all entries from R that also exist in S. In our example, a subtraction SPORTS_CLUB\PHOTO_CLUB would result in a relation containing only the members Murphy and Stewart. Howard would be eliminated, since he is also a member of the PHOTO_CLUB. The set difference operator therefore allows us to find all members of the sport club that are not also part of the photo club.

The basic relationship between the set intersection operator and the set difference operator can be expressed as a formula:

$$R \cap S = R \backslash (R \backslash S).$$

The determination of set intersections is therefore based on the calculation of set differences as can be seen in our example with the sports and photography club members.

The last remaining set operator is the Cartesian product of two arbitrary relations R and S that do not have to be union-compatible. The Cartesian product R×S of two relations R and S is the set of all possible combinations of tuples from R with tuples from S.

To illustrate this, Fig. 3.6 shows a table COMPETITION containing a combination of members of (SPORTS_CLUB \ PHOTO_CLUB) × PHOTO_CLUB, i.e., all possible combinations of sports club members (that are not also members of the photo club) and photo club members. It shows a typical competition constellation for the two clubs. Of course, Howard as a member of both clubs cannot compete against himself and enters on the photography club side due to the set difference SPORTS_CLUB \ PHOTO_CLUB.

This operation is called a Cartesian product because all respective entries of the original tables are multiplied with those of the other. For two arbitrary relations R and S with m and n entries, respectively, the Cartesian product R×S has m times n tuples.

COMPETITION = (SPORTS_CLUB\ PHOTO_CLUB)×PHOTO_CLUB

E#	Name	Street	City	E#	Name	Street	City
E1	Murphy	Murray Road	Kent	E4	Bell	S Water Street	Kent
E1	Murphy	Murray Road	Kent	E7	Howard	Lorain Avenue	Cleveland
E19	Stewart	E Main Street	Stow	E4	Bell	S Water Street	Kent
E19	Stewart	E Main Street	Stow	E7	Howard	Lorain Avenue	Cleveland

Fig. 3.6 COMPETITION relation as an example of Cartesian products

3.2.3 Relation Operators

The relation-based operators complement the set operators. A projection $\pi_a(R)$ with the project operator π forms a subrelation of the relation R based on the attribute names defined by a. For instance, given a relation R with the attributes (A,B,C,D), the expression $\pi_{A,C}(R)$ reduces R to the attributes A and C. The attribute names in a projection do not have to be in order; e.g., $R' := \pi_{C,A}(R)$ means a projection of R = (A,B,C,D) onto $R' = (C,A)$.

The first example in Fig. 3.7, $\pi_{City}(EMPLOYEE)$, lists all places of residence from the EMPLOYEE table in a single-column table without any repetitions. The second example, $\pi_{Sub,Name}(EMPLOYEE)$, results in a subtable with all department numbers and names of the respective employees.

The select operator σ in an expression $\sigma_F(R)$ extracts a *selection of tuples from the relation R based on the formula F*. F consists of a number of attribute names and/or value constants connected by comparison operators, such as $<$, $>$, or $=$, or by logical operators, e.g., AND, OR, or NOT. $\sigma_F(R)$ therefore includes all tuples from R that meet the selection condition F.

This is illustrated by the examples for selection of tuples from the EMPLOYEE table in Fig. 3.8: In the first example, all employees meeting the condition City=Kent, i.e., living in Kent, are selected. The second example with the condition "Sub=D6" picks out only those employees working in department D6. The third and last example combines the two previous selection conditions with a logical connective, using the formula "City=Kent AND Sub=D6." This results in a singleton relation, since only employee Bell lives in Kent and works in department D6.

Of course, the operators of relational algebra as described above can also be combined with each other. For instance, if we first do a selection for employees of department D6 by $\sigma_{Sub=D6}(EMPLOYEE)$ and then project on the City attribute using the operator $\pi_{City}(\sigma_{Sub=D6}(EMPLOYEE))$, we get a result table with the two towns of Stow and Kent.

EMPLOYEE

E#	Name	Street	City	Sub
E19	Stewart	E Main Street	Stow	D6
E1	Murphy	Murray Road	Kent	D3
E7	Howard	Lorain Avenue	Cleveland	D5
E4	Bell	S Water Street	Kent	D6

π_{City} (EMPLOYEE)

City
Stow
Kent
Cleveland

$\pi_{Sub,Name}$ (EMPLOYEE)

Sub	Name
D6	Stewart
D3	Murphy
D5	Howard
D6	Bell

Fig. 3.7 Sample projection on EMPLOYEE

Next is the *join operator*, which merges two relations into a single one. The join $R|\times|_P S$ of the two relations R and S by the predicate P is a *combination of all tuples from R with all tuples from S where each meets the join predicate P* the join operator combines a Cartesian product with a selection over predicate P, hence the symbol. The join predicate contains one attribute from R and one from S. Those two attributes are correlated by a comparison operator ($<$, $>$, or $=$) so that the relations R and S can be combined. If the join predicate P uses the relational operator $=$, the result is called an *equi-join*.

The join operator often causes misunderstandings which may lead to wrong or unwanted results. This is mostly due to the predicate for the combination of the two tables being left out or ill-defined.

For example, Fig. 3.9 shows two join operations with and without a defined join predicate. By specifying EMPLOYEE $|\times|_{Sub=D\#}$DEPARTMENT, we join the EMPLOYEE and DEPARTMENT tables by expanding the employee information with their respective departments.

Should we forget to define a join predicate in the example from Fig. 3.9 and simply specify EMPLOYEE $\times$ DEPARTMENT, we get the Cartesian product of the two tables EMPLOYEE and DEPARTMENT. This is a rather meaningless combination of the two tables, since all employees are juxtaposed with all departments, resulting in combinations of employees with departments they are not actually part of (see also the COMPETITION table in Fig. 3.6).

$\sigma_{City=Kent}$ (EMPLOYEE)

E#	Name	Street	City	Sub
E1	Murphy	Murray Road	Kent	D3
E4	Bell	S Water Street	Kent	D6

$\sigma_{Sub=D6}$ (EMPLOYEE)

E#	Name	Street	City	Sub
E19	Stewart	E Main Street	Stow	D6
E4	Bell	S Water Street	Kent	D6

$\sigma_{City=Kent\ AND\ Sub=D6}$ (EMPLOYEE)

E#	Name	Street	City	Sub
E4	Bell	S Water Street	Kent	D6

Fig. 3.8 Examples for selection operations

As shown by the examples in Fig. 3.9, the join operator |×| with the join predicate P is merely a limited Cartesian product.

In fact, a join of two tables R and S without a defined join predicate P expresses the Cartesian product of the R and S tables, i.e., for an empty predicate P={}

$$R \ |\times|_{P=\{\}} \ S = R \times S.$$

Using a join predicate as the selection condition in a select operation yields

$$R \ |\times|_{P} \ S = \sigma_{P} \ (R \times S).$$

This general formula demonstrates that each join can be expressed using first a Cartesian product and second a selection.

Referring to the example from Fig. 3.9, we can calculate the intended join EMPLOYEE $|\times|_{Sub=D\#}$ DEPARTMENT with the following two steps: First we generate the Cartesian product of the two tables EMPLOYEE and DEPARTMENT. Then all entries of the preliminary result table meeting the join predicate Sub=D# are determined using the selection $\sigma_{Sub=D\#}$(EMPLOYEE × DEPARTMENT). This gives us the same tuples as calculating the join EMPLOYEE $|\times|_{Sub=D\#}$ DEPART-MENT directly (see the tuples marked in yellow in Fig. 3.9).

EMPLOYEE

E#	Name	Street	City	Sub
E19	Stewart	E Main St.	Stow	D6
E1	Murphy	Murray Road	Kent	D3
E7	Howard	Lorain Ave.	Cleveland	D5
E4	Bell	S Water St.	Kent	D6

DEPARTMENT

D#	DepartmentName
D3	IT
D5	HR
D6	Accounting

EMPLOYEE |×|$_{Sub=D\#}$ DEPARTMENT

E#	Name	Street	City	Sub	D#	DepartmentName
E19	Stewart	E Main St.	Stow	D6	D6	Accounting
E1	Murphy	Murray Road	Kent	D3	D3	IT
E7	Howard	Lorain Ave.	Cleveland	D5	D5	HR
E4	Bell	S Water St.	Kent	D6	D6	Accounting

EMPLOYEE × DEPARTMENT

E#	Name	Street	City	Sub	D#	DepartmentName
E19	Stewart	E Main St.	Stow	D6	D3	IT
E19	Stewart	E Main St.	Stow	D6	D5	HR
E19	Stewart	E Main St.	Stow	D6	D6	Accounting
E1	Murphy	Murray Road	Kent	D3	D3	IT
E1	Murphy	Murray Road	Kent	D3	D5	HR
E1	Murphy	Murray Road	Kent	D3	D6	Accounting
E7	Howard	Lorain Ave.	Cleveland	D5	D3	IT
E7	Howard	Lorain Ave.	Cleveland	D5	D5	HR
E7	Howard	Lorain Ave.	Cleveland	D5	D6	Accounting
E4	Bell	S Water St.	Kent	D6	D3	IT
E4	Bell	S Water St.	Kent	D6	D5	HR
E4	Bell	S Water St.	Kent	D6	D6	Accounting

Fig. 3.9 Join of two relations with and without a join predicate

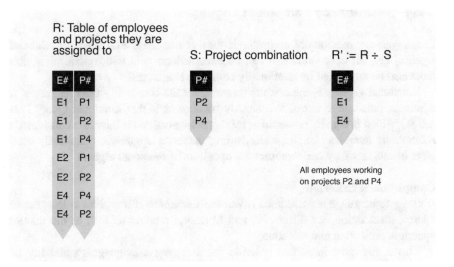

Fig. 3.10   Example of a divide operation

A *division* of the relation R by the relation S is only possible if S is contained within R as a subrelation. The divide operator R÷S calculates a subrelation R′ from R, which has the property that *all possible combinations* of the tuples r′ from R′ with the tuples s from S are part of the relation R, i.e., the Cartesian product R′×S must be contained within R.

Table R in Fig. 3.10 shows which employees work on which projects. Assuming we want to determine who works on all projects from S, i.e., projects P2 and P4, we first define the table S with the project numbers P2 and P4. S is obviously contained in R, so we can calculate the division R′ := R÷S. The result of this division is the table R′ with the two employees E1 and E4. A quick check shows that E1 and E4 do indeed work on both P2 and P4, since the table R contains the tuples (E1,P2), (E1, P4), (E4,P2), and (E4,P4).

A divide operation can also be expressed through project and set difference operators and a Cartesian product, which makes the divide operator the third substitutable operator in relational algebra besides the set intersection and the join operator.

In summary, set union, set difference, Cartesian product, projection, and selection make up the minimal set of operators that renders relational algebra fully functional: Set intersection, join, and division can all be expressed using those five operators of relational algebra, although sometimes circuitously.

The operators of relational algebra not only are theoretically significant but also have a firm place in practical application. They are used in the language interfaces of relational database systems for the purpose of optimization (see Sect. 5.3.2) as well as in the construction of database computers: The operators of relational algebra and their derivatives do not have to be realized in software—they can be implemented directly in hardware components.

3.2.4   Relationally Complete Languages

Languages are relationally complete if they are at least equivalent to relational algebra, i.e., all operations that can be executed on data with relational algebra must also be supported by relationally complete languages.

Relational algebra is the orientation point for the commonly used languages of relational database systems. We already mentioned SQL (Structured Query Language), which is equally powerful as relational algebra and is therefore considered a *relationally complete language*. Regarding database languages, relationally complete means that they can represent the operators of relational algebra.

Completeness Criterion
A database language is considered *relationally complete* if it enables at least the set operators set union, set difference, and Cartesian product as well as the relation operators projection and selection.

This is the most important criterion for assessing a language's suitability for relational contexts. Not every language working with tables is relationally complete. If it is not possible to combine multiple tables via their shared attributes, the language is not equivalent to relational algebra and can therefore not be considered relationally complete.

Relational algebra is the foundation for the query part of relational database languages. Of course, it is also necessary to be able to not only analyze but also manipulate tables or individual parts. Manipulation operations include, among others, insertion, deletion, or changes to tuple sets. Database languages therefore need the following functions in order to be practically useful:

- It has to be possible to define tables and attributes.
- Insert, change, and delete operations must be possible.
- Aggregate functions such as addition, maximum and minimum determination, or average calculation should be included.
- Formatting and displaying tables by various criteria must be possible, e.g., including sorting orders and control breaks for table visualization.
- Languages for databases must include elements for assigning user permissions and for protecting the databases (see Sect. 4.2).
- Arithmetic expressions and calculations should preferably be supported.
- Multi-user access should be supported (transaction principle; see Sects. 4.4 and 4.5), and commands for data security should be included.

The definition of relational algebra has given us the formal framework for relational database languages. However, this formal language is not per se used in practice; rather, it has been a long-standing approach to try and make *relational database languages as user-friendly as possible*. Since the algebraic operators in their pure form are beyond most database users, they are represented by more accessible language elements. The following sections will give examples from SQL in order to illustrate this.

3.3   Relational Language SQL

In the 1970s, the language SEQUEL (Structured English QUEry Language) was created for IBM's System R, one of the first working relational database systems. The concept behind SEQUEL was to create a relationally complete query language based on *English words*, such as "select," "from," "where," "count," "group by," etc., rather than mathematical symbols. A derivative of that language named SQL (Structured Query Language) was later standardized first by ANSI and then internationally by ISO. For years, SQL has been the leading language for database queries and interactions.

A tutorial for SQL can be found on the website accompanying this book, www. sql-nosql.org. The short introduction given here covers only a small part of the existing standards; modern SQL offers many extensions, e.g., for programming, security, object orientation, and analysis.

Before we can query data, we must be able to enter data into the database. Therefore, we will first start with how to create a database schema starting from the table structure and fill it with data.

3.3.1   Creating and Populating the Database Schema

SQL provides the CREATE TABLE command for defining a new table. The EMPLOYEE table would be specified as follows. The first column, which consists of six characters, is called *E#* and cannot be empty; The second column called Name can contain up to 20 characters, and so on.[1]

```
CREATE TABLE      EMPLOYEE
( E#    CHAR(6) NOT NULL,
Name    VARCHAR(20),
...)
```

---

[1]The column name *E#* without double quotes is used here for illustrative purposes. In standard SQL, unquoted object names may contain only letters (A–Z and a–z), numbers (0–9), and the underscore character. Thus, a column name such as *E#* is not a legal name unless you enclose it in double quotes (called a quoted identifier in the SQL standard), but if you do that, you have to reference it as "*E#*" everywhere it is referenced. The names can also be modified to something like E_ID if readers would like to run the examples throughout the book.

The SQL language allows to define characteristics and tables (data definition language or DDL). The SQL standard specifies different formats as data types:

- CHARACTER(n) or CHAR(n) means a sequence of letters of fixed length.
- CHARACTER VARYING or VARCHAR allows the specification of letter sequences of any length.
- Numeric data is specified with the data types NUMERIC or DECIMAL, where size and precision must be specified.
- Integers can be specified by INTEGER or SMALLINT.
- The data type DATE gives dates by YEAR, MONTH, and DAY. Different formats are used, e.g., (yyyy,mm,dd) for year, month, and day (see Sect. 6.3 about temporal databases).
- The TIME data type returns time information in HOUR, MINUTE, and SECOND.
- The TIMESTAMP data type is a combination of the DATE and TIME types. Additionally, the precision of the time and the time zone can be specified.
- There are also other data types for bit strings (BIT or BIT VARYING) and for large objects (CHARACTER LARGE OBJECT or BINARY LARGE OBJECT).
- In addition, the integration of complex objects with XML (eXtensible Markup Language) and JSON (JavaScript Object Notation) is supported.

The opposite command, DROP TABLE, is used to delete table definitions. It is important to note that this command also eliminates all table contents and assigned user permissions (see Sect. 4.2).

Once a table is defined, the following command can be used to insert new tuples:

```
INSERT INTO EMPLOYEE VALUES
('E20', 'Mahoney', 'Market Ave S', 'Canton', 'D6'),
('E21', 'Baker', O Street', Lincoln, 'D5');
```

In practice, the INSERT command of SQL is rather suitable for modest data volumes. For larger data volumes (cf. big data), SQL database systems often offer special NoSQL language extensions that support efficient loading of large data volumes (so-called bulk loads).[2] In addition, extract-transform-load (ETL) tools and application programming interfaces (API) exist for this purpose.

Existing tables can be manipulated using UPDATE statements:

---

[2]Examples are the LOAD command in MySQL and the COPY command in PostgreSQL.

```
UPDATE  EMPLOYEE
SET     City = 'Cleveland'
WHERE   City = 'Cuyahoga Heights'
```

This example replaces the value Cuyahoga Heights for the City attribute with the new name Cleveland in all matching tuples of the EMPLOYEE table. The UPDATE manipulation operation is set-based and can edit a multi-element set of tuples.

The content of entire tables or parts of tables can be removed with the help of DELETE statements:

```
DELETE FROM EMPLOYEE
WHERE City = 'Cleveland'
```

DELETE statements usually affect sets of tuples if the selection predicate applies to multiple entries in the table. Where referential integrity is concerned, deletions can also impact dependent tables.

3.3.2   Relational Operators

As described in Sect. 1.2.2, the basic structure of SQL looks like this:

```
SELECT  selected attributes       (Output)
FROM    tables to be searched     (Input)
WHERE   selection condition       (Processing)
```

In the following, we will look at the individual relational operators and their implementation in SQL.

Projection

The SELECT clause corresponds to the project operator of relational algebra, in that it defines a list of attributes. In SQL, the equivalent of the project operator $\pi_{Sub, Name}(EMPLOYEE)$ as shown in Fig. 3.7 is simply

```
SELECT Sub, Name
FROM   EMPLOYEE
```

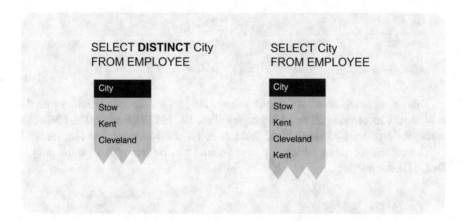

Fig. 3.11   Projection with and without elimination of duplicates

If a list of places of residence according the EMPLOYEE table is to be compiled, the following instruction will suffice:

```
SELECT  Place
FROM    EMPLOYEE;
```

The result table is a single-column table with the localities Stow, Kent, Cleveland, and Kent, as shown in Fig. 3.11 to the right.

Correctly, it must be added here that the result table of query is not a relation at all in the sense of the relation model, since every relation is a set by definition and hence does not allow duplicates. Since SQL, unlike relation algebra, does not eliminate duplicates, the word DISTINCT must be added to the SELECT clause (cf. Fig. 3.11).

Cartesian Product
The FROM clause lists all tables to be used. For instance, the Cartesian product of EMPLOYEE and DEPARTMENT is expressed in SQL as

```
SELECT  E#, Name, Street, City, Sub, D#, Department_Name
FROM    EMPLOYEE, DEPARTMENT
```

This command generates the cross-product table from Fig. 3.9, similar to the equivalent operators

$$\text{EMPLOYEE}| \times |_{P=\{\}}\text{DEPARTMENT}$$

and

$$\text{EMPLOYEE} \times \text{DEPARTMENT}.$$

Join

By setting the join predicate "Sub=$D\#$" in the WHERE clause, we get the equi-join of the EMPLOYEE and DEPARTMENT tables in SQL notation:

```
SELECT E#,Name,Street,City,Sub,D#,Department_Name
FROM    EMPLOYEE, DEPARTMENT
WHERE   Sub=D#
```

An alternative way of expressing this is the following:

```
SELECT *
FROM    EMPLOYEE,
JOIN    DEPARTMENT
ON      Sub=D#
```

An asterisk (*) in the SELECT clause means that all attributes in the table are selected, i.e., the result table contains all the attributes $E\#$, Name, Street, City, and Sub (Subordinate).

Selection

Qualified selections can be expressed by separate statements in the WHERE clause being connected by the logical operators AND or OR. The SQL command for the selection of employees $\sigma_{City=Kent\ AND\ Sub=D6}(\text{EMPLOYEE})$ as shown in Fig. 3.8 would be

```
SELECT *
FROM    EMPLOYEE
WHERE   City='Kent' AND Sub='D6'
```

The WHERE clause contains the desired selection predicate. Executing the above query would therefore give us all information of the employee Bell from Kent working in department D6.

Union

The set-oriented operators of the relation algebra find their equivalent in the SQL standard. For example, if one wants to unite the union-compatible tables SPORTCLUB with FOTOCLUB, this is done in SQL with the keyword UNION:

```
SELECT *
FROM SPORTCLUB
    UNION
SELECT *
FROM FOTOCLUB;
```

Since the two tables are union-compatible, the results table contains all sports and photo club members, eliminating duplicates.

Difference

If you want to find out all sport club members who are not in the photo club at the same time, the query is done with the difference operator EXCEPT:

```
SELECT *
FROM SPORTCLUB
    EXCEPT
SELECT *
FROM PHOTOCLUB;
```

Intersection

For union-compatible tables, intersections can be formed. If you are interested in members who participate in both the sports club and the photo club, the INTER-SECT keyword comes into play:

```
SELECT *
FROM SPORTCLUB
    INTERSECT
SELECT *
FROM FOTOCLUB;
```

3.3.3   Built-In Functions

In addition to the common operators of relational algebra, SQL also contains *built-in functions* that can be used in the SELECT clause.

Aggregate Functions

These include the aggregate functions which calculate a scalar value based on a set, namely, COUNT for counting, SUM for totaling, AVG for calculating the average, MAX for determining the maximum, and MIN for finding the minimum value.

For example, all employees working in department D6 can be counted. In SQL, this request is as follows:

```
SELECT COUNT (M#)
FROM EMPLOYEE
WHERE Sub='D6'
```

The result is a one-element table with a single value 2, which according to the table excerpt in Fig. 3.7 stands for the two persons Stewart and Bell.

Grouping

The results of aggregations can also be grouped by values of variables. For example, all employees working in each department can be counted. In SQL, this prompt is as follows:

```
SELECT Sub, COUNT (E#)
FROM EMPLOYEES
GROUP BY Sub
ORDER BY COUNT(E#)DESC
```

The result is a table with one row per department number together with the corresponding number of employees.[3] With the last line of the statement, the result is sorted by the number of employees in descending order.

Nested Queries

It is allowed and sometimes necessary to formulate another SQL call within an SQL statement. In this context, one speaks of nested queries. Such queries are useful, for example, when searching for the employee with the highest salary:

---

[3] COUNT(*) can also be used, the difference being COUNT(*) counts all rows that pass any filters while COUNT(column_name) only counts rows where the column name specified is not NULL, cf. Sect. 3.3.4.

```
SELECT M#, Name
FROM EMPLOYEE
WHERE Salary >= ALL (SELECT Salary
                     FROM EMPLOYEE);
```

This statement contains another SQL statement within the WHERE clause to select the salaries of all employees. This is called an inner SQL expression or subquery. In the outer SQL statement, the PERSONNEL table is consulted again to get the employee with *M#* and name who earns the highest salary. The keyword ALL means that the condition must be valid for all results of the subquery.

The existence quantifier of the propositional logic is expressed in the SQL standard by the keyword EXISTS. This keyword is set to "true" in an SQL evaluation if the subsequent subquery selects at least one element or row.

As an example of a query with an EXISTS keyword, we can refer to the project affiliation INVOLVED, which shows which employees work on which projects. If we are interested in the employees who are not doing project work, the SQL statement is as follows:

```
SELECT M#, Name, Street, City
FROM EMPLOYEES e
WHERE NOT EXISTS (SELECT *
                  FROM INVOLVED i
                  WHERE e.E# = i.E#);
```

In the outer statement, the names and addresses of the employees who do not belong to a project are selected from the table EMPLOYEES. For this purpose, a subquery is formulated to get all employees' project affiliations (relations). In the exclusion procedure (NOT EXISTS), we obtain the desired employees who do not perform project work.

In this query, we can see once again how useful substitute names (aliases) are when formulating SQL statements.

3.3.4   Null values

The work with databases regularly entails situations where individual data values for tables are not (yet) known. For instance, it may be necessary to enter a new employee in the EMPLOYEE table before their full address is available. In such cases, instead of entering meaningless or maybe even wrong filler values, it is advisable to use null values as placeholders.

A null value represents an as yet unknown data value within a table column.

Null values, illustrated in Fig. 3.12 as "?", must not be confused with the number 0 (zero) or the value ""(space). These two values express specific situations in

EMPLOYEE

E#	Name	Street	City	Sub
E19	Stewart	E Main Street	Stow	D6
E1	Murphy	?	?	D3
E7	Howard	Lorain Avenue	Cleveland	D5
E4	Bell	?	?	D6

```
SELECT   *
FROM      EMPLOYEE
WHERE    City = 'Kent'
     UNION
SELECT   *
FROM      EMPLOYEE
WHERE    NOT City = 'Kent'
```

RESULTS_TABLE

E#	Name	Street	City	Sub
E19	Stewart	E Main Street	Stow	D6
E7	Howard	Lorain Avenue	Cleveland	D5

Fig. 3.12 Unexpected results from working with null values

relational databases, while the keyword NULL is a placeholder (with meaning unknown).

Figure 3.12 shows the EMPLOYEE table with null values for the attributes Street and City. Of course, not all attribute categories may contain null values; otherwise, conflicts are unavoidable. Primary keys must not contain null values by definition; in our example, that applies to the employee number $E\#$. For the foreign key "Sub," the database architect can make that decision at their discretion and based on their practical experiences.

Working with null values can be somewhat problematic, since they form a new logic state UNKNOWN (?) in addition to TRUE (1) and FALSE (0). We therefore have to leave behind the classical binary logic in which any statement is either true or false. Truth tables for logical connectives such as AND, OR, or NOT can also be derived for three truth values. As shown in Fig. 3.13, combinations of true or false statements with propositions of unknown truth value return null values, which may lead to counter-intuitive results as in the example in Fig. 3.12.

OR	1	?	0
1	1	1	1
?	1	?	?
0	1	?	0

AND	1	?	0
1	1	?	0
?	?	?	0
0	0	0	0

NOT	
1	0
?	?
0	1

Fig. 3.13 Truth tables for three-valued logic

The query in Fig. 3.12, which selects all employees from the EMPLOYEE table who live either in Kent or not in Kent, returns a result table containing only a subset of the employees in the original table. The reason is that some places of residence of employees are unknown. Therefore, the truth of both comparisons, City='Kent' and NOT City='Kent', is unknown and therefore not true.

This clearly goes against the conventional logical assumption that a union of the subset "employees living in Kent" with its complement "employees NOT living in Kent" should result in the total set of all employees.

Sentential logic with the values TRUE, FALSE, and UNKNOWN is commonly called three-valued logic for the three truth values a statement can take. This logic is less known and poses a special challenge for users of relational databases, since analyses of tables with null values are hard to interpret. In practice, null values are therefore largely avoided. Sometimes, DEFAULT values are used instead. For instance, the company address could be used to replace the yet unknown private addresses in the EMPLOYEE table from our example. The function COALESCE (X, Y) replaces all X attributes with a null value with the value Y. If null values have to be allowed, attributes can be checked for unknown values with specific comparison operators, IS NULL or IS NOT NULL, in order to avoid unexpected side effects.

Foreign keys are usually not supposed to take null values; however, there is an exception for foreign keys under a certain rule of referential integrity. For instance, the deletion rule for the referenced table DEPARTMENT can specify whether existing foreign key references should be set to NULL or not. The referential integrity constraint "set NULL" declares that foreign key values are set to NULL if their referenced tuple is deleted. For example, deleting the tuple (D6, Accounting) from the DEPARTMENT table in Fig. 3.12 with the integrity constraint rule "set NULL" results in null values for the foreign keys of employees Stewart and Bell in the EMPLOYEE table. For more information, see also Sect. 4.3.1.

Null values also exist in graph-based languages. As we will see in the following section, handling null values with IS NULL and COALESCE is done in the Cypher language as well, which we will cover in detail in the next section.

3.4   Graph-Based Language Cypher

Graph-based database languages were first developed toward the end of the 1980s. The interest in high-performance *graph query languages* has grown with the rise of the Internet and social media, which produce more and more graph-structured data.

Graph databases store data in graph structures and provide options for data manipulation on a graph transformation level. As described in Sect. 1.4.1, graph databases consist of property graphs with nodes and edges, with each graph storing a set of key-value pairs as properties. Graph-based database languages build on that principle and enable the use of a computer language to interact with graph structures in databases and program the processing of those structures.

Like relational languages, graph-based languages are set-based. They work with graphs, which can be defined as sets of vertices and edges or paths. Graph-based languages allow for filtering data by predicates, similar to relational languages; this filtering is called a *conjunctive query*. Filtering a graph returns a subset of nodes and/or edges of the graph, which form a partial graph. The underlying principle is called subgraph matching, the task of finding a partial graph matching certain specifications within a graph. Graph-based languages also offer features for aggregating sets of nodes in the graph into scalar values, e.g., counts, sums, or minimums.

In summary, the advantage of graph-based languages is that the language constructs directly target graphs, and thus the language definition of processing graph-structured data is much more direct. As a language for graph databases, we focus on the graph-based language Cypher in this work.

Cypher is a declarative query language for graph databases. It provides pattern matching on property graphs. It was developed by Andrés Taylor in 2011 at Neo4J, Inc. With openCypher, the language was made available to the general public as an open-source project in 2015. It is now used in more than ten commercial database systems. In 2019, the International Organization for Standardization (ISO) decided to further develop openCypher into an international standard under the name GQL by 2023.

The graph database Neo4J[4] (see also Cypher tutorial and Travelblitz case study with Neo4J on www.sql-nosql.org) uses the language Cypher to support a language interface for the scripting of database interactions.

Cypher is based on a *pattern matching* mechanism. Cypher has language commands for data queries and data manipulation (*data manipulation language*, DML); however, the schema definition in Cypher is done implicitly, i.e., node and edge types are defined by inserting instances of them into the database as actual specific nodes and edges.

Cypher also includes direct linguistic elements for security mechanisms, similar to relational languages, with statements such as GRANT and REVOKE (see Sect. 4.2). Below, we will take a closer look at the Cypher language.

---

[4]http://neo4j.com

3.4.1 Creating and Populating the Database Schema

Schema definition in Cypher is done implicitly, i.e., abstract data classes (metadata) such as node and edge types or attributes are created by using them in the insertion of concrete data values. The following example inserts new data into the database:

```
CREATE
 (p:Product {
 productName:'Alice's Adventures in Wonderland'})
-[:PUBLISHER]->
 (o:Organization {
 name:'Macmillan'})
```

This instruction deserves special consideration because it implicitly extends the schema. Two new nodes are created and connected to each other. The first node, p, stores the record for the Alice in Wonderland product. The second node, o, defines the record for the Macmillan publishing house. This implicitly creates a new node type, "Organization," since it did not exist before.

Attribute-value pairs are inserted into the new nodes. Since the attribute "name" did not exist before, it is also implicitly added in the schema without the need for an additional command.

In addition, an edge is created between the book node and the publisher node with edge type "PUBLISHER." Assuming that this is a new edge type, it is also implicitly added to the database schema.

To change data, then the command MATCH ... WHERE ... SET can be used. The following example shows an expression that resets the price of the specified product:

```
MATCH (p:Product)
WHERE p.productName = 'Alice's Adventures in Wonderland'
SET p.unitPrice = 13.75
```

With DELETE, it is possible to eliminate nodes and edges as specified. Since graph databases ensure referential integrity (see Sect. 4.3), vertices can only be deleted if they have no edges attached. Before being able to remove a node, the user therefore has to delete all incoming and outgoing edges.

Below is an expression that first recognizes all edges connected to the product selected by name, then eliminates those edges, and finally deletes the node of the product itself.

```
MATCH
 ()-[r1]->(p:Product),
 (p)-[r2]->()
WHERE p.productName = 'Alice's Adventures in Wonderland'
DELETE r1, r2, p
```

3.4.2 Relation Operators

As described in Sect. 1.4.2, Cypher has three basic commands:

- MATCH for defining search patterns
- WHERE for conditions to filter the results by
- RETURN for outputting properties, vertices, relationships, or paths

Even though Cypher operates on graphs, property graphs can be mapped congruently to relations. Therefore, it is possible to analyze the relational operators of Cypher.

Selection and Projection

The following example returns the node with the specified product name. This corresponds to a relational selection, which is specified in the WHERE clause.

```
MATCH (p:Product)
WHERE p.productName = 'Alice's Adventures in Wonderland'
RETURN p
```

The RETURN clause can output either vertices or property tables. The return of entire nodes is similar to "SELECT *" in SQL. Cypher can also return properties as attribute values of nodes and edges in the form of tables:

```
MATCH (p:Product)
WHERE p.unitPrice > 55
RETURN p.productName, p.unitPrice
ORDER BY p.unitPrice
```

This query includes a selection, a projection, and a sorting. The MATCH clause defines a pattern matching filtering the graph for the node of the "Product" type; the WHERE clause selects all products with a price greater than 55; and the RETURN clause projects those nodes on the product name and price, with the ORDER BY clause sorting the products by price.

Cartesian Product and Join

The Cartesian product of two nodes can be generated in Cypher with the following syntax:

```
MATCH (p:Product), (c:Category)
RETURN p.productName, c.categoryName
```

This command lists all possible combinations of product names and category names. A join of nodes, i.e., a selection on the Cartesian product, is executed graph-based by matching path patterns by edge types:

```
MATCH (p:Product) -[:PART_OF]-> (c:Category)
RETURN p.productName, c.categoryName
```

For each product, this query lists the category it belongs to, by only considering those product and category nodes connected by edges of the PART_OF type. This equals the inner join of the "Product" node type with the "Category" node type via the edge type PART_OF.

3.4.3   Built-In Functions

In Cypher, there are built-in functions which can be applied to properties and data sets. These functions, as a supplement to selection, projection, and join, are central for the usability in practice. An important category for data analysis are the aggregate functions.

Aggregate Functions

An important category of built-in functions for data analysis are the aggregating functions like COUNT, SUM, MIN, MAX, and AVG, which Cypher supports.

Suppose we want to generate a list of all employees, together with the number of subordinates. To do this, we match the pattern MATCH (e:Employee)<-[: REPORTS_TO]-(sub) and get a list of employees where the number of subordinates is greater than zero:

```
MATCH (e:Employee) <-[:REPORTS_TO]-(sub)
RETURN e.employeeID, COUNT(sub.employeeID)
```

There are node types where only a subset of the nodes has an edge of a specific edge type. For instance, not every employee has subordinates, i.e., only a subset of the nodes of the "Employee" type has an incoming REPORTS_TO type edge.

An OPTIONAL MATCH clause allows to list all employees including those without subordinates:

```
MATCH (e:Employee)
OPTIONAL MATCH (e)<-[:REPORTS_TO]-(sub)
RETURN e.employeeID, COUNT (sub.employeeID)
```

With OPTIONAL MATCH, connected attributes that are not connected remain empty (NULL). Cypher is based on three-valued logic. Handling null values with IS NULL and COALESCE is analogous to SQL (see Sect. 3.3.4). To filter records with null values, the additional code WHERE sub.employeeID IS NULL can be used. With the function COALESCE(sub.employeeID, "not available"), the null values can be replaced.

Other aggregates are sum (SUM), minimum (MIN), and maximum (MAX). An interesting non-atomic aggregate is COLLECT, which generates an array from the available data values. Thus, the expression in the previous example lists all employees by first name and abbreviated last name, along with a list of the employee numbers of their subordinates.

Data Operators
Cypher supports functions on data values. The following query returns the full first name and the last name initial for each employee, along with the number of subordinates:

```
MATCH (e:Employee)
OPTIONAL MATCH (e)<-[:REPORTS_TO]-(sub)
RETURN
 e.firstName + " "
 + LEFT(e.lastName, 1) + "." as name,
 COUNT(sub.employeeID)
```

The operator + can be used on "text" type data values to string them together. The operator LEFT returns the first n characters of a text.

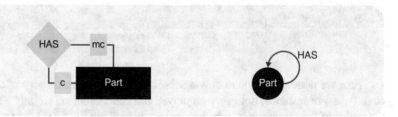

Fig. 3.14 Recursive relationship as entity-relationship model and as graph with node and edge types

3.4.4   Graph Analysis

Graph-based languages offer additional analysis mechanisms for paths within graphs. An area of special interest is the search for patterns directly in the paths of a graph, which can be done with dedicated language elements. A *regular path query* allows to describe path patterns in a graph with regular expressions in order to find matching records in the database (see the Cypher tutorial on www.sql-nosql.org for more information).

Figure 3.14 illustrates this using an entity-relationship model of item parts. It shows a recursive relationship, where parts (e.g., product parts) can potentially have multiple subparts and at the same time also potentially be a subpart to another, superordinate part. If we want to query all subparts contained in a part *both directly and indirectly*, a simple join is not sufficient. We have to recursively go through all subparts of subparts, etc. in order to get a complete list.

For a long time, this kind of query could not even be defined in SQL. Only with the SQL:1999 standard did recursive queries become possible via common table expressions (CTEs); however, their formulation is still highly complicated. Defining the query for all direct and indirect subparts with a (recursive) SQL statement is rather cumbersome:

```
with recursive
r_path (partID, hasPartId, length) - CTE definition
as (
   select partID, hasPartId, 1 -- Initialization
   from part
   union all
   select r.partID, p.hasPartId, r.length+1
   from part p
   join r_path r - Recursive join of CTE
   on (r.hasPartId = p.partID)
)
select
distinct path.partID, path.hasPartId, path.length
from r_path -- Selection via recursive defined CTE
```

This query returns a list of all subparts for a part, plus the degree of nesting, i.e., the length of the path within the tree from the part to any (potentially indirect) subpart.

A regular path query in a graph-based language allows for simplified filtering of path patterns with regular expressions. For instance, the regular expression HAS* using a Kleene star (*) defines the set of all possible concatenations of connections with the edge type HAS (called the Kleene hull). This makes defining a query for all indirectly connected vertices in a graph-based language much easier. The example below uses the graph-based language Cypher to declare the same query for all direct and indirect subparts as the SQL example above, but in only two lines:

```
MATCH path = (p:Part) <-[:HAS*]- (has:Part)
RETURN p.partID, has.partID, LENGTH(path)
```

In addition to the data manipulation we know from SQL, Cypher also supports operations on paths within the graph. In the following example, an edge of the type BASKET is generated for all product pairs that have been ordered together. This edge shows that those two products have been included in at least one order together. Once that is done, the shortest connection between any two products through shared orders can be determined with a *shortestPath* function:

```
MATCH
  (p1:Product)<--(o:Order)-->(p2:Product)
CREATE
  p1-[:BASKET{order:o.orderID}]->p2,
  p2-[:BASKET{order:o.orderID}]->p1;

MATCH path =
  shortestPath(
  (p1:Product)-[b:BASKET*]->(p2:Product))
RETURN
  p1.productName, p2.productName, LENGTH(path),
  EXTRACT(r in RELATIONSHIPS(path) | r.order)
```

In addition to the names of the two products, the RETURN clause also contains the length of the shortest path between them and a list of the order numbers indirectly connecting them.

It should be noted here that, while Cypher offers some functions for analyzing paths within graphs (including the Kleene hull for edge types), it does not support the full range of Kleene algebra for paths in graphs, as required in the theory of graph-based languages. Nevertheless, Cypher is a language well-suited for practical use.

3.5   Document-Oriented Language MQL

The MongoDB Query Language (MQL) is a JSON-based language for interacting
with document databases. MQL provides methods that are parameterized with JSON
objects. These methods can be used to create, edit, and query collections of
documents.

3.5.1   Creating and Filling the Database Schema

Document databases like MongoDB[5] are schema-free. This does not mean that their
records do not follow a schema. A schema is always necessary to structure records.
Schema freedom simply means that database users are free to use any schema they
want for structuring without first reporting it to the database system and without
requiring that the schemas of records within a collection be uniform. It is thus a
positive freedom to use any schema within a collection. The database schema in a
document database is an *implicit schema.*

Therefore, all that is needed to populate a document database schema is a JSON
document. We propose that an entity-relationship model be used to structure the
JSON records, as described in Sect. 2.5. For example, to insert a document about an
employee into the database according to the structure in Fig. 2.25, we use the
insertOne() method on the EMPLOYEE collection as follows:

```
db.EMPLOYEES.insertOne( {
  { "EMPLOYEE":
   { "Name": "Steward",
     "City": { "Stow",
     "DEPARTMENT": { "Designation": "Finance" },
     }, { "PROJECTS":
      [ { "Title": "DWH", "Workload": 0.3 },
        { "Title": "Strat", "Workload": 0.5 } ] } }
 )
```

If the used collection does not exist yet, it will be created implicitly. To insert
multiple documents, the method insertMany() can be applied.

To adapt an existing document, the method updateOne() can be applied. In the
following example for employee Steward, the department is changed to "IT":

---

[5]https://www.mongodb.com

```
db.EMPLOYEES.updateOne(
{ "EMPLOYEE.Name": "Steward" },
{ $set: {
"EMPLOYEE.DEPARTMENT.Designation": "IT" }})
```

The updateOne() method can use several update operators. The $set operator sets a new value for a field or adds the field if it does not already exist. With $unset, a field can be removed; with $rename, it is renamed. Other operators are available, such as $inc, which increments the field value by the specified value.

UpdateOne changes the first document that matches the filter criterion. Similar to insertion, multiple documents can be changed at once with the updateMany() method.

The deleteOne() method is used to delete a document that matches a filter criterion. If there are several documents that match the filter, the first one is deleted. To delete several documents at once, the deleteMany() method can be used. In the following example, we delete all documents related to employees named "Smith."

```
db.EMPLOYEES.deleteMany(
{ "EMPLOYEE.Name": "Smith" } )
```

Once we have inserted data into the database, we can query that data. The relational operators, which exist in a similar form for MQL, are used for this purpose.

3.5.2 Relation Operators

MQL operates on sets of JSON-structured records. However, JSON documents can be mapped to tuples. Therefore, relational algebra can serve as a theoretical model for MQL. Assuming the model in Sect. 2.5.1, we will emulate relational operators with MQL in the following paragraphs.

Selection
To select employees, the find() method is applied to the EMPLOYEES collection. In the following example, the filter "location = Kent" is given as a parameter in JSON syntax.

```
db.EMPLOYEES.find({
"EMPLOYEES.City": "Kent"})
```

Different filter criteria can be combined with the Boolean operators $and, $or, and $not, even over multiple attributes, as shown in the following example. Here, employees are selected who live in Kent and work in IT.

```
db.EMPLOYEES.find(
{$and: [
{"EMPLOYEE.city": "Kent"},
{"EMPLOYEE.DEPARTMENT.Designation": "IT"
} ] } )
```

Projection
Document sets (collections) can be projected to attributes. For this purpose, a second parameter can be given to the find() method, specifying a list of properties of the document to be returned by the database. In the following example, the fields name and city are shown for the employees from Kent. This is called an *inclusion projection*.

```
db.EMPLOYEES.find({
"EMPLOYEE.City": "Kent"},
{_id:0,
"EMPLOYEE.Name": 1,
"EMPLOYEE.City": 1})
```

The _id field is an automatically generated identification key for documents, which is output by default (cf. Sect. 4.3.3). This can be changed by using the *exclusion projection* with the value 0. However, the _id field is the only field that allows mixing exclusion and inclusion.

Join
By definition, documents are complete with respect to a subject. For certain evaluations, it can be nevertheless meaningful to join document sets. This is basically possible in MQL with the $lookup aggregation. The operation performs a kind of left outer join because all documents of the parent (left) collection are returned, even if they do not match the filter criteria. However, the operation is not performant and should be used with caution.

The following example associates the employees (according to Fig. 2.25) with the departments (according to Fig. 2.29) using the "Designation" field, thus adding the name of the department head. We are looking for the departments whose name matches the department of the corresponding employee. The statements in the pipeline field are used here to modify the connected documents with the $project operator. The department documents are projected to a single "Name" field, which stores the name of the department head. The $ operator before the property name on the fourth to last line eliminates the nested field properties and reduces the JSON structure to the value of the corresponding field.

```
db.EMPLOYEES.aggregate([{
$lookup: {
from: "DEPARTMENTS",
localField: "EMPLOYEE.DEPARTMENT.name",
foreignField: "DEPARTMENT.Designation",
pipeline: [
{ $project: { _id:0, "name":
"$DEPARTMENT.EMPLOYEES.DEPARTMENT_HEAD.Name"
}}],
as: "STAFF.DEPARTMENT.Head"
}}]);
```

Pipelines show the advantage of using root elements in JSON objects, as suggested by rule D1 (Sect. 2.5.2). By specifying the entity set in the field path, we can more easily understand which document types and properties are referenced. In fact, MQL pipelines can get much more complicated in practice. Therefore, it pays to name the fields so that the field origin is clear. Below we show the return of the above query for the document in Fig. 2.23. The _id field is the automatic primary key mentioned above. The $lookup operation was used to insert a new field "Head" with the name of the department head from the DEPARTMENTS collection in the field EMPLOYEE.DEPARTMENT:

```
{ _id: ObjectId("62aa3c16c1f35d9cedb164eb"),
  EMOPLOYEE:
    { Name: 'Murphy',
      Place: 'Kent',
      DEPARTMENT: { Designation: 'IT',
        'Head': [ { Name: 'Miller' } ] },
      PROJECTS:
        [ { Title: 'WebX', Workload: 0.55 },
          { Title: 'ITorg', Workload: 0.45 } ] } }
```

The $lookup operator always returns the associated documents and values are as an array, even if there is only one corresponding document. Therefore, this value is enclosed in square brackets. With further operations, this single value could be unpacked.

Cartesian Product

Similarly, we can use the $lookup operation to derive a kind of Cartesian product by omitting the join predicates localField and foreignField. This cross join is only listed here for the sake of completeness. The operation is inefficient even for small data sets.

For example, the names of all department heads could be stored in a new field "Bosses":

```
db.EMPLOYEES.aggregate([{
$lookup: {
from: "DEPARTMENTS",
pipeline: [
{ $project: { _id:0, "Name":
"$DEPARTMENT.EMPLOYEE.DEPARTMENT.Designation"
}}],
as: "EMPLOYEES.Bosses"
}}]);
```

Union

To unify collections as sets of documents, the aggregation operator $unionWith is available. In the following example, all documents of the collection SPORTS_CLUB are united with all documents of the collection PHOTO_CLUB. However, it is not a true set operator because $unionWith does not remove the duplicates. It is more like the SQL command UNION ALL.

```
db.SPORTS_CLUB.aggregate([
    { $unionWith: { coll: "PHOTO_CLUB"} }
])
```

Similar operators for intersections or difference sets at the collection level do not exist. We see that MQL is relationally incomplete, since basic set operators are missing. However, MQL provides a rich set of built-in functions, some of which we look at below.

3.5.3   Built-In Functions

In MQL terminology, the term aggregation is used in a more general sense. Therefore, aggregation functions such as $count or $sum are called aggregation accumulators in MQL to distinguish them from other aggregations such as $lookup or $unionWith.

Accumulation Aggregations

With the $count accumulator, we can count documents in a collection. In the following, we count the number of employees:

```
db.EMPLOYEES.aggregate([ {
    $count: "Result"
} ] )
```

Other accumulators include average ($avg), minimum ($min), and maximum ($max). These accumulator aggregations can be used together with a $group aggregation, which corresponds to a grouping of aggregated values according to the characteristics of a variable.

Grouping

An accumulator aggregation such as sum, count, or average cut can be grouped using a variable. For each value of this variable, a corresponding partial result is calculated. In the following example, we ask for the number of employees per location:

```
db.EMPLOYEES.aggregate( [ {
    $group: {
        _id: "$employee.location",
        Number_of_employees: { $count: { } }
} } ] )
```

The output of this query is one JSON object per department, with the name of the department in the "_id" field and the number of employees in the "Number_of_employees" field. If records for employees are stored in the database analogous to Fig. 1.3, this results in the following output in Mongo Shell (mongosh):

```
{ _id: 'Stow', count: 1 }
{ _id: 'Kent', count: 1 }
{ _id: 'Cleveland', count: 2 }
```

The $group aggregation can be used with all the above aggregation accumulators like $sum, $avg, $count, $max, and $min.

Output Valid JSON Syntax

The Mongo Shell return value above is oriented on JSON, but it deviates from the JSON standard. Properties are not quoted, and values are represented in single quotes. To produce valid JSON as output, the JSON.stringify() method can be used on a conversion of the result set as an array, as shown in the following example:

```
JSON.stringify(
db.EMPLOYEES.aggregate( [ {
    $group: {
        _id: "$EMPLOYEE.City",
        count: { $count: { } }
} } ] )
.toArray())
```

Nested Queries with Pipelines

The step-by-step processing of aggregation functions is called pipeline in MQL. These allow to combine several query steps. Any number of processing steps can be declared sequentially in a pipeline. Operators for pipelines are, for example, $unwind, $group, $lookup, and $project, as already shown above. Other options include $match to filter results, $sort for sorting, or $limit to limit results.

When using accumulators and groupings, arrays (lists of field values) can lead to unexpected results. For example, the $sum accumulator in the $group aggregation treats numeric values inside arrays as non-numeric. Therefore, they will not be summed. The array must first be unwound as individual values using $unwind.

For example, if we want to know the sum of project stints per department in a document structure shown in Fig. 2.25, we face the problem that stints may be contained multiple times in arrays. Therefore, applying the $sum accumulator to the field EMPLOYEES.PROJECTS.WORKLOAD would return the value 0. Therefore, to unwind the array of project stints, we write the following query:

```
db.EMPLOYEES.aggregate([
  { $unwind: "$EMPLOYEES.PROJECTS" },
  { $group: {
      _id:"$EMPLOYEES.DEPARTMENT.Designation",
      "s": {"$sum":"$EMPLOYEES.PROJECTS.Workload"}
  }}
])
```

For the sum of the workloads stored within an array of projects for the employees, in addition to the grouping, the unwinding of the array structure with $unwind is necessary.

3.5.4 Null Values

In MQL field values can remain unknown explicitly. For this purpose, the keyword "null" is used (the lower case is relevant). The special feature of the schema-free document model is that even the omission of an object field can logically be a null value.

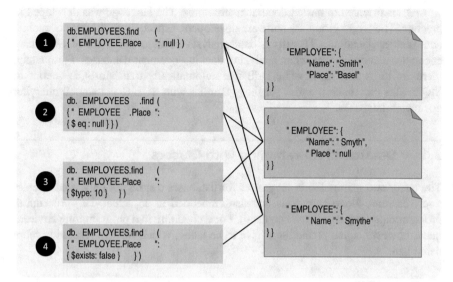

Fig. 3.15 Null values in MQL

In a three-valued first-order logic, it is the same whether one specifies a field with a property whose value is "null," which means explicitly unknown, or whether the field is omitted altogether and is thus implicitly unknown. However, in three-valued second-order logic, the former is a *known* unknown, but the latter is an *unknown unknown*. MQL treats both variants as equivalent.

As an example, let's look at the documents for employees Smith, Smyth, and Smythe in Fig. 3.15. While we know the Place is Basel for Smith, it is unknown for the other two. For Smyth, we explicitly mark this as a null value in the object field with property "Place"; for Smythe, we omit the field with property "Place." This now leads to different ways of filtering with null values.

- In query (1) in Fig. 3.15, we use "null" directly as a filter criterion. This means that the criterion itself is unknown, and therefore it is not applied at all—so all employees are returned.
- In query (2) in Fig. 3.15, we filter on whether the "Place" property is equal to "null." In this case, documents are returned that either have such a field with explicit value "null"—as with Smyth—or do not have such a field, as with Smythe.
- In query (3) in Fig. 3.15, we explicitly select for values of data type 10 (BSON Type Null). Thus, only documents are returned that have a field with property "Place" and an explicit value "null," like Smyth.
- In query (4) in Fig. 3.15, we ask for documents in the collection EMPLOYEES for which no field with property "Place" exists. This is only true for Smythe.

MQL is oriented to nested document structures. The language was developed in practice. The target group are software developers, especially in the area of mobile and Web applications. Therefore, data analysts used to the logic of SQL may encounter some surprises when analyzing data in document databases. Fortunately, there are tools such as Apache Drill that automatically translate SQL queries to MQL. This can make it easier for those familiar with SQL to get started querying document databases.

3.6   Database Programming with Cursors

The query and manipulation languages for databases can be not only used interactively as stand-alone languages but also embedded in an actual, i.e., procedural, programming language (host language). For embedding in a programming environment, however, some precautions have to be taken, which we will discuss in more detail here.

Cursor Concept
A cursor is a pointer that can traverse a set of records in a sequence specified by the database system. Since a sequential program cannot process an entire set of records in one fell swoop, the cursor concept allows a record-by-record, iterative approach.

In the following, we take a closer look at the embedding of SQL, Cypher, and MQL in procedural languages with cursors.

3.6.1   Embedding of SQL in Procedural Languages

The concept of embedded languages will first be explained using SQL as an example. For a program to read a table by a SELECT statement, it must be able to access the table from one tuple to the next, for which a cursor concept is required. For the selection of a table, a cursor can be defined in the program as follows:

```
DECLARE cursor-name CURSOR FOR <SELECT-statement>
```

This allows to process the individual records in a table, i.e., tuple by tuple. If necessary, it is also possible to modify some or all data values of the current tuple. If the table has to be processed in a specific sequence, the above declaration must be amended by an ORDER BY clause.

Multiple cursors can be used within one program for navigation reasons. They have to be declared and then activated and deactivated by OPEN and CLOSE commands. The actual access to a table and the transmission of data values into the corresponding program variables happen via a FETCH command. The types of the variables addressed in the programming language must match the formats of the respective table fields. The FETCH command is phrased as

```
FETCH cursor-name INTO host-variable {,host-variable}
```

Each FETCH statement moves the CURSOR forward by one tuple. If no further tuples are found, a corresponding status code is returned to the program.

Cursor concepts allow the *embedding of set-oriented query and manipulation languages into a procedural host language.* For instance, the same linguistic constructs in SQL can be either used interactively or embedded. This has additional advantages for testing embedded programming sections, since the test tables can be analyzed and checked with interactive SQL at any point.

Stored Procedures and Stored Functions
From SQL:1999 onward, SQL standards offered the possibility to embed SQL in internal database procedures and functions. Since those are stored in the data dictionary on the database server, they are called stored procedures or, if they return values, stored functions. Such linguistic elements enable the procedural processing of record sets via CURSORs and the use of branches and loops. The procedural linguistic elements of SQL were only standardized long after the language's intro-duction, so many vendors developed separate proprietary formats. Procedural pro-gramming with SQL is therefore largely product-specific.

The following example of a stored function calculates the first quartile[6] of all employee salaries:

---

[6]Quartiles of ranked data sets are the points between the quarters of the set.

```
CREATE FUNCTION SalaryQuartile()
RETURNS INTEGER DETERMINISTIC
BEGIN
 DECLARE cnt int;
 DECLARE i int;
 DECLARE tmpSalary int;
 DECLARE employeeCursor CURSOR FOR
 SELECT Salary
 FROM Employee
 ORDER BY Salary ASC;
 SELECT COUNT(*)/4 INTO cnt FROM Employee;
 SET i := 0;
 OPEN employeeCursor;
 employeeLoop: LOOP
 FETCH employeeCursor INTO tmpSalary;
 SET i := i + 1;
 IF i >= cnt THEN
 LEAVE employeeLoop;
 END IF;
 END LOOP;
 RETURN tmpSalary;
```

This function opens a cursor on the employee table sorted by salary (low to high), loops through each row, and returns the value of the Salary column from the row where COUNT(*)/4 iterations of the loop have been run. This value is the first quartile, i.e., the value separating the lowest 25% of values in the set. The result of the function can then be selected with the statement

```
Select SalaryQuartile();
```

Embedding SQL in External Programming Languages
Recently, the Python programming language has become popular. Especially for data analysis, but also for Web and mobile applications, the language is very common. Therefore, let's take a look at the cursor concept in the following example in the Python language:

```
import mysql.connector as mysql
db = mysql.connect(
host="localhost", user="root", passwd=" ")
cursor = db.cursor()
cursor.execute("SELECT * FROM EMPLOYEES")
for record in cursor:print(record[1])
```

First, the program library for the database is imported, which is product-specific. Then a connection to the database is opened with appropriate access information (see Sect. 4.2) and stored in the variable db. Finally, a cursor is opened on a SQL-SELECT query, which is run sequentially in a FOR loop. In this simple example, only the record is printed with print(); any processing logic could now be inserted here.

3.6.2   Embedding Graph-Based Languages

Graph-based languages, since they are also set-oriented, can be embedded in host languages using the same principle with the use of the cursor concept. One receives a result set back under execution of an embedded Cypher statement, which can be processed arbitrarily in a loop.

Python is also used more and more in the area of graph databases. For this reason, there is also the possibility to embed Cypher in Python scripts. In the following example, we see a corresponding example with Python:

```
from neo4j import GraphDatabase
driver = GraphDatabase.driver(
"bolt://localhost:7687",
auth=("neo4j", "password"))
session = driver.session()
query = "MATCH (p:Product) RETURN p.productName"
result = session.run(query)
for r in result: print(r)
```

First, the program library is imported. Then a driver is instantiated that contains the access information. With this, a database session can be opened. With the run command, a Cypher query can be executed on the database server. The processing of the CURSOR is done in a FOR loop.

3.6.3   Embedding Document Database Languages

We have now seen the embedding of the set-oriented database languages SQL and Cypher. However, MQL is actually a program library that is controlled with JSON parameters. Therefore, MQL is not embedded as a separate language in procedural host languages. The find, insert, update, and delete commands are applied directly as routines of the corresponding APIs and parameterized accordingly. Below we see an example of using MQL in Python:

```
import pymongo
uri = "mongodb://localhost:27017"
client = pymongo.MongoClient(uri)
database = client['Company']
collection = database['EMPLOYEES']
result = collection.find({},{"Name" : 1})
for r in result: print(r)
```

Again, after importing the program library, a connection to the database is established, a query is executed, and the result is processed sequentially in a cursor.

In this example, we see an advantage of the Python language: its proximity to JSON with the object constructor {}. The filter criterion can thus be specified directly in the JSON syntax.

We have now introduced some basic principles of database languages for relational, graph, and document databases. These have been related to the insertion and processing of data. We now devote a separate chapter to a central category of language elements: security functions. Therefore, the following chapter will apply the CIA triad of information security to databases and analyze in detail the corresponding language elements in the area of access control, integrity conditions, and consistency assurance for the three database types with SQL, Cypher, and MQL.

Bibliography

Codd, E.F.: A relational model of data for large shared data banks. Commun. ACM. **13**(6), 377–387 (1970)

Chamberlin, D.D., Boyce, R.F.: SEQUEL: a structured English query language. In: Proceedings of the 1974 ACM SIGFIDET (Now SIGMOD) Workshop on Data Description, Access and Control, pp. 249–264 (1974)

Kemper, A., Eikler, A.: Datenbanksysteme – Eine Einführung. DeGruyter (2015)

Melton, J., Simon, A.R.: SQL1999 – Understanding Relational Language Components. Morgan Kaufmann (2002)

MongoDB, Inc.: MongoDB Documentation. https://www.mongodb.com/docs/ (2022)

Neo4J, Inc.: (2022). Neo4j Documentation. Neo4j Graph Data Platform. https://neo4j.com/docs/ (2022)

Panzarino, O.: Learning Cypher. Packt Publishing Ltd., Birmingham (2014)

Perkins, L., Redmond, E., Wilson, J.R.: Seven Databases in Seven Weeks: A Guide to Modern Databases and the Nosql Movement, 2nd edn. O'Reilly UK Ltd., Raleigh, NC (2018)

Database Security

4

4.1 Security Goals and Measures

As soon as a database system is put into operation, it is exposed to risks. For example, data can be lost, unintentionally or maliciously changed, or disclosed. In order to ensure the long-term functioning of a database system, the general objectives of information security as classically defined by the CIA triad are followed:

- **Confidentiality**: Protecting privacy from unauthorized access to information
- **Integrity**: Ensuring the correctness and accuracy of information
- **Availability**: Maintaining the functional state of the information system

Database security is based on the basic security of the data center, the computers, and the network in which the database server is operated. Computers must use the latest version of all software components to close security gaps. The network must be protected with firewall rules and geo-IP filters. And the data center must physically protect hardware from access. We do not go into these basics of cybersecurity here, but refer to relevant literature. We focus on the technical functions that a database system can use to achieve the security goals.

Figure 4.1 lists necessary measures for databases for each of the three CIA goals. The security measures in Fig. 4.1 build on each other. To achieve integrity, confidentiality must also be ensured, and the measures for integrity are also necessary but not sufficient for availability. In the following, we provide a brief overview of the general security measures before we discuss the special features in the database environment in the following sections.

To ensure confidentiality, privacy protection is central. Authentication uses accounts and passwords to verify that users are who they say they are. With appropriate password policies, users are encouraged to choose passwords with a sufficiently large number of characters (e.g., 9) with upper and lower case, including numbers and special characters, and to change them regularly. Authorization rules

© The Author(s), under exclusive license to Springer Nature Switzerland AG 2023
M. Kaufmann, A. Meier, *SQL and NoSQL Databases*,
https://doi.org/10.1007/978-3-031-27908-9_4

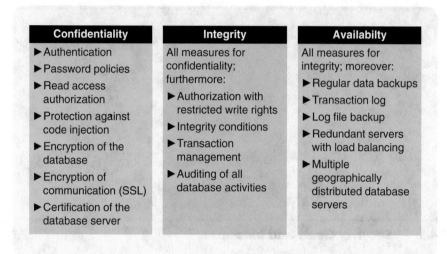

Fig. 4.1 Database security measures for confidentiality, integrity, and availability

restrict access rights and give users exactly the access they need. However, even with the best access protection, injection attacks can inject executable code into user interfaces to read or modify the database without permission. This must be prevented with appropriate measures (e.g., prepared statements). Encryption of the database and communication with the database server prevents unauthorized reading. The certification of the server ensures that information is entrusted to one's own system and not unintentionally revealed to a "person in the middle."

Many of the measures mentioned above serve to ensure the integrity of the data as well, i.e., to protect it from unintentional modification. In the case of authorization, additional care must be taken to be particularly restrictive in terms of write permissions. Furthermore, database auditing can be used to record who has performed which action on the database and when, which allows errors to be traced and corrected. A special feature of database management systems is that they can partially check the integrity of the data automatically. For this purpose, conditions under which the data is correct, so-called integrity constraints, can be formulated. Inconsistencies can also occur in multi-user operation if data records are modified simultaneously. Transaction management provides mechanisms to protect the integrity of data from side effects and version conflicts.

To ensure the availability of the services of a database system, further measures are needed. A system of multiple servers with load balancing ensures availability even with a large number of requests. The geographical distribution of redundant, identical database systems protects against interruptions caused by natural disasters and other major events. Regular backups of the database ensure that all data remains available in the event of damage. A transaction log records all changes to the database and ensures that all transactions are completed consistently in the event of a crash. To do this, the log files must be copied and backed up regularly.

In the following sections, we will deal with security measures for which the database management system provides specific mechanisms: access control, integrity conditions, and transaction management.

4.2 Access Control

4.2.1 Authentication and Authorization in SQL

Data protection is the prevention of access to and manipulation of data by unauthorized persons. Protective measures include procedures for the positive identification of a person or for the assignment of user permissions for specific data access as well as cryptographic methods for confidential data storage and transmission. In contrast, *data security* means the hardware and software solutions that help to protect data from falsification, destruction, and loss.

The relational model facilitates the implementation of reliable restrictions to ensure data protection. A major data protection mechanism in relational databases is to provide users with only those tables and table sections they need for their work.

To create a user account for authentication, we use the CREATE USER command. The following example creates a user account for employee Murphy with a relatively secure password that does not contain words, but lowercase and uppercase letters, numbers, and special characters:

```
CREATE USER murphy
IDENTIFIED BY 'jd7k_Ddjh$1';
```

Similar to other database objects, user accounts can be modified and deleted with ALTER USER and DROP USER.

The GRANT command is used to authorize users for actions on tables. The following command authorizes user Murphy for all actions on the STAFF table (see Fig. 4.2).

```
GRANT ALL ON STAFF TO murphy;
```

What is awarded with GRANT can be taken back with REVOKE:

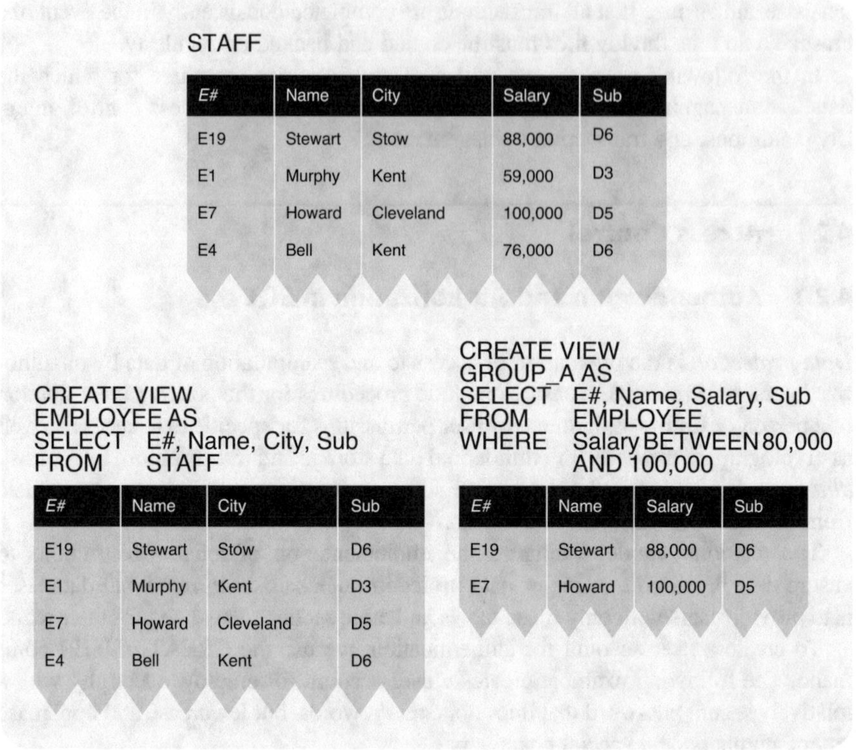

STAFF

E#	Name	City	Salary	Sub
E19	Stewart	Stow	88,000	D6
E1	Murphy	Kent	59,000	D3
E7	Howard	Cleveland	100,000	D5
E4	Bell	Kent	76,000	D6

```
CREATE VIEW
EMPLOYEE AS
SELECT   E#, Name, City, Sub
FROM     STAFF
```

E#	Name	City	Sub
E19	Stewart	Stow	D6
E1	Murphy	Kent	D3
E7	Howard	Cleveland	D5
E4	Bell	Kent	D6

```
CREATE VIEW
GROUP_A AS
SELECT   E#, Name, Salary, Sub
FROM     EMPLOYEE
WHERE    Salary BETWEEN 80,000
         AND 100,000
```

E#	Name	Salary	Sub
E19	Stewart	88,000	D6
E7	Howard	100,000	D5

Fig. 4.2 Definition of views as part of data protection

```
REVOKE ALL ON STAFF FROM murphy;
```

To simplify the assignment of rights for several users, reusable roles can be defined. In the following example, a role "hr" is created. This role will be authorized to perform read and write actions on the table STAFF.

```
CREATE ROLE hr;
GRANT SELECT, INSERT, UPDATE on STAFF to hr;
GRANT hr TO murphy;
```

However, the GRANT command only allows access control at the level of entire database objects, such as tables. In many cases, we may want to further restrict access to columns and rows of a table. This is done with table *views*, each of which is based on either one or multiple physical tables and is defined using a SELECT statement:

```
CREATE VIEW view-name AS <SELECT-statement>
```

However, view security is only effective when users are granted privileges on the views rather than on the base tables.

Figure 4.2 shows two example views based on the STAFF table. The EMPLOYEE view shows all attributes except for the salary information. The view GROUP_A shows only those employees with their respective salaries who earn between USD 80,000 and 100,000 annually. Other views can be defined similarly, e.g., to allow HR to access confidential data per salary group.

The two examples in Fig. 4.2 demonstrate important protection methods: On the one hand, tables can be limited for specific user groups by projection; on the other hand, access control can also be value-based, e.g., for salary ranges, via corresponding view definitions in the WHERE clause.

As on tables, it is possible to formulate queries on views; however, manipulation operations cannot always be defined uniquely. If a view is defined as a join of multiple tables, change operations may be denied by the database system under certain circumstances.

Updateable views allow for insert, delete, and update operations. The following criteria determine whether a view is updateable:

- The view contains content from only one table (no joins allowed).
- That base table has a primary key.
- The defining SQL expression contains no operations that affect the number of rows in the result set (e.g., *aggregate*, *group by*, *distinct*, etc.).

It is important to note that for different views of a single table, the data are managed uniformly in the base table; rather, merely the definitions of the views are stored. Only when the view is queried with a SELECT statement are the corresponding result tables generated from the view's base tables with the permitted data values.

Using views, it is now possible to grant only reading privileges for a subset of columns of the STAFF table with the EMPLOYEE view from Fig. 4.2:

```
GRANT SELECT ON EMPLOYEE TO PUBLIC
```

Instead of listing specific users, this example uses PUBLIC to assign reading privileges to all users so they can look at the limited EMPLOYEE view of the base table.

For a more selective assignment of permissions, for instance, it is possible to authorize only a certain HR employee with the user ID ID37289 to make changes to a subset of rows in the GROUP_A view from Fig. 4.2:

```
GRANT UPDATE ON GROUP_A TO ID37289
WITH GRANT OPTION
```

User ID37289 can now modify the GROUP_A view and, thanks to the GRANT OPTION, even assign this authorization or a limited reading privilege to others and take it back. This concept allows to define and manage dependencies between privileges.

The complexity of managing the assignment and removal of permissions when giving end users access to a relational query and manipulation language is not to be underestimated, even if the data administrators can use GRANT and REVOKE commands. In reality, daily changes and the monitoring of user authorizations require additional management tools (e.g., auditing). Internal or external controlling instances and authorities may also demand special measures to constantly ensure the proper handling of especially sensitive data (see also the legal data protection obligations for your jurisdiction).

SQL Injection

One security aspect that plays an increasingly important role in the age of the Web in the area of databases is the prevention of so-called SQL injections. When Web pages are programmed on the server side and connected to an SQL database, server scripts sometimes generate SQL code to interface with the database (see Sect. 3.6). If the code contains parameters that are entered by users (e.g., in forms or as part of the URL), additional SQL code can be injected there, the execution of which exposes or modifies sensitive information in the database.

As an explanatory example, let's assume that after logging into the user account of a Web store, the payment methods are displayed. The Web page that displays the user's saved payment methods has the following URL:

```
http://example.net/payment?uid=117
```

Let's assume that in the background, there is a program in the Java programming language that fetches the credit card data (name and number) from the database via

Java Database Connectivity (JDBC). The Java servlet uses embedded SQL and a cursor (see Sect. 3.6.1). Then the data is displayed on the Web page using HTML:

```
Connection connection = DriverManager.getConnection(
        "jdbc:mysql://127.0.0.1:3306/ma",
        "user",
        "password");

ResultSet cursor =
  connection.createStatement().executeQuery(
      "SELECT credit card number, name+
      + "FROM PAYMENT"
      + "WHERE uid = "
      + request.getParameter("uid"));

while (cursor.next()) {
  out.println(
      resultset.getString("credit_card_number ")
      + "<br/>" +
          + resultset.getString("name");
}
```

For this purpose, an SQL query of the PAYMENT table is generated on lines 6 and following of the Java code above. It is parameterized via the user input via URL using a get request (request.getParameter). This type of code generation is vulnerable to SQL injection. If the parameter uid is added to the URL as follows, all credit card data of all users will be displayed on the Web page:

```
http://example.net/payment?uid=117%20OR%201=1
```

The reason for this is that the servlet shown above generates the following SQL code based on the GET parameter:

```
SELECT credit_card_number, name
FROM PAYMENT
WHERE uid = 117 OR 1=1;
```

The additional SQL code "OR 1=1" inserted, the SQL injection, causes the search filter to become inactive with the user identification in the generated query, since 1=1 is always true, and an OR operation is always true even if only one of the conditions is true. Therefore, in this simple example, the website is exposing protectable data due to this SQL injection.

SQL injection is a security vulnerability that should not be underestimated. Hackers repeatedly succeed in attacking even well-known websites via this mechanism. There are several ways to protect a website from this. SQL code generation can be outsourced to typed stored functions in the database (see Sect. 3.6.1). In the example above, a server-side function can accept a user ID as input as a numeric value and then return the credit card information as output. If this function were given a text instead of a number, an error message would be generated. As a client-side option, the Java code could be modified to use so-called prepared statements instead of inserting the input string directly into the query text:

```
PreparedStatement ps = con.prepareStatement(
"SELECT credit_card_number, name FROM PAYMENT" +
"WHERE uid = "?");
ps.setString(1, + request.getParameter("uid"));
ResultSet resultset = ps.executeQuery();
```

In summary, SQL databases provide comprehensive protection mechanisms with the GRANT and REVOKE and CREATE VIEW constructs. However, these control mechanisms can be leveraged with code injection in the larger context of Web-based information systems. The situation is similar for NoSQL databases, as we will see in the following sections.

4.2.2   Authentication in Cypher

Newer versions of Cypher provide mechanisms for authentication and authorization of users. The CREATE USER command can be used to create a user account for Murphy. The password must be changed the first time the user logs in.

```
CREATE USER murphy
SET PASSWORD 'jd7k_Ddjh$1'
CHANGE REQUIRED;
```

With SHOW USERS, all existing user accounts can be displayed. To rename a user account, use the command RENAME USER:

```
RENAME USER murphy TO murphy.kent
```

An account can be changed with the command ALTER USER, e.g., to reset the password. With the addition CHANGE NOT REQUIRED, the specified password can be reused.

```
ALTER USER murphy.kent
SET PASSWORD 'j83hd_:sdfD'
CHANGE NOT REQUIRED;
```

For authorization, Cypher offers the GRANT command. There are predefined roles for the role-based access control (RBAC):

- **PUBLIC** can access its own HOME database and perform all functions there. All user accounts have this role.
- **reader** can read data from all databases.
- **editor** can read databases and modify contents.
- **publisher** can read and edit and add new node and edge types and property names.
- **architect** has in addition to publisher the ability to manage indexes and integrity constraints.
- **admin** can manage databases, users, roles, and permissions in addition to the architect role.

The following command assigns the role architect to user account murphy.kent:

```
GRANT ROLE architect TO murphy.kent;
```

With REVOKE, authorizations can be removed again:

```
REVOKE ROLE architect FROM murphy.kent;
```

Privileges can also be set in a fine-grained way. The following command allows reading all node types (*) of the "company" graph for user account muprh.

```
GRANT MATCH {*} ON GRAPH company NODE *
TO murphy.kent
```

Authorization works similarly for relationship types. The following Cypher code creates a new role project.admin, gives it the ability to create relationships of type Team, and grants permissions to this role to murphy.kent.

```
CREATE ROLE project.admin;

GRANT WRITE {*} ON GRAPH company RELATIONSHIP Team
TO project.admin;

GRANT ROLE project.admin TO murphy.kent;
```

Cypher supports the division of access rights at the level of individual properties. The following ensures that the role project.admin can read all nodes and edges, but cannot see the property wage of the table personnel.

```
GRANT MATCH {*} ON GRAPH company NODE *
TO project.admin;

GRANT MATCH {*} ON GRAPH company RELATIONSHIP *
TO project.admin;

DENY READ {Wage} ON GRAPH Company NODE Personnel
TO project.admin;
```

If a user account is forbidden to read a property, it can be queried in a Cypher request without error message, but the return value remains empty (NULL, cf. Sect. 3.3.4).

Cypher Injection
Cypher injection is an attack using specifically formatted input from users to perform unexpected operations on the database, read, or modify data without permission. Let's assume that a Web application allows to insert new records about projects into the database. To do this, a Web server executes the following Java code:

```
String query = "CREATE (p:project)"
  + "SET p.name = '"
  + user_input + "'"
session.run(query);
```

This code is vulnerable to Cypher injection. Users could write the following input to the Web form:

```
"Anything' WITH true as x MATCH (p:project) DELETE p//"
```

Cypher code has been injected in this user input. If this string is interpreted in the Java code above, the following Cypher command is generated:

```
CREATE (p:project)
SET p.name = 'Anything'
WITH true as x
MATCH (p:Project) DETACH DELETE p //'
```

It doesn't matter what other code comes directly before the quotation mark that terminates the string. The WITH statement after the CREATE command allows in Cypher to append a MATCH and DELETE statement. This deletes all project data here. All other strings are reduced to comments with the double crossbar //, and are therefore not executed as code.

To work around this problem, user input can be passed as parameters in Cypher. This way the query is precompiled, and the parameter inputs are not interpreted by the DBMS.

```
HashMap<String,Object> params = new HashMap();
params.put( "name", <user input> );
String qry = "CREATE (p:project) SET p.name = $name";
System.out.println(qry);
session.run(qry, params);
```

In summary, Cypher databases provide a comprehensive protection mechanism using the GRANT and REVOKE constructs, even at the level of individual node types, edge types, and properties. When embedding Cypher in programming languages, care must be taken to prevent injection attacks.

4.2.3   Authentication and Authorization in MQL

Sophisticated concepts of access control are present in MQL. The basis is to create a user account for authentication with the createUser() method:

```
use Company
db.createUser(
   {
     user: "murphy",
     pwd: passwordPrompt(),
     roles: [
         { role: "read", db: "Company" },
     ]
   }
)
```

This request creates a user account "murphy" in the database "Company" With the passwordPrompt() specification, the password is not passed as plain text, but by command prompt. This has security advantages. The password is not visible on the screen, is not saved as a file, does not appear in the command history of the command line, and is invisible to other processes of the operating system. However, the createUser() function can be passed the password in plain text if necessary.

```
db.changeUserPassword("murphy",
"KJDdfgSD$_3")
```

To authorize accounts for database actions, database-level roles can be communicated in the roles field of the createUser() method. There are built-in roles in MongoDB that cover the typical requirements:

- **read**: read access
- **readWrite**: read and write access
- **dbAdmin**: rights for indexes and statistics
- **userAdmin**: rights to create user accounts and define and assign roles
- **dbOwner**: combines the rights of all above roles

These roles each apply to all collections in a database. In order to set the user rights on the level of collections, user-defined roles can be created. For example, to give a user account write access to the "Staff" collection, a "staffAdmin" role can be created using the "createRole()" method:

```
use admin
db.createRole(
    {
       role: "staffAdmin",
       privileges: [
          {
             actions: [ "insert", "remove", "update" ],
             resource: { db: "Company",
                          collection: "Staff" }
          }
       ],
       roles: [] } )
```

This command gives the "staffAdmin" role the privileges to perform the insert, remove, and update actions on the "Staff" collection. This role can now be assigned to individual user accounts using the "grantRolesToUser()" method.

```
use Company
db.grantRolesToUser(
    "murphy",
    [
       { role: "staffAdmin", db: "Company" } ] )
```

With the opposite function "revokeRolesFromUser()," roles can be taken away again:

```
use reporting
db.revokeRolesFromUser(
    }, "murphy",
    [
       { role: "read", db: "Company" } ] )
```

MQL does not offer the possibility to grant privileges to user accounts individually. All access rights are distributed via roles. Roles allow to distribute access rights on collections level. To restrict read access to individual fields and to subsets of documents, MQL can define views.

```
Use Company;
db.createView(
   "vStaff",
   "Staff",
   [
        { $match: { Salary:
        { $gte : 80000, $lte : 160000} } },
        { $project: { Salary: 0 } }
   ] )
```

This view shows only employees with salaries between 80,000 and 160,000, but without the exact salary information, because the field was expanded in the view definition with an exclusion projection.

Subsequently, a user-defined role can be authorized to read this view instead of the original collection:

```
use Company
db.grantPrivilegesToRole(
   "staffAdmin",
   [
      {
         resource: {
                db: "Company",
                collection: "vStaff" },
         actions: [ "find" ]
      }
   )
```

JavaScript Injection

Although MQL is not interpreted as a language, but is parameterized with JSON objects, NoSQL injection attacks are certainly possible with MongoDB. Let's assume, for example, that the user name and password for authentication in a Web application with MongoDB are passed as Get parameters via the URL:

```
https://example.org/login?user=u526&password=123456
```

Let's further assume that in the background, this URL request to the Web server is forwarded to the MongoDB database in a Python program to check if the combination of user and password is present in the database:

```
result = collection.find({"$where":
"this.user == '"
              + parse_qs(urlparse(url).query)['user'][0]
    + "' && this.pw == '"
              + parse_qs(urlparse(url).query)['pw'][0]
    + "'" })
```

Given the input parameters, this Python program generates and executes the following MQL query:

```
Db.users.find({'$where':
"this.user == 'u526'
    && this.pw == '123456'" } )
```

The $where operator in MQL, in the current version 5.0 of MongoDB, allows a JavaScript expression to be checked for document selection. The operator is vulnerable to JavaScript injection.

If an attacker injects JavaScript code into the URL, it could look like this:

```
'https://example.org/login?user=u526&pw=%27%3B%20return%20tr
ue%2B%27
```

In this URL, special characters like single quotes (%27), a semicolon (%3B), spaces (%20), and a plus sign (%2B) have been injected together with JavaScript code like "return true." The server generates the following query to MongoDB from this:

```
Db.users.find({'$where':
"this.user == 'u526'
    && this.pw == ''; return true+'" } )
```

By injecting the statement "return true," the filter predicate for checking users and passwords becomes a tautology, so it is always true. Thus, we can bypass the password in this example.

A real authentication is certainly not implemented this way. We simply want to show here that the injection is principally possible in MQL. This simple example should suffice for that.

MongoDB does not provide stored procedures or prepared statements to prevent injections. However, server-side execution of JavaScript can be disabled. In addition, every input must be checked via user interface. There are sanitizing libraries that provide additional security. For example, special characters can be escaped.

4.3   Integrity Constraints

The integrity of a database is a fundamental security objective that the database management system must support.

The term integrity or consistency refers to the absence of contradictions in databases. A database is considered to have integrity or consistency if the stored data is recorded without errors and correctly reflects the desired information content. Data integrity, on the other hand, is violated when ambiguities or contradictory facts come to light. For a consistent representation of employees in a database, we assume, for example, that the names of the employees, street names, location information, etc. are correct and exist in reality.

The rules that apply to insert or change operations at any time are called integrity constraints. It makes sense not to specify such rules individually in each program, but to specify them comprehensively once in the database schema. Depending on the maturity level, the DBMS can automatically check compliance with the rules defined by the integrity constraints. A distinction is made between declarative, procedural, and transactional integrity conditions. Declarative integrity conditions for ensuring integrity are those rules that can be expressed by the database schema itself. Procedural conditions are defined by programs with sequences of statements. Transactional consistency rules refer to consistency across multiple individual actions.

The following classes of integrity conditions are essential to database management systems:

- **Uniqueness constraint:** An attribute value can exist at most once within a given class of records.
- **Existence constraint:** An attribute has to exist at least once within a given class of records and must not be empty.
- **Key constraint:** An attribute value has to exist exactly once within a given set of records, and the corresponding attribute has to be present for each record of a class. The key condition combines uniqueness and existence constraints. Keys can also be defined on attribute combinations.
- **Primary key constraint:** If multiple attributes exist that satisfy the key condition, at most one of them can be defined as primary.
- **Domain constraint:** The set of possible values of an attribute can be restricted, for example, using data types, enumerations, and checking rules.
- **Referential integrity constraint:** Attributes within a data set that refer to other data sets must not point to nothing, i.e., the referenced data sets must exist.

In the following, we will compare examples of possible integrity conditions for relational databases, graph databases, and document databases using the SQL, Cypher, and MQL languages.

4.3.1   Relational Integrity Constraints

Integrity or consistency of data means that stored data does not contradict itself. A database has integrity/consistency if the stored data is free of errors and accurately represents the anticipated informational value. Data integrity is impaired if there are ambiguities or conflicting records. For example, a consistent EMPLOYEE table requires that the names of employees, streets, and cities really exist and are correctly assigned.

Declarative integrity constraints are defined during the generation of a new table in the CREATE TABLE statement using the data definition language. Constraints can be added to, changed, and removed from existing tables using the ALTER TABLE statement. In the example in Fig. 4.3, the primary key for the DEPART-MENT table is specified as an integrity constraint with PRIMARY KEY. Primary and foreign key of the EMPLOYEE table are defined similarly.

The various types of declarative integrity constraints are:

- **Primary key definition**: PRIMARY KEY defines a unique primary key for a table. Primary keys must, by definition, not contain any NULL values.
- **Foreign key definition**: FOREIGN KEY can be used to specify a foreign key, which relates to another table in the REFERENCES clause.
- **Uniqueness**: The uniqueness of an attribute can be determined by the UNIQUE constraint. Unlike primary keys, unique attributes may contain NULL values.
- **Existence**: The NOT NULL constraint dictates that the respective attribute must not contain any NULL values. For instance, the attribute Name in the EMPLOYEE table in Fig. 4.3 is set to NOT NULL, because there must be a name for every employee.
- **Check constraint**: Such rules can be declared with the CHECK command and apply to every tuple in the table. For example, the CHECK Salary >30,000 statement in the STAFF table in Fig. 4.3 ensures that the annual salary of each employee is at least USD 30,000.
- **Set to NULL for changes or deletions**: ON UPDATE SET NULL or ON DELETE SET NULL declares for dependent tables that the foreign key value of a dependent tuple is set to NULL when the corresponding tuple in the referenced table is modified or removed.
- **Restricted changes or deletion**: If ON UPDATE RESTRICT or ON DELETE RESTRICT is set, tuples cannot be manipulated or deleted while there are still dependent tuples referencing them.
- **Cascading changes or deletion**: ON UPDATE CASCADE or ON DELETE CASCADE defines that the modification or removal of a reference tuple is extended to all dependent tuples.

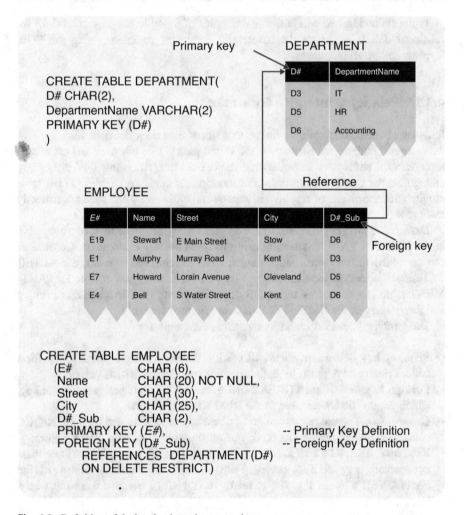

Fig. 4.3 Definition of declarative integrity constraints

In Fig. 4.3, a restrictive deletion rule has been specified for the two tables DEPARTMENT and EMPLOYEE. This ensures that individual departments can only be removed if they have no dependent employee tuples left. The command

```
DELETE FROM Department WHERE D# = 'D6'
```

would therefore return an error message, since the employees Stewart and Bell are listed under the accounting department.

Aside from delete operations, declarative integrity constraints can also affect insert and update operations. For instance, the insert operation

```
INSERT INTO EMPLOYEE
VALUES ('E20','Kelly','Market Ave S','Canton','D7')
```

will also return an error message: Department D7 is not yet listed in the referenced table DEPARTMENT, but due to the foreign key constraint, the DBMS checks whether the key D7 exists in the referenced table before the insertion.

Declarative, or static, integrity constraints can be defined during table generation (CREATE TABLE statement). On the other hand, procedural, or dynamic, integrity constraints compare database states before and after a change, i.e., they can only be checked during runtime. The triggers are an alternative to declarative integrity constraints because they initiate a sequence of procedural branches via instructions. Triggers are mostly defined by a trigger name, a database operation, and a list of subsequent actions:

```
CREATE TRIGGER NoCuts  -- trigger name
BEFORE UPDATE ON Employee   -- database operation
FOR EACH ROW BEGIN              -- subsequent action
IF NEW.Salary < OLD.Salary
THEN set NEW.Salary = OLD.Salary
END IF;
END
```

The example above shows a situation where employees' salaries must not be cut, so before updating the EMPLOYEE table, the trigger checks whether the new salary is lower than the old one. If that is the case, the integrity constraint is violated, and the new salary is reset to the original value from before the update. This is a very basic example meant to illustrate the core concept. In a production environment, the user would also be notified.

Working with triggers can be tricky, since individual triggers may prompt other triggers, which raises the issue of terminating all subsequent actions. In most commercial database systems, the simultaneous activation of multiple triggers is prohibited to ensure a clear action sequence and the proper termination of triggers.

4.3.2 Integrity Constraints for Graphs in Cypher

In graph databases, implicit and explicit integrity constraints exist. The graph database model implicitly checks referential integrity by ensuring that all edges are connected to existing nodes. The four consistency conditions that Cypher explicitly supports are the following:

- Unique node property constraints
- Relationship property existence constraints
- Node property existence constraints
- Node key constraints

Uniqueness Constraint for Node Properties
Node properties in the graph can be defined to be unique for a node type, i.e., to occur only once per node type. For example, the following integrity condition specifies that the e-mail address of employees must be unique:

```
CREATE CONSTRAINT EMPLOYEE_EMailAddress
ON (e:EMPLOYEE)
ASSERT e.EMailAddress IS UNIQUE
```

With the opposite command DROP CONSTRAINT, the integrity condition can be deleted again:

```
DROP CONSTRAINT EMPLOYEE_EMailAddress
```

Existence Constraint for Node Properties
An integrity condition can be defined to ensure that a property must exist for each node of a node type. For example, the following condition enforces that all employees receive a social security number (Ssn):

```
CREATE CONSTRAINT EMPLOYEE_Svn
ON (m:EMPLOYEE)
ASSERT EXISTS (m.Ssn)
```

Existence Constraint for Edge Attributes (Relationship Property)
For edge attributes, we can define that they must exist at each edge of an edge type. For example, we can ensure that a workload is specified for each project assignment of employees:

```
CREATE CONSTRAINT PROJECT_EMPLOYMENT_Workload
ON ()- [R:PROJECT ASSIGNMENT]-()
ASSERT EXISTS (R.Workload)
```

Node Key Condition

For a node type, it can be defined that a property or a combination of properties is a key. This means that the property or combination is always present for that node type and that it is unique for that node type. For example, the following integrity condition specifies that for collaborators, the Number property is a key:

```
CREATE CONSTRAINT EMPLOYEE_Number
ON (e:EMPLOYEE)
ASSERT (e.Number) IS NODE KEY
```

There can be more than one key for a node type. The key condition is simply a combination of the existence and uniqueness conditions.

Value Range Conditions

Cypher provides schema-free data types for properties. This means that the same property within the same node type may have different data types at individual nodes. The same is true for edge properties. Thus, there are no range conditions for properties in Cypher. For example, the following query is allowed:

```
CREATE (:EMPLOYEE { Ssn: 1 });
CREATE (:EMPLOYEE { Ssn: "A" });
```

These statements insert two EMPLOYEE nodes with the Ssn property, first with type Integer and then with type String. In terms of schema freedom, this is possible. However, schema freedom does not mean that Cypher has no datatypes. The apoc. meta.type() function can be used to output the list of data types it stores for an input:

```
MATCH (n) RETURN distinct apoc.meta.type(n.Ssn)
```

Referential Integrity

As a graph database language, Cypher implicitly checks all edges for referential integrity, i.e., neither primary nor foreign keys need to be explicitly declared for linking nodes to directed edges. The database management system ensures that edges refer to existing nodes in all cases. Nodes can therefore only be deleted if there are no edges associated with them. In addition, it is not possible to insert edges without nodes. Edges must always be created as triples together with source and target nodes. If necessary, the connected nodes can also be created directly during the insertion of the edge.

4.3.3   Integrity Constraints in Document Databases with MQL

The MongoDB database system, with its concept of schema freedom, offers a flexible insertion of new data. This means that any data structure can be inserted into all collections by default. This is especially useful for dealing with heterogeneous data (Big Data variety). Nevertheless, it is possible to ensure data integrity in MQL in various ways.

Primary Key Conditions

In MongoDB, each document in a collection has a unique field with property "_id" (cf. Sect. 3.5.2). This satisfies the conditions of a primary key for the document. Users can assign their own unique value to the "_id" field, or the database management system can automatically generate a unique object identity.

Uniqueness Constraints

It is possible in MQL to create an index for a property that ensures the uniqueness of the property values. For example, the following statement prevents records from being inserted into the EMPLOYEE collection if the value of the EMPLOYEE. EMailAddress field already exists.

```
db.EMPLOYEES.createIndex(
{ "EMPLOYEE.EMailAddress": 1},
{ unique: true } )
```

Existence Constraints

MQL supports validation of input documents with JSON Schema (see Sect. 2.5.1). This is the variant of schema validation recommended by the manufacturer. For example, JSON Schema can be used to specify which properties must be present for a document. The following example creates a collection EMPLOYEE with validator that sets an existence condition for the fields EMPLOYEE.Name and EMPLOYEE. Status. Thus, only documents can be inserted which have at least these two fields.

```
db.createCollection("EMPLOYEE", {
    validator: {
        $jsonSchema: {
            required: [ "EMPLOYEE.Name", "EMPLOYEE.Status" ]
        }
    }
})
```

Domain Constraints

In addition to JSON Schema, MQL supports validation rules which allow filters with all existing filter operators, with few exceptions. This allows sophisticated value range conditions to be defined. For example, the following statement creates a new collection EMPLOYEE with a validator that checks if titles are of type string and restricts the Status field to three possible values.

```
db.createCollection( "PROJECTS",
    { validator: { $and:[
        { PROJECTS.title: { $type: "string" } },
        { PROJECTS.status: { $in:
            [ "Requested", "Active", "Performed"]
} } ] } } )
```

Referential Integrity Constraints

MQL assumes, based on the document definition (see Sect. 1.5), that records are complete in themselves, so there is no way in MQL to define relationships, between documents or foreign keys, in the database schema. This is a deliberate choice, as assuming completeness of documents allows for faster queries and easier partitioning of the database for very large data sets.

In summary, we see that despite foregoing referential integrity checking in favor of scalability for Big Data, MQL has comprehensive and flexible mechanisms for checking integrity constraints.

4.4 Transaction Consistency

4.4.1 Multi-user Operation

The terms consistency and integrity of a database describe a state in which the stored data does not contradict itself. Integrity constraints are to ensure that data consistency is maintained for all insert and update operations.

One potential difficulty arises when multiple users simultaneously access a database and modify contained data. This can cause conflicts involving blocking each other (deadlocks) or even consistency violations. Depending on the use case, breaches of consistency rules are absolutely unacceptable. A classic example are posting transactions in banking, where the principles of double-entry bookkeeping must always be observed and must not be violated.

Transaction management systems ensure that consistent database states are only changed to other consistent database states. These systems follow an all-or-none rule to prevent transactions from executing partial changes to the database. Either all requested changes are applied or the database is not modified at all. Pessimistic or optimistic concurrency control methods are used to guarantee that the database remains in a consistent state at any time.

However, with comprehensive Web applications, it has been shown that striving for full consistency is not always desirable. This is due to the CAP theorem, which states that any database can, at most, have two out of three: consistency, availability, or partition tolerance. Therefore, if the focus is on availability and partition tolerance, temporarily inconsistent database states are unavoidable.

4.4.2 ACID

Ensuring the integrity of data is a major requirement for many database applications. The *transaction management* of a database system *allows conflict-free simultaneous work by multiple users*. Changes to the database are only applied and become visible if all integrity constraints as defined by the users are fulfilled.

The term *transaction* describes database operations bound by integrity rules, which update database states while maintaining consistency. More specifically, a transaction is a sequence of operations that has to be atomic, consistent, isolated, and durable.

- **Atomicity (A)**: Transactions are either applied in full or not at all, leaving no trace of its effects in the database. The intermediate states created by the individual operations within a transaction are not visible to other concurrent transactions. A transaction can therefore be seen as a *unit for the resettability* of incomplete transactions.
- **Consistency (C)**: During the transaction, integrity constraints may be temporarily violated; however, at the end of the transaction, all of them must be met again. A transaction therefore always results in moving the database from one consistent state into another and ensures the integrity of data. It is considered a *unit for maintaining consistency*.
- **Isolation (I)**: The concept of isolation requires that parallel transactions generate the same results as transactions in single-user environments. Isolating individual transactions from transactions executed simultaneously protects them from unwanted side effects. This makes transactions a *unit for serializability*.

- **Durability (D)**: Database states must remain valid and be maintained until they are changed by a transaction. In case of software errors, system crashes, or errors on external storage media, durability retains the effects of a correctly completed transaction. In relation to the reboot and recovery procedures of databases, transactions can be considered a unit for recovery.

These four principles, *Atomicity* (A), *Consistency* (C), *Isolation* (I), and *Durability* (D), describe the *ACID concept of transactions*, which is the basis of several database systems and guarantees that all users can only make changes that lead from one consistent database state to another. Inconsistent interim states remain invisible externally and are rolled back in case of errors.

4.4.3 Serializability

A major aspect in the definition of operation systems and programming languages is the coordination or synchronization of active processes and the mutual exclusion of simultaneous processes. For database systems, too, concurrent accesses to the same data objects must be serialized in order for database users to be able to work independently from each other.

Concept of Serializability
A system of simultaneous transactions is synchronized correctly if there is a serial execution creating the same database state.

The principle of serializability ensures that the results in the database are identical, whether the transactions are executed one after the other or in parallel. The focus in defining conditions for serializability is on the READ and WRITE operations within each transaction, i.e., the operations which *read and write records in the database*.

Banking provides typical examples of concurrent transactions. The basic integrity constraint for posting transactions is that debit and credit have to be balanced. Figure 4.4 shows two simultaneously running posting transactions with their READ and WRITE operations in chronological order. Neither transaction on its own changes the total amount of the accounts a, b, and c. The transaction TRX_1 credits account a with 100 units of currency and, at the same time, debits account b with 100 units of currency. The posting transaction TRX_2 similarly credits account b and debits account c for 200 currency units each. Both transactions therefore fulfill the integrity constraint of bookkeeping, since the ledgers are balanced.

However, if both transactions are executed simultaneously, a *conflict* arises: The transaction TRX_1 misses the credit b := b+200[1] done by TRX_2, since this change is not immediately written back, and reads a "wrong" value for account b. After both

---

[1] The notation b := b+200 means that the current balance of account b is increased by 200 currency units.

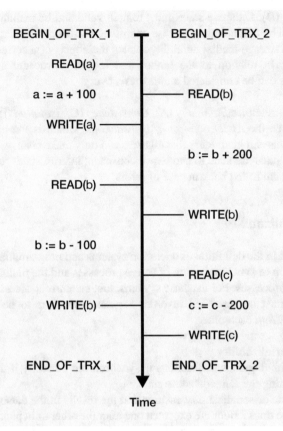

Fig. 4.4 Conflicting posting transactions

transactions are finished, account a holds the original amount + 100 units (a+100), the amount in account b is reduced by 100 units (b−100), and c holds 200 units less (c−200). Due to the Transaction TRX_1 missing the b+200 step for account b and not calculating the amount accordingly, the total credits and debits are not balanced, and the integrity constraint is violated.

Potential conflicts can be discovered beforehand. To do so, those READ and WRITE operations affecting a certain object, i.e., a single data value, a record, a table, or sometimes even an entire database, are filtered from all transactions. The *granularity* (relative size) of the object decides how well the picked transactions can be synchronized. The larger the granularity, the smaller the degree of transaction synchronization and vice versa. All READ and WRITE operations from different transactions that apply to a specific object are therefore listed in the *log* of the object x, short LOG(x). The LOG(x) of object x contains, in chronological order, all READ and WRITE operations accessing the object.

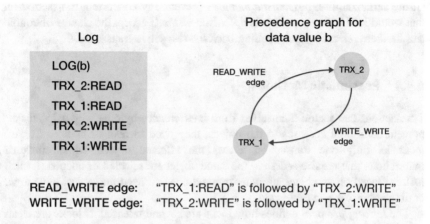

Fig. 4.5 Analyzing a log using a precedence graph

In our example of the concurrent posting transactions TRX_1 and TRX_2, the objects in question are the accounts a, b, and c. As shown in Fig. 4.5, the log for object b, for instance, contains four entries (see also Fig. 4.4). First, TRX_2 reads the value of b, and then TRX_1 reads the same value, before TRX_2 gets to write back the modified value of b. The last log entry is caused by TRX_1 when it overwrites the value from TRX_2 with its own modified value for b. Assessing the logs is an easy way to analyze conflicts between concurring transactions. A *precedence graph* represents the transactions as nodes and possible READ_WRITE or WRITE_WRITE conflicts as directed edges (arched arrows). For any one object, WRITE operations following READs or WRITEs can lead to conflicts, while multiple READ operations are generally not a conflict risk. The precedence graph does therefore not include any READ_READ edges.

Figure 4.5 shows not only the log of object b for the posting transactions TRX_1 and TRX_2 but also the corresponding precedence graph. Starting from the TRX_1 node, a READ on object b is followed by a WRITE on it by TRX_2, visualized as a directed edge from the TRX_1 node to the TRX_2 node. According to the log, a WRITE_WRITE edge goes from the TRX_2 node to the TRX_1 node, since the WRITE operation by TRX_2 is succeeded by another WRITE on the same object by TRX_1. The precedence graph is therefore cyclical, in that there is a directed path from a node that leads back to the same node. This cyclical dependency between the transactions TRX_1 and TRX_2 shows that they are not serializable.

Serializability Condition

A set of transactions is serializable if the corresponding precedence graphs contain no cycles.

The serializability condition states that multiple transactions have to yield the same results in a multi-user environment as in a single-user environment. In order to ensure serializability, *pessimistic methods* prevent any concurrent transaction runs that would lead to conflicts, while *optimistic methods* accept the chance of conflicts and fix them retroactively by rolling back the respective transactions.

4.4.4 Pessimistic Methods

Transactions can secure themselves from interferences by others by using locks to prevent additional accesses to the objects they need to read or update. *Exclusive locks* let only one transaction access the affected object, while concurring transactions that require access to the same object are rejected or queued. If such a lock is placed on an object, all other transactions that need this object have to wait until the object is released again.

The *locking protocol* defines how locks are set and released. If locks are cleared too early or without proper care, non-serializable sequences can arise. It is also necessary to prevent multiple transactions from blocking each other and creating a deadlock.

The exclusive locking of objects requires the operations LOCK and UNLOCK. Every object has to be locked before a transaction can access it. While an object x is blocked by a LOCK(x), no other transaction can read or update it. Only after the lock on object x has been released by UNLOCK(x) can another transaction place a new lock on it.

Normally, locks follow a well-defined protocol and cannot be requested or released arbitrarily.

Two-Phase Locking Protocol
Two-phase locking (2PL) prevents a transaction from *requesting an additional LOCK after the first UNLOCK.*

Transactions under this locking protocol are always executed in two phases: During the *expanding phase*, all locks are requested and placed; during the *shrinking phase*, the locks are released one by one. This means that during the expanding phase of a transaction with 2PL, LOCKs can only be placed, gradually or all at once, but never released. UNLOCK operations are only allowed during the shrinking phase, again individually or in total at the end of the transaction. Two-phase locking effectively prohibits an intermix of creating and releasing locks.

Figure 4.6 shows a possible 2PL protocol for the posting transaction TRX_1. During the expanding phase, first account a is locked and then account b, before both accounts are released again in the same order. It would also be possible to have both locks in this example created right at the beginning of the transaction instead of one after the other. Similarly, they could both be released at once at the end of the transaction, rather than progressively.

However, requesting the locks on the objects a and b one by one during the expanding phase and releasing them individually during the shrinking phase increase the degree of synchronization for TRX_1. If both locks were set at the beginning and

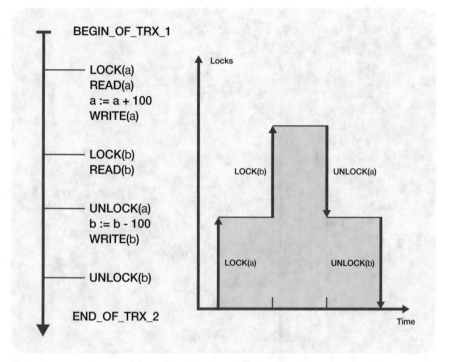

Fig. 4.6 Sample two-phase locking protocol for the transaction TRX_1

only lifted at the end of the transaction, concurring transactions would have to wait the entire processing time of TRX_1 for the release of objects a and b.

Overall, two-phase locking ensures the serializability of simultaneous transactions.

Pessimistic concurrency control

With the help of two-phase locking, any set of concurring transactions is serializable. Due to the strict separation of expanding and shrinking phase, the 2PL protocol prevents any cyclical dependencies in all precedence graphs from the start; the concurring transactions remain free of conflict. In case of the two posting transactions TRX_1 and TRX_2, that means that with properly planned locking and unlocking, they can be synchronized without any violation of the integrity constraint.

Figure 4.7 shows how such a conflict-free parallel run of TRX_1 and TRX_2 can be achieved. LOCKs and UNLOCKs are set according to 2PL rules, so that, for instance, account b is locked by TRX_2 and can only be unlocked during the transaction's shrinking phase, while TRX_1 has to wait to get its own lock on b. Once TRX_2 releases account b via UNLOCK(b), TRX_1 requests access to and a lock on b. In this run, TRX_1 reads the correct value for b, i.e., b+200. The two transactions TRX_1 and TRX_2 can therefore be executed simultaneously.

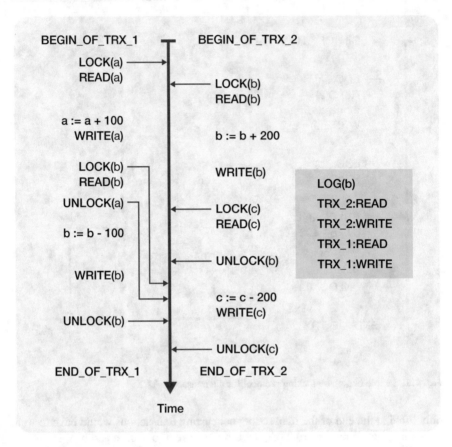

Fig. 4.7 Conflict-free posting transactions

2PL causes a slight delay in the transaction TRX_1, but after both transactions are finished, integrity is retained. The value of account a has increased by 100 units (a +100), as has the value of account b (b+100), while the value of account c has been reduced by 200 units (c−200). The total amount across all three accounts has therefore remained the same.

A comparison between the LOG(b) from Fig. 4.7 and the previously discussed log from Fig. 4.5 shows a major difference: It is now strictly one read (TRX_2: READ) and one write (TRX_2: WRITE) by TRX_2 before TRX_1 gets access to account b and can also read (TRX_1: READ) and write (TRX_1:WRITE) on it. The corresponding precedence graph contains neither READ_WRITE nor WRITE_WRITE edges between the nodes TRX_1 and TRX_2, i.e., it is free of cycles. The two posting transactions therefore fulfill the integrity constraint.

In many database applications, the demand for high serializability prohibits the use of entire databases or tables as locking units. Consequently, it is common to define smaller locking units, such as database excerpts, parts of tables, tuples, or even individual data values. Ideally, *locking units* are defined in a way that allows for *hierarchical dependencies* in lock management. For instance, if a set of tuples is locked by a specific transaction, the superordinate locking units such as the containing table or database must not be completely blocked by other transactions during the lock's validity. When an object is put under an exclusive lock, locking hierarchies can be used to automatically evaluate and mark superordinate objects accordingly.

Various locking modes are also important: The most basic classification of locks is the dichotomy of read and write locks. Read locks (or shared locks) grant read-only access for the object to a transaction, while write locks (or exclusive locks) permit read and write access to the object.

Another pessimistic method ensuring serializability are timestamps that allow for strictly ordered object access according to the age of the transactions. Such time tracking methods preserve the chronological order of the individual operations within the transactions and therefore avoid conflicts.

4.4.5 Optimistic Methods

Optimistic methods are based on the assumption that conflicts between concurring transactions will be rare occurrences. No locks are set initially in order to increase the degree of synchronization and reduce wait times. Before transactions can conclude successfully, they are validated retroactively.

Transactions with *optimistic concurrency control* have three parts: *read phase*, *validation phase*, and *write phase*. During the read phase, all required objects are read, saved to a separate transaction workspace, and processed there, without any preventative locks being placed. After processing, the validation phase is used to check whether the applied changes conflict with any other transactions. The goal is to check currently active transactions for compatibility and absence of conflicts. If two transactions block each other, the transaction currently in the validation phase is deferred. In case of successful validation, all changes from the workspace are entered into the database during the write phase.

The use of transaction-specific workspaces increases concurrency in optimistic methods, since reading transactions do not impede each other. Checks are only necessary before writing back changes. This means that the read phases of multiple transactions can run simultaneously without any objects being locked. Instead, the validity of the objects in the workspace, i.e., whether they still match the current state of the database, must be confirmed in the validation phase.

For the sake of simplicity, we will assume that validation phases of different transactions do not overlap. To ensure this, the time the transaction enters the validation phase is marked. This allows for both the start times of validation phases and the transactions themselves to be sorted chronologically. Once a transaction enters the validation phase, it is checked for serializability.

The procedure to do so in optimistic concurrency control is as follows: Let TRX_t be the transaction to be validated and TRX_1 to TRX_k be all concurrent

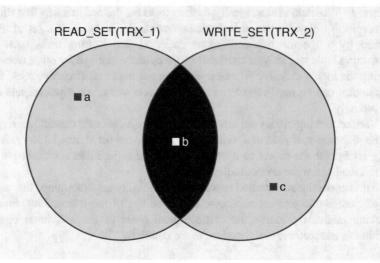

Fig. 4.8 Serializability condition for TRX_1 not met

transactions that have already been validated during the read phase of TRX_t. All other transactions can be ignored since they are handled in strict chronological order. All objects read by TRX_t must be validated, since they could have been modified by any of the critical transactions TRX_1 to TRX_k in the meantime. The set of objects read by TRX_t is labeled READ_SET(TRX_t), and the set of objects written by the critical transactions is labeled WRITE_SET(TRX_1,...,TRX_k). This gives us the following serializability condition:

Optimistic Concurrency Control
In order for the transaction TRX_t to be serializable in optimistic concurrency control, the sets READ_ SET(TRX_t) and WRITE_SET(TRX_1,...,TRX_k) must be *disjoint*.

For a more practical example, we will revisit the two posting transactions TRX_1 and TRX_2 from Fig. 4.4, with the assumption that TRX_2 has been validated before TRX_1. To assess whether TRX_1 is serializable in this scenario, we compare the objects read by TRX_1 and those written by TRX_2 (Fig. 4.8) to see that object b is part of both sets, i.e., READ_SET(TRX_1) and WRITE_SET (TRX_2) overlap, thereby violating the serializability condition. The posting transaction TRX_1 has to be rolled back and restarted.

Optimistic methods can be improved by preventatively ensuring the disjointness of the sets READ_SET and WRITE_SET, using the validation phase of a transaction TRX_t to check whether it will modify any objects that have already been read by other transactions. This assessment method limits the validation effort to transactions that actually make changes to database contents.

4.4.6 Recovery

Various errors can occur during database operation and will normally be mitigated or corrected by the database system itself. Some error cases, such as integrity violations or deadlocks, have already been mentioned in the sections on concurrency control. Other issues may be caused by operating systems or hardware, for instance, when data remains unreadable after a save error on an external medium.

The *restoration of a correct database state after an error* is called recovery. It is essential for recovery to know where an error occurred: in an application, in the database software, or in the hardware. In case of integrity violations or after an application program "crashes," it is sufficient to roll back and then repeat one or several transactions. With severe errors, it may be necessary to retrieve earlier saves from backup archives and restore the database state by partial transaction re-runs.

In order to roll back transactions, the database system requires certain information. Usually, a copy of an object (called *before image*) is written to a *log file*[2] before the object is modified. In addition to the object's old values, the file also contains markers signaling the beginning and end of the transaction. In order for the log file to be used efficiently in case of errors, *checkpoints* are set either based on commands in the application program or for certain system events. A system-wide checkpoint contains a list of the transactions active up until that time. If a restart is needed, the database system merely has to find the latest checkpoint and reset the unfinished transaction.

This procedure is illustrated in Fig. 4.9: After system failure, the log file must be read backward until the last checkpoint. Of special interest are those transactions that had not been able to indicate their correct conclusion with an EOT (end of transaction) marker, such as the transactions TRX_2 and TRX_5 in our example. For them, the previous database state has to be restored with the help of the log file (*undo*). For TRX_5, the file has to be read back until the BOT (beginning of transaction) marker in order to retrieve the transaction's before image. Regardless of the type of checkpoint, the newest state (*after image*) must be restored for at least TRX_4 (*redo*).

The recovery of a database after a defect in an external storage medium requires a backup of the database and an inventory of all updates since the creation of the backup copy. Backups are usually made before and after the end-of-day processing, since they are quite time-consuming. During the day, changes are recorded in the log file, with the most up-to-date state for each object being listed.

Securing databases requires a clear-cut *disaster prevention* procedure on the part of the responsible database specialists. Backup copies are usually stored in generations, physically separate, and sometimes redundant. The creation of backup files and the removal of old versions have to be fully documented. In case of errors or for disaster drills, the task is to restore current data from backup files and logged changes within a reasonable timeframe.

---

[2]This log file is not to be confused with the log from Sect. 4.2.2.

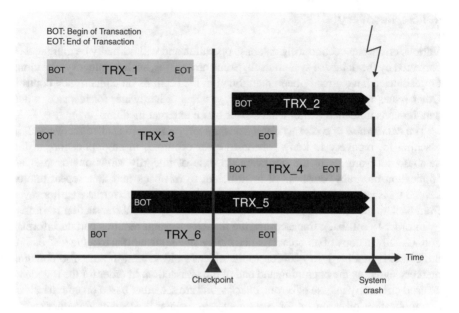

Fig. 4.9 Restart of a database system after an error

4.5   Soft Consistency in Massive Distributed Data

4.5.1   BASE and the CAP Theorem

It has become clear in practice that for large and distributed data storage systems, consistency cannot always be the primary goal; sometimes, availability and partition tolerance take priority.

In relational database systems, transactions at the highest isolation level are always atomic, consistent, isolated, and durable (see ACID, Sect. 4.4.2). Web-based applications, on the other hand, are geared toward high availability and the ability to continue working if a computer node or a network connection fails. Such partition-tolerant systems use replicated computer nodes and a softer consistency requirement called BASE (Basically Available, Soft state, Eventually consistent): This allows replicated computer nodes to temporarily hold diverging data versions and only be updated with a delay.

During a symposium in 2000, Eric Brewer of the University of California, Berkeley, presented the hypothesis that the three properties of consistency, availability, and partition tolerance cannot exist simultaneously in a massive distributed computer system.

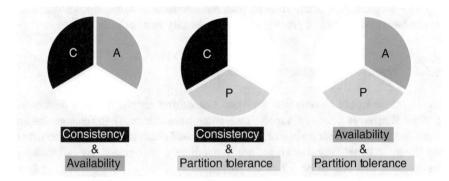

Fig. 4.10 The three possible combinations under the CAP theorem

- **Consistency (C)**: When a transaction changes data in a distributed database with replicated nodes, all reading transactions receive the current state, no matter from which node they access the database.
- **Availability (A)**: Running applications operate continuously and have acceptable response times.
- **Partition tolerance (P)**: Failures of individual nodes or connections between nodes in a replicated computer network do not impact the system as a whole, and nodes can be added or removed at any time without having to stop operation.

This hypothesis was later proven by researchers at MIT in Boston and established as the CAP theorem.

CAP Theorem

The CAP theorem states that in any massive distributed data management system, only two of the three properties consistency, availability, and partition tolerance can be ensured. In short, massive distributed systems can have a combination of either consistency and availability (CA), consistency and partition tolerance (CP), or availability and partition tolerance (AP); but it is impossible to have all three at once (see Fig. 4.10). Use cases of the CAP theorem may include:

- Stock exchange systems requiring consistency and availability (CA), which are achieved by using relational database systems following the ACID principle.
- Country-wide networks of ATMs, which still require consistency, but also partition tolerance, while somewhat long response times are acceptable (CP); distributed and replicated relational or NoSQL systems supporting CP are best suited for this scenario.
- The Internet service Domain Name System (DNS) is used to resolve URLs into numerical IP addresses in TCP/IP (Transmission Control Protocol/Internet Protocol) communication and must therefore be always available and partition tolerant

(AP), a task that requires NoSQL data management systems, since a relational database system cannot provide global availability and partition tolerance.

4.5.2   Nuanced Consistency Settings

Ideally, there would be only one approach to ensuring consistency in a distributed system: Whenever a change is made, all reading transactions see the change and are certain to get the current state. For instance, if a hotel chain offers online reservation via their website, any bookings are immediately recognized by all reading transactions, and double bookings are prevented.

However, the CAP theorem has taught us that in networks of replicated computer nodes, only two out of three corresponding properties can be achieved at any time. International hotel chains commonly focus on AP, meaning they require high availability and partition tolerance. In exchange, they accept that bookings are made according to the BASE principle. There are other possible refinements that can be configured based on the following parameters:

- N = number of replicated nodes or number of copies in the cluster
- R = number of copies to be read (successful read)
- W = number of copies to be written (successful write)

With these three parameters N, R, and W, it is possible to formulate four basic options for nuanced consistency control. Figure 4.11 gives an overview over those variants for a sample case of three replicated nodes ($N=3$). Initially, all nodes hold the object version A, before some nodes are subsequently overwritten with the new version B. The issue at hand is how reading programs can identify current versions if writing programs make modifications.

The first option is formulated as $W+R \leq N$. In the example in Fig. 4.11 (top left), the parameters are set to $N=3$, $W=1$, and $R=2$. $W=1$ means that at least one node must be written successfully, while R2 requires at least two nodes to be read successfully. In the node accessed by the writing program, the old version A is replaced with the new version B. In the worst case scenario, the reading program accesses the other two nodes and receives the old version A from both of them. This option is therefore an example for eventual consistency.

One alternative is "consistency by writes," in which W must match the number of replicated nodes, i.e., $W=N$ (Fig. 4.11, top right). Successful write operations replace version A with the new version B in all three nodes. When a reading program accesses any node, it will always get the current version B.

Option 3 is called "consistency by reads," since the number of reads equals the number of nodes (Fig. 4.11, bottom left). The new version B is only written on one node, so the consultation of all three nodes by a reading operation returns both the current version B and the old version A. When a transaction receives multiple read results, such as versions A and B in this case, it has to establish the chronological order of the results, i.e., whether it is A before B ($A<B$) or B before A ($B<A$), in

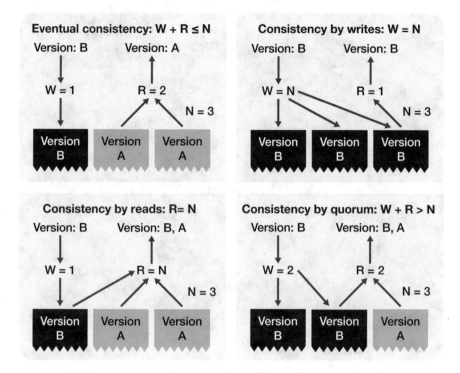

Fig. 4.11 Ensuring consistency in replicated systems

order to determine which is the newest. This is done with the help of vector clocks (see Sect. 4.5.3).

The fourth and final case is "consistency by quorum" with the formula W+R>N (Fig. 4.11, bottom right). In our example, both parameters W and R are set to two, i.e., W=2 and R=2. This requires two nodes to be written and two nodes to be read successfully. The read operation once again definitely returns both versions A and B so that the chronological order has to be determined using vector clocks.

4.5.3 Vector Clocks for the Serialization of Distributed Events

In distributed systems, various events may occur at different times due to concurring processes. Vector clocks can be used to bring some order into these events. They are not time-keeping tools, but counting algorithms allowing for a partial chronological ordering of events in concurrent processes.

Below, we will look at concurrent processes in a distributed system. A vector clock is a vector with k components or counters C_i with i=1,...,k, where k equals the number of processes. Each process P_i therefore has a vector clock $V_i=[C_1,...,C_k]$ with k counters.

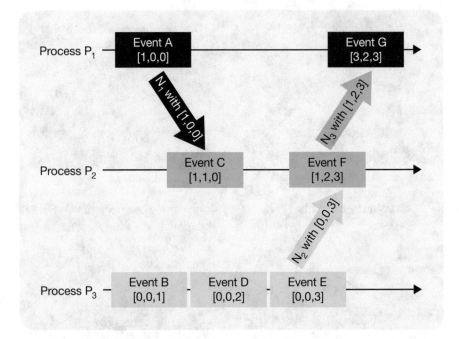

Fig. 4.12 Vector clocks showing causalities

A vector clock works along the following steps:

- Initially, all vector clocks are set to zero, i.e., $V_i=[0,0,...,0]$, for all processes P_i and counters C_k.
- In each interprocess message, the sender includes its own vector clock for the recipient.
- When a process receives a message, it increments its own counter C_i in its vector by one, i.e., $C_i=C_i+1$. It also merges its own updated vector V_i with the received vector W component by component by keeping the higher of two corresponding counter values, i.e., $V_i[j]=max(V_i[j],W[j])$, for all $j=1,...,k$.

Figure 4.12 shows a possible scenario with three concurrent processes P1, P2, and P3. Process P_3 includes the three events B, D, and E in chronological order. It increments its own counter C_3 in its vector clock by one for each event, resulting in the vector clocks [0,0,1] for event B, [0,0,2] for event D, and [0,0,3] for event E.

In process P_1, event A occurs first, and the process' counter C_1 is raised by one in its vector clock V_1, which is then [1,0,0]. Next, P_1 sends a message M_1 to process P_2, including its current vector clock V_1. Event C in process P_2 first updates the process' own vector clock V_2 to [0,1,0] before merging it with the newly received vector clock $V_1=[1,0,0]$ into [1,1,0].

Similar mergers are executed for the messages M_2 and M_3: First, the processes' vector clocks V_2/V_1 are incremented by one in the process' own counter, and then the maximum of the two vector clocks to be merged is determined and included. This results in the vector clocks $V_2=[1,2,3]$ (since $[1,2,3]=max([1,2,0],[0,0,3])$) for event F and $V_1=[3,2,3]$ for event G.

Causality can be established between two events in a distributed system: Event X happened before event Z if the vector clock $V(X)=[X_1,X_2,...,X_k]$ of X is less than the vector clock $V(Y)=[Y_1,Y_2,...,Y_k]$ of Y. In other words:

Causality Principle Cased on Vector Clocks
Event X happened before event Y (or X<Y) if $X_i<Y_i$ for all $i=1,...,k$ and if there is at least one j where $X_j<Y_j$.

In Fig. 4.12, it is clear that event B took place before event D, since the corresponding vector clocks $[0,0,1]$ and $[0,0,2]$ meet the abovementioned condition.

Comparing the events F and G, we can also see from their vector clocks $[1,2,3]$ and $[3,2,3]$ that F happened before G. The first counter of the vector clock $V(F)$ is less than the first counter of $V(G)$ and the other components are identical, and $[1,2,3]$ $<[3,2,3]$ in the vector clocks means a causality F<G.

Now assume two fictional vector clocks $V(S)=[3,1,1]$ for an event S and $V(T)=$ $[1,1,2]$ for an event T: These two vector clocks are not comparable, since neither S<T nor T<S is true. The two events are concurrent and no causality can be established.

Vector clocks are especially suitable for massive distributed and replicated computer structures. Since actual time clocks are hard to synchronize in global networks, vector clocks are used instead, including as many components as there are replicas.

During the distribution of replicas, vector clocks allow to determine which version is the newer and therefore more current one. For the two options "consistency by reads" and "consistency by quorum" in Sect. 4.3.2, read operations returned both the versions A and B. If these two versions have vector clocks, the causality condition described above can be applied to conclude that A<B, i.e., B is the newer version.

4.5.4   Comparing ACID and BASE

There are some major differences between the ACID (Atomicity, Consistency, Isolation, Durability) and BASE (Basically Available, Soft state, Eventually consistent) approaches, as summarized in Fig. 4.13.

Most SQL and NoSQL database systems are strictly based on ACID, meaning that consistency is ensured at any time in both centralized and distributed systems. Distributed database systems require a coordinating program that implements all changes to table contents in full and creates a consistent database state. In case of errors, the coordinating program makes sure that the distributed database is not affected in any way and the transaction can be restarted.

ACID	BASE
Consistency is the top priority (strong consistency)	Consistency is ensured only eventually (weak consistency)
Mostly pessimistic concurrency control methods with locking protocols	Mostly optimistic concurrency control methods with nuanced setting options
Availability is ensured for moderate volumes of data	High availability and partition tolerance for massive distributed data storage
Some integrity restraints (e.g. referential integrity) are ensured by the database schema	Some integrity restraints (e.g. referential integrity) are ensured by the database schema

Fig. 4.13 Comparing ACID and BASE

Some NoSQL systems support ensuring consistency in various ways. Generally, changes in massive distributed data storage systems are written on the source node and replicated to all other nodes. However, this replication may come at a slight delay, so it is possible for nodes to not have the current database state available when accessed by user queries. Individual nodes in the computer network are usually accessible (basically available), but may not have been properly updated yet (eventually consistent), i.e., they may be in a soft state.

Most SQL and NoSQL database systems commonly use pessimistic concurrency control procedures which require locks to be placed and released according to the two-phase locking protocol (see Sect. 4.4.4) for the operations of a transaction. If database applications execute disproportionately fewer changes than queries, optimistic methods (see Sect. 4.4.5) may be deployed. If conflicts arise, the respective transactions have to be restarted.

Massively distributed data management systems focused on availability and partition tolerance can only provide consistent states with a delay according to the CAP theorem. Moreover, placing and removing locks on replicated nodes would be an exorbitant effort. Some NoSQL systems therefore use optimistic concurrency control.

In terms of availability, relational database systems are on par with their alternatives up to a certain amount of data and distribution. Applications with a very high data volume, however, are generally based on NoSQL systems that offer high availability in addition to partition tolerance. Examples are column family databases (e.g., Apache Cassandra) or key-value databases (e.g., Riak).

Some NoSQL systems allow for more nuanced settings on how to ensure consistency, resulting in some fuzzy lines between ACID and BASE.

4.6 Transaction Control Language Elements

4.6.1 Transaction Control in SQL

To declare a series of operations in SQL as one transaction, they should be marked with BEGIN TRANSACTION. They end either with COMMIT (success) or ROLL-BACK (failure). Start and end of a transaction indicate to the database system which operations form a unit and must be protected by the ACID concept.

The SQL statement COMMIT applies the changes from the transaction. They remain until changed by another successfully completed transaction. In case of an error during the transaction, the entire transaction can be undone with the SQL command ROLLBACK.

The SQL standard allows for the degree of consistency enforced by the database system to be configured by setting an isolation level with the following expression:

```
SET TRANSACTION ISOLATION LEVEL <isolation level>
```

There are four isolation levels:

- READ UNCOMMITTED (no consistency enforcement)
- READ COMMITTED (only applied changes can be read by other transactions)
- REPEATABLE READ (read queries give the same result repeatedly)
- SERIALIZABLE (full serializable ACID consistency enforced)

Each of these isolation levels provides a different degree of consistency. Only SERIALIZABLE guarantees ACID-consistency. But it uses extensive locking to do so, which slows down concurrent processing. Figure 4.14 visualizes with warning triangles which of the three common version conflicts can occur in which isolation level.

Dirty read refers to reading data that originate from transactions that have not yet been successfully completed. Non-repeatable read occurs when the repetition of the same read operation within a transaction produces different results. And phantom read means that the read operation returns data that is no longer current because it has been modified by other transactions.

Let's look at this using an example in Fig. 4.15. In a table ACCOUNTS, accounts are stored with their balances. Two parallel processes A and B are running simultaneously. Process B wants to transfer 100 currency units to account 2 in one transaction. This requires two UPDATE commands, which are executed atomically as a whole and can be reversed in the event of an error. Process A inserts amounts to accounts 1 (300 currency units) and 2 (200 currency units) in a first transaction. Then it starts a new transaction with isolation level REPEATABLE READ. This reads the balance of account 2 three times in succession in substeps 4, 6, and 8 to test exactly when the changes made by process B running in parallel become visible. After the

Isolation level	Dirty reads	Non-repeatable reads	Phantom reads
Read Uncommitted	▲	▲	▲
Read Committed		▲	▲
Repeatable Read			▲
Serializable			

Fig. 4.14 Risks of consistency errors with different isolation levels

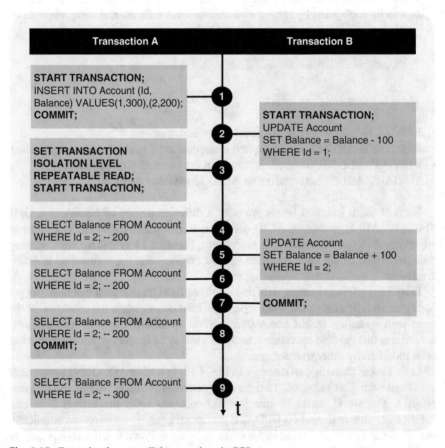

Fig. 4.15 Example of two parallel transactions in SQL

transaction is complete, process A reads this balance again in step 9. Which balances does process A read at times 4, 6, 8, and 9?

At point 4, the balance of account 2 is unchanged at 200, represented in Fig. 4.15 by the SQL comment --.200, which is what process A reads. Due to the REPEAT-ABLE READ isolation level, subsequent read operations within the same transaction will continue to receive this value of 200, i.e., even at point 8, when process B has already committed (COMMIT) the change. Only after the completion of the transaction at point 9, process A sees the change in account 2, namely, the balance of 300.

These read operations are repeatable, but not serializable, because the result does not correspond to what a serial execution would have produced. Since process B started the transaction at time 2 before process A, a correctly timed serialized execution would have first run process B completely. Only then would process A have been started. Process A would therefore have already read the changed balance of 300 at time no. 8. The value of 200 at time no. 8 in process A can therefore be described as a phantom.

Since process B started the transaction first, sequential execution of the two processes would result in process A reading the new balance of 300 from account 2 from the beginning. This is indeed the case with isolation level SERIALIZABLE. However, this is only possible with a lock, with which process A would have to wait for process B to complete the transaction, which would increase the execution time.

If we had chosen the isolation level READ COMMITTED, process A would have already read the new balance at eventNo. 8. Thus, the read operation of time points #4 and #6 would not have been repeatable.

With the isolation level READ UNCOMMITTED, which actually does not isolate at all, process A would have already read the changed balance at time point 6. This would correspond to a "dirty read," since B had not yet completed the transaction with a COMMIT at this point.

4.6.2 Transaction Management in the Graph Database Neo4J and in the Cypher Language

To protect data integrity, the Neo4j database system supports transactions that basically comply with the ACID principle. All database operations that access graphs, indexes, or the schema must be performed in a transaction. Deadlock detection is also integrated into the central transaction management. However, data retrieved by graph traversal is not protected from modification by other transactions.

Individual Cypher queries are executed within one transaction each. Changes made by updating queries are held in memory by the transaction until committed, at which time the changes are saved to disk and visible to other transactions. If an error occurs, either during query evaluation (e.g., division by zero) or during commit, the transaction is automatically rolled back, and no changes are saved. Each updating query is always either completely successful or not successful at all. Thus, a query that makes many updates consumes large amounts of memory because the transaction holds changes in memory.

Isolation Levels

Transactions in the Neo4j database system use the READ COMMITTED isolation level. Transactions see data changes once they have been committed, and they do not see data changes that have not yet been committed. This type of isolation is weaker than serializability but offers significant performance advantages. It is sufficient for most cases. However, non-repeatable reads may occur because locks are only maintained until the end of a transaction.

If this is not sufficient, the Neo4j Java API allows explicit locking of nodes and relationships. One can manually set up write locks on nodes and relationships to achieve the higher isolation level of serializability by explicitly requesting and releasing locks. For example, if a lock is placed on a shared node or relationship, all transactions on that lock will be serialized if the lock is maintained.

Transactions in Cypher

Cypher does not support explicit language elements for transaction management. By default, each individual Cypher statement runs as a separate transaction. This means that, for example, UPDATE commands in a transaction run atomically using the ACID principle, even if they modify many nodes and edges simultaneously. However, it is currently not directly possible with Cypher to run multiple separate statements as a single transaction.

To start multiple statements as one transaction in the Neo4J database management system, there are several other ways. The easiest way to do this is usually via an API, e.g., via HTTP or Java. Also in the command line program Cypher shell, it is possible with the commands :begin, :commit, and :rollback the transaction control; however, the commands are not part of the Cypher language. The following example will illustrate this. Suppose the following sequence of commands is executed as a batch script via Cypher shell. What result will be returned by the last line?

```
CREATE (k:Account {Id:1}) SET k.Balance = 1;
CREATE (k:Account {Id:2}) SET k.Balance = 2;

MATCH (k:Account {Id:1}) SET k.Balance = 3;
MATCH (k:Account {Id:2}) SET k.Balance = 4/0;

:begin
MATCH (k:account {Id:1}) SET k.balance = 5;
MATCH (k:account {Id:2}) SET k.balance = 6/0;
:commit
:rollback

MATCH(k:Account) RETURN k;
```

The following is returned as the result: Account with Id 1 has balance 3, and Account with Id 2 has balance 2. Why? The first two statements create two nodes of type Account with Id 1 and 2 and set the balance to 1 and 2, respectively. The third statement sets Balance to 3 for Account with Id 1. Each of these statements is successfully executed as a single transaction.

The fourth statement, which is again a separate transaction, is not completed successfully due to division by zero. Therefore, the property of Account with Id 2 is not reset.

Subsequently, a new transaction is started in the Cypher shell with :begin. Now the next Cypher statements up to the :commit command are executed as an atomic transaction. Due to the division by zero, both statements are not processed successfully. The :commit command results in an error message. The :rollback command, in turn, rolls back all uncommitted changes. Due to the transaction over both statements, the balance of the account with Id 1 was not changed either. Therefore, we get the following result with the last statement:

```
neo4j@neo4j> MATCH(k:account) RETURN k;
+-----------------------------+
| k |
+-----------------------------+
| (:account {id: 1, balance: 3}) |
| (:account {id: 2, balance: 2}) |
+-----------------------------+
```

In summary, Cypher provides support for transactions having an isolation level READ COMMITTED. However, the language does not provide different isolation levels nor language elements for starting and ending transactions. This is a gap that the Current Development of Cypher to the International Standard GQL—Graph Query Language—aims to close from 2023. In the current GQL draft, serializability is required as a standard isolation level and language commands for transaction control such as START TRANSACTION, COMMIT, and ROLLBACK are planned.

4.6.3   Transaction Management in MongoDB and MQL

In the MongoDB database system, changes to a single document are always atomic. Single document transactions are very efficient to process. Since all relevant entities for a subject can be aggregated into a single document type (see Sect. 2.5), the need for multiple document transactions is eliminated in many use cases. If atomic reads and writes are needed across multiple documents, in different collections, or across different machines, MongoDB supports distributed transactions. However, this is associated with performance penalties.

Atomicity of Transactions
When a transaction is committed, all data changes made in the transaction are stored and visible outside the transaction. As long as a transaction is not committed, the data changes made in the transaction are not visible outside the transaction. When a

transaction commits, all changes made in the transaction are discarded without ever becoming visible. If a single action in the transaction fails, the entire transaction is rolled back.

Transactions in the Mongo Shell
The MongoDB Query Language (MQL) provides the following language elements for transaction control:

- Starting a new transaction with startTransaction()
- Committing a transaction with commitTransaction()
- Aborting a transaction with abortTransaction()

Let's look at this with an example.[3] If we assume that on the database named "db" the collection named "ACCOUNT" is empty, what will be the return of the command on the last line, and why?

```
s = db.getMongo().startSession()
c = s.getDatabase('db').getCollection('ACCOUNT')
c.createIndex( { "Key": 1 }, { "unique": true } )
c.insertMany([{"Key":1, "Val":1},{" Key":1, "Val":2}])
s.startTransaction( )
c.insertMany([{"Key3, "Val":3},{" Key":3, "Val":4}])
s.commitTransaction( )
c.find({},{_id:0})
```

Let's go through the above example step by step:

- The first line starts a new session. Transactions are bound to sessions in MongoDB.
- The second line instantiates the collection ACCOUNT within the session so that the following transactions are linked to it. Since the collection does not yet exist, it is newly created.
- The third line sets a uniqueness constraint for the "Key" field to test transaction behavior in terms of integrity.
- The fourth line tries to insert two documents with the same "Key" which is not possible because of the uniqueness condition. Since this happens outside of a distributed transaction, the statement over two documents is not executed atomically. Therefore, the first document with "Key"=1 and "Val"=1 is successfully committed. The second document generates an error due to the duplicate "Key" and is discarded.
- The fifth line starts a transaction with s.startTransaction().

---

[3] Transactions work in MongoDB only within replica sets. So the database server (mongod) must be started first with the corresponding option --replSet <name>. In addition, the command rs.initiate() must then be executed in the Mongo Shell (mongo).

- The sixth line again wants to insert two documents with the same "Key," this time within the transaction started above. The statement is now executed atomically according to the all-or-nothing principle. An error occurs, because duplicates in the "Key" field are not accepted due to the unique index.
- The seventh line terminates the transaction with s.commitTransaction().
- On the eighth line, we ask for all documents in the collection, excluding the object id. We then see the following output:

```
rs0:PRIMARY> c.find({},{_id:0})
{ "Key" : 1, "Val" : 1 }
```

Within the distributed transaction, the insertion of both documents on the sixth line has been rolled back, even though only the one document with "Key"=3 and "Balance"=4 generated an error due to the duplicate. The example shows how atomicity is ensured within a transaction across multiple documents.

Isolation of Distributed Transactions Across Multiple Computers
The isolation level of transactions in MongoDB on a single machine is read-committed, i.e., changes to a transaction become visible to all transactions, including those already running, exactly when they are committed. This can lead to consistency problems due to lack of isolation, such as non-repeatable reads (see Sect. 4.6.1).

To ensure availability under heavy load, MongoDB servers can be replicated. Then, a replica can step in when as a computer is overloaded. However, this makes transaction management more complex. This is because changes on one node in the redundant computer cluster must be propagated to all replicas. Due to network latency, the replicas will have different, i.e., inconsistent, data states for a certain period of time, until the changes have been tracked everywhere. This is called eventual consistency (see Sect. 4.5) and is the default behavior of MongoDB. If causal consistency is required, this can be set using the "read concern" parameters when starting a transaction.

Transactions whose "read concern" parameter is set to the "local" level (default setting) can see the result of write operations before they have been traced on all replica servers. The "majority" level can be used to ensure that only data is read that has already been committed and confirmed on a majority of replica servers. The consistency levels for read and write operations can be set as follows:

```
session = db.getMongo().startSession()
session.startTransaction({
    "readConcern": { "level": "majority" },
    "writeConcern": { "w": "majority" }
})
```

In summary, MQL provides a language tool for managing transactions in distributed databases that rely on soft consistency requirements based on the BASE principle.

Bibliography

Basta, A., Zgola, M.: Database Security. Cengage Learning (2011)

Bowman, A.: Protecting Against Cypher injection. Neo4j Knowledge Base. https://neo4j.com/developer/kb/protecting-against-cypher-injection/ (n.d.). Accessed 4 July 2022

Brewer E.: Keynote – Towards Robust Distributed Systems. In: 19th ACM Symposium on Principles of Distributed Computing, Portland, Oregon, 16–19 July 2000

Dindoliwala, V.J., Morena, R.D.: Comparative study of integrity constraints, storage and profile management of relational and non-relational database using MongoDB and Oracle. Int. J. Comp. Sci. Eng. **6**(7), 831–837 (2018) https://www.ijcseonline.org/pdf_paper_view.php?paper_id=2520&134-IJCSE-04376.pdf

Eswaran, K.P., Gray, J., Lorie, R.A., Traiger, I.L.: The notion of consistency and predicate locks in a data base system. Commun. ACM. **19**(11), 624–633 (1976)

Gilbert, S., Lynch, N.: Brewer's Conjecture and the Feasibility of Consistent, Available, Partition-Tolerant Web Services. Massachusetts Institute of Technology, Cambridge (2002)

Gray, J., Reuter, A.: Transaction Processing – Concepts and Techniques. Morgan Kaufmann (1992)

Härder, T., Reuter, A.: Principles of transaction-oriented database recovery. ACM Comput. Surv. **15**(4), 287–317 (1983)

MongoDB, Inc.: MongoDB Documentation. https://www.mongodb.com/docs/ (2022)

Neo4J, Inc.: Neo4j Documentation. Neo4j Graph Data Platform. https://neo4j.com/docs/ (2022)

Onyancha, B.H.: Securing MongoDB from External Injection Attacks. Severalnines. https://web.archive.org/web/20210618085021/https://severalnines.com/database-blog/securing-mongodb-external-injection-attacks (2019)

Papiernik, M.: How To Use Transactions in MongoDB. DigitalOean. https://www.digitalocean.com/community/tutorials/how-to-use-transactions-in-mongodb (2019)

Riak: Open Source Distributed Database. siehe http://basho.com/riak/

Redmond, E., Wilson, J.R.: Seven Databases in Seven Weeks – A Guide to Modern Databases and the NoSQL Movement. The Pragmatic Bookshelf (2012)

Spiegel, P.: NoSQL Injection – Fun with Objects and Arrays. German OWASP-Day, Darmstadt. https://owasp.org/www-pdf-archive/GOD16-NOSQL.pdf (2016)

Vogels, W.: Eventually consistent. Commun. ACM. **52**(1), 40–44 (2009)

Weikum, G., Vossen, G.: Transactional Information Systems – Theory, Algorithms, and the Practice of Concurrency Control and Recovery. Morgan Kaufmann (2002)

System Architecture

5

5.1   Processing of Homogeneous and Heterogeneous Data

Throughout the 1950s and 1960s, file systems were kept on secondary storage media (tape, drum memory, magnetic disk), before database systems became available on the market in the 1970s. Those file systems allowed for random, or direct, access to the external storage, i.e., specific records could be selected by using an address, without the entirety of records needing to be checked first. The access address was determined via an index or a hash function (see Sect. 5.2).

The mainframe computers running these file systems were largely used for technical and scientific applications (computing numbers). With the emergence of database systems, computers also took over in business contexts (computing numbers and text) and became the backbone of administrative and commercial applications, since database systems support consistency in multi-user operation (see ACID, Sect. 4.4.2). Today, many information systems are based on the relational database technology which replaced most of the previously used hierarchic or network-like database systems. More and more NoSQL database systems such as graph databases or document databases are being used for Big Data applications. This applies not only to large data volumes but also to a large variety of different structured and unstructured data (variety) and fast data streams (velocity).

Relational database systems use only tables to store and handle data. A table is a set of records that can flexibly process structured data. *Structured data* strictly adheres to a well-defined data structure with a focus on the following properties:

- **Schema**: The structure of the data must be communicated to the database system by specifying a schema (see the SQL command CREATE TABLE in Chap. 3). In addition to table formalization, integrity constraints are also stored in the schema (cf., e.g., the definition of referential integrity and the establishment of appropriate processing rules).
- **Data types**: The relational database schema guarantees that for each use of the database, the data manifestations always have the set data types (e.g.,

M. Kaufmann, A. Meier, *SQL and NoSQL Databases*,
https://doi.org/10.1007/978-3-031-27908-9_5

CHARACTER, INTEGER, DATE, TIMESTAMP, etc.; see also the SQL tutorial at www.sql-nosql.org). To do so, the database system consults the system tables (schema information) at every SQL invocation. Special focus is on authorization and data protection rules, which are checked via the system catalog (see VIEW concept and privilege assignment via GRANT and REVOKE in Sect. 4.2.1).

Relational databases therefore mostly process structured and formatted data. In order to meet specific requirements in the fields of office automation, technology, and Web applications (among others), SQL has been extended by data types and functions for alphabetical strings (CHARACTER VARYING), bit sequences (BIT VARYING, BINARY LARGE OBJECT), and text fragments (CHARACTER LARGE OBJECT). The integration of XML (eXtensible Markup Language) is also supported. These additions resulted in the definition of semi-structured and unstructured data.

Semi-structured data is defined as follows:

- They consist of a set of data objects whose structure and content are subject to continuous changes.
- Data objects are either atomic or composed of other data objects (complex objects).
- Atomic data objects contain data values of a specified data type.

Data management systems for semi-structured data work without a fixed database schema, since structure and content change constantly. A possible use case are content management systems for websites which can flexibly store and process Web pages and multimedia objects. Such systems require extended relational database technology (see Chap. 6), XML databases, or NoSQL databases (see Chap. 7).

A *data stream* is a continuous flow of digital data with a variable data rate (records per unit of time). Data within a data stream is sorted chronologically and often given a timestamp. Besides audio and video data streams, this can also be a series of measurements which are analyzed with the help of analysis languages or specific algorithms (language analysis, text analysis, pattern recognition, etc.). Unlike structured and semi-structured data, data streams can only be analyzed sequentially.

Figure 5.1 shows a simple use case for data streams. The setting is a multi-item auction via an electronic bidding platform. In this auction, bidding starts at a set minimum. Participants can make multiple bids that have to be higher than the previous highest bid. Since electronic auctions have no physical location, time and duration of the auction are set in advance. The bidder who makes the highest bid during the set time wins the auction.

Any AUCTION can be seen as a relationship set between the two entity sets OBJECT and BIDDER. The corresponding foreign keys $O\#$ and $B\#$ are complemented by a timestamp and the offered sum (e.g., in USD) per bid. The data stream is used to show bidders the current standing bids during the auction. After the auction is over, the highest bids are made public, and the winners of the

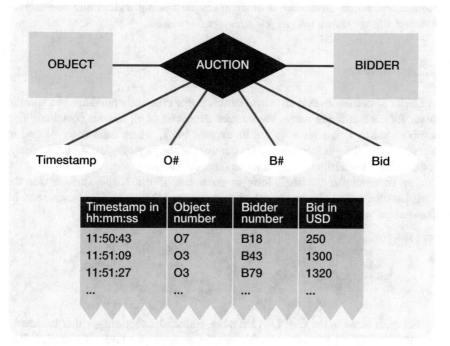

Fig. 5.1 Processing a data stream

individual items are notified. The data stream can then be used for additional purposes, for instance, bidding behavior analyses or disclosure in case of legal contestation.

Unstructured data are digital data without any fixed structure. This includes multimedia data such as continuous text, music files, satellite imagery, or audio/video recordings. Unstructured data is often transmitted to a computer via digital sensors, for example, in the data streams explained above, which can sequentially transport structured and/or unstructured data.

The processing of unstructured data or data streams calls for special adapted software packages. NoSQL databases or specific data stream management systems are used to fulfill the requirements of Big Data processing.

The next sections discuss several architectural aspects of SQL and NoSQL databases.

5.2 Storage and Access Structures

Storage and access structures for relational and non-relational database systems should be designed to manage data in secondary storage as efficiently as possible. For large amounts of data, the structures used in the main storage cannot simply be reproduced on the background memory. It is necessary to instead optimize the storage and access structures in order to enable reading and writing contents *on external storage media with as few accesses as possible.*

5.2.1   Indexes

An *index* of one attribute is an access structure that efficiently provides, in a specific order for each attribute value, the internal addresses of all records containing that attribute value. It is similar to the index of a book, where each entry—listed in alphabetical order—is followed by the numbers of the pages containing it. Similarly, indexes exist for attribute combinations (cf. Sect. 5.2.5).

For an example, we shall look at an index of the Name attribute for the EMPLOYEE table. This index, which remains invisible to standard users, can be constructed with the following SQL command:

```
CREATE INDEX IX1
ON EMPLOYEE(NAME)
USING HASH;
```

For each name in the EMPLOYEE table, sorted alphabetically, either the identification key *E#* or the internal address of the employee tuple is recorded. The database system uses this index of employee names for increasing access speed of corresponding queries or when executing a join. In this case, the Name attribute is the *access key*.

In this example, USING HASH is used to create a hash index (see Sect. 5.2.3) that is optimized for equality queries.

Another possibility is to use balanced trees (B-trees; see Sect. 5.2.2) for indexes. These are suitable for range queries such as "greater than" or "less than."

```
CREATE INDEX IX1
ON EMPLOYEE(year)
USING BTREE;
```

5.2.2   Tree Structures

Tree structures can be used to store records or access keys and to *index* attributes in order to increase efficiency. For large amounts of data, the root, internal, and leaf nodes of the tree are not assigned individual keys and records, but rather entire *data pages*. In order to find a specific record, the tree then has to be searched.

With central memory management, the database system usually uses binary trees in the background in which *the root node and each internal node have two subtrees.*

Such trees cannot be used unlimitedly for storing access keys or records for extensive databases, since their height grows exponentially for larger amounts of data; large trees, however, are impractical for searching and reading data content on external storage media, since they require too many page accesses.

The *height of a tree*, i.e., the distance between the root node and the leaves, is an *indicator for the number of accesses* required on external storage media. To keep the number of external accesses as low as possible, it is common to make the storage tree structures for database systems grow in width instead of height. One of the most important of those tree structures is the *B-tree* (see Fig. 5.2).

A B-tree is a tree whose *root node and internal nodes generally have more than two subtrees*. The data pages represented by the individual internal and leaf nodes should not be empty, but ideally filled with key values or entire records. They are therefore usually required to be filled at least halfway with records or keys (except for the page associated with the root node).

B-Tree

A tree is a *B-tree of the nth order* if:

- It is fully balanced (the paths from the root to each leaf have the same length)
- Each node (except for the root node) has at least n and at the most 2*n entries in its data page

That second condition also means that, since every node except the root node has at least n entries, each node has at least n subtrees. On the other hand, each node has a maximum of 2*n entries, i.e., no node of a B-tree can have more than 2*n subtrees.

Assume, for instance, that the key *E#* from the EMPLOYEE table is to be stored in a B-tree of the order n=2 as an access structure, which results in the tree shown in Fig. 5.2.

Nodes and leaves of the tree cannot contain more than four entries due to the order 2. Apart from the keys, we will assume that the pages for the nodes and leaves hold not only key values but also pointers to the data pages containing the actual records. This means that the tree in Fig. 5.2 represents an access tree, not the data management for the records in the EMPLOYEE table.

In our example, the root node of the B-tree contains the four keys E1, E4, E7, and E19 in numerical order. When the new key E3 is added, the root node must be split because it cannot hold any more entries. The split is done in a way that produces a balanced tree. The key E4 is declared the new root node, since it is in between two equal halves of the remaining key set. The left subtree is formed of key values that meet the condition "*E#* lower than E4" (in this case E1 and E3); the right subtree consists of key values where "*E#* higher than E4" (i.e., E7 and E19). Additional keys can be inserted in the same way, while the tree retains a fixed height.

The database system searches for individual keys top-down, e.g., if the candidate key E15 is requested from the B-tree B4 in Fig. 5.2, it checks against the entries in the root node. Since E15 lies between the keys E4 and E18, it selects the corresponding subtree (in this case, only one leaf node) and continues the search

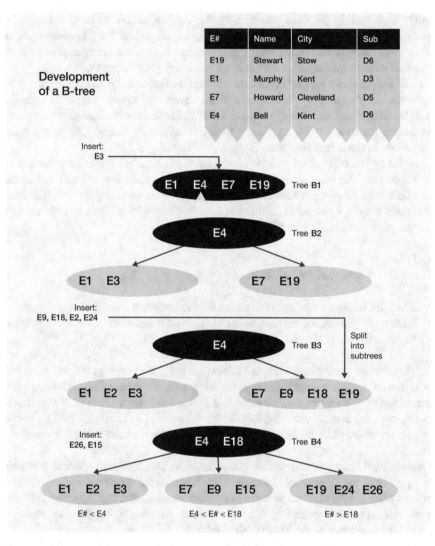

Fig. 5.2 B-tree with dynamic changes

until it finds the entry in the leaf node. In this simple example, the search for E15 requires only two page accesses, one for the root node and one for the leaf node.

The height of a B-tree determines the access times for keys as well as the data associated with a (search) key. The access times can be reduced by increasing the branching factor of the B-tree.

Another option is a *leaf-oriented B-tree* (commonly called B*-Tree), where the actual records are never stored in internal nodes but only in leaf nodes. The internal roots contain only key entries in order to keep the tree as low as possible.

5.2.3 Hashing Methods

Key hashing or simply hashing is an address determination procedure that is at the core of any distributed data and access structures. *Hash functions* map a set of keys on a set of addresses forming a contiguous address space.

A simple hash function assigns a number between 1 and n to each key of a record as its address. This address is interpreted as a relative page number, with each page holding a set number of key values with or without their respective records.

Hash functions have to meet the following requirements:

- It must be possible to follow the transformation rule with simple calculations and little resources.
- The assigned addresses must be distributed evenly across the address space.
- The probability of assignment collisions, i.e., the use of identical addresses for multiple keys, must be the same for all key values.

There is a wide variety of hash functions, each of which has its pros and cons. One of the simplest and best-known algorithms is the division method.

The Division Method of Hashing
Each key is interpreted as an integer by using bit representation. The *hash function H for a key k and a prime number p* is given by the formula

$$H(k) := k \bmod p.$$

The integer "k mod p"—the remainder from the division of the key value k by the prime number p—is used as a relative address or page number. In the division method, the choice of the prime number p determines the memory use and the uniformity of distribution.

Figure 5.3 shows the EMPLOYEE table and how it can be mapped to different pages with the division method of hashing.

In this example, each page can hold four key values. The prime number chosen for p is 5. Each key value is now divided by 5, with the remaining integer determining the page number.

Inserting the key E14 causes problems, since the corresponding page is already full. The key E14 is placed in an *overflow area*. A link from page 4 to the overflow area maintains the affiliation of the key with the co-set on page 4.

There are multiple methods for handling overflows. Instead of an overflow area, additional hash functions can be applied to the extra keys. Quickly growing key ranges or complex delete operations often cause difficulties in overflow handling. In order to mitigate these issues, dynamic hashing methods have been developed.

Such *dynamic hash functions* are designed to keep memory use independent from the growth of keys. Overflow areas or comprehensive redistribution of addresses is mostly rendered unnecessary. The existing address space for a dynamic hash function can be extended either by a specific choice of hashing algorithm or by the

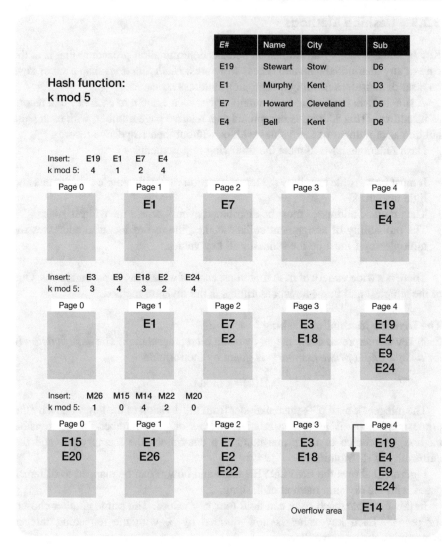

Fig. 5.3 Hash function using the division method

use of a page assignment table kept in the main memory, without the need to reload all keys or records already stored.

5.2.4   Consistent Hashing

Consistent hashing functions belong to the family of distributed address calculations (see hashing methods in the previous section). A storage address or hash value is calculated from a set of keys in order to store the corresponding record.

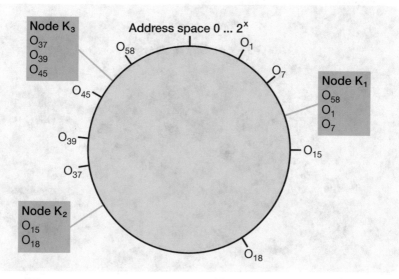

Fig. 5.4 Ring with objects assigned to nodes

In Big Data applications, the key-value pairs are assigned to different nodes in the computer network. Based on the keys (e.g., term or day), their values (e.g., frequencies) are stored in the corresponding node. The important part is that with consistent hashing, address calculation is used for both the node addresses and the storage addresses of the objects (key-value).

Figure 5.4 provides a schematic representation of consistent hashing. The address space of 0 to 2^x key values is arranged in a circle; then a hash function is selected to run the following calculations:

- **Calculation of node addresses**: The nodes' network addresses are mapped to storage addresses using the selected hash function and then entered on the ring.
- **Calculation of object addresses**: The keys of the key-value pairs are transformed into addresses with the hashing algorithm, and the objects are entered on the ring.

The key-value pairs are stored on their respective storage nodes according to a simple assignment rule: The objects are assigned to the next node (clockwise) and managed there.

Figure 5.4 shows an address space with three nodes and eight objects (key-value pairs). The positioning of the nodes and objects results from the calculated addresses. According to the assignment rule, objects O_{58}, O_1, and O_7 are stored on node K_1; objects O_{15} and O_{18} on node K_2; and the remaining three objects on node K_3.

The strengths of consistent hashing best come out in flexible computer structures, where nodes may be added or removed at any time. Such changes only affect objects directly next to the respective nodes on the ring, making it unnecessary to recalculate

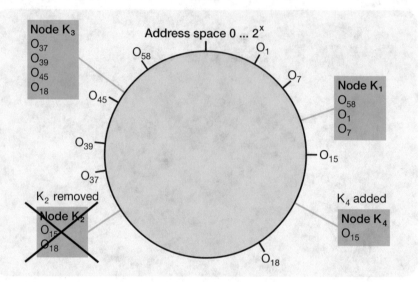

Fig. 5.5 Dynamic changes in the computer network

and reassign the addresses for a large number of key-value pairs with each change in the computer network.

Figure 5.5 illustrates two changes: Node K_2 is removed, and a new node K_4 is added. After the local adjustments, object O_{18}, which was originally stored in node K_2, is now stored in node K_3. The remaining object O_{15} is transferred to the newly added node K_4 according to the assignment rule.

Consistent hashing can also be used for replicated computer networks. The desired copies of the objects are simply given a version number and entered on the ring. This increases partition tolerance and the availability of the overall system.

Another option is the introduction of virtual nodes in order to spread the objects across nodes more evenly. In this method, the nodes' network addresses are also assigned version numbers in order to be represented on the ring.

Consistent hashing functions are used in many NoSQL systems, especially in implementations of key-value store systems.

5.2.5 Multi-dimensional Data Structures

Multi-dimensional data structures support access to records with multiple access key values. The combination of all those access keys is called *multi-dimensional key*. A multi-dimensional key is always unique, but does not have to be minimal.

A data structure that supports such multi-dimensional keys is called a *multi-dimensional data structure*. For instance, an EMPLOYEE table with the two key parts Employee Number and Year of Birth can be seen as a two-dimensional data structure. The employee number forms one part of the two-dimensional key, but remains unique in itself. The Year attribute is the second part and serves as an additional access key, without having to be unique.

Unlike tree structures, multi-dimensional data structures are designed so that no one key part controls the storage order of the physical records. A multi-dimensional data structure is called *symmetrical* if it permits access with multiple access keys without favoring a certain key or key combination. For the sample EMPLOYEE table, both key parts, Employee Number and Year of Birth, should be equally efficient in supporting access for a specific query.

One of the most important multi-dimensional data structures is the grid file or bucket grid.

Grid File

A grid file is a multi-dimensional data structure with the following properties:

- It supports access with a *multi-dimensional access key* symmetrically, i.e., no key dimension is dominant.
- It enables reading any record with only *two page accesses*, one on the grid index and the second on the data page itself.

A grid file consists of a grid index and a file containing the data pages. The grid index is a multi-dimensional space with each dimension representing a part of the multi-dimensional access key. When records are inserted, the index is partitioned into cells, alternating between the dimensions. Accordingly, the example in Fig. 5.6 alternates between Employee Number and Year of Birth for the two-dimensional access key. The resulting division limits are called the scales of the grid index.

One *cell of the grid index* corresponds to one data page and contains at least n and at the most 2*n entries, n being the number of dimensions of the grid file, where n is the number of dimensions of the grid file. Empty cells must be combined with other cells so that the associated data pages can have the minimum number of entries. In our example, data pages can hold no more than four entries (n=2).

Since the grid index is generally large, it has to be stored in secondary memory along with the records. The set of scales, however, is small and can be held in the main memory. The procedure for accessing a specific record is therefore as follows: The system searches the scales with the k key values of the k-dimensional grid file and determines the interval in which each individual part of the search key is located. These intervals describe a cell of the grid index which can then be accessed directly. Each index cell contains the number of the data page with the associated records, so that one more access, to the data page of the previously identified cell, is sufficient to find whether there is a record matching the search key or not.

The two-disk-access maximum, i.e., no more than two accesses to secondary memory, is guaranteed for the search for any record. The first access is to the appropriate cell of the grid index and the second to the associated data page. As an example, the employee with number E18, born in 1969, is searched in the grid file G4 from Fig. 5.6: The employee number E18 is located in the scale interval E15 to E30, i.e., in the right half of the grid file. The year 1969 can be found between the

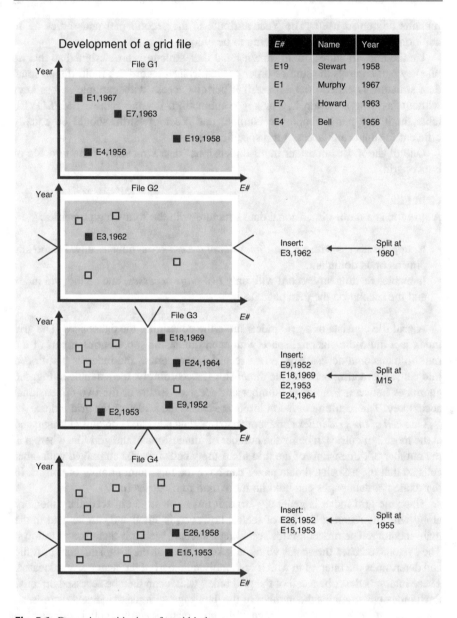

Fig. 5.6 Dynamic partitioning of a grid index

scales 1960 and 1970 or in the top half. With those scales, the database system finds the address of the data page in the grid index with its first access. The second access, to the respective data page, leads to the requested records with the access keys (E18, 1969) and (E24, 1964).

A k-dimensional grid file supports queries for individual records or record areas. *Point queries* can be used to find a specific record with k access keys. It is also possible to formulate partial queries specifying only a part of the key. With a *range query*, on the other hand, users can examine a range for each of the k key parts. All records whose key parts are in the defined range are returned. Again, it is possible to only specify and analyze a range for part of the keys (partial range query).

The search for the record (E18, 1969) described above is a typical example of a point query. If only the employee's year of birth is known, the key part 1969 is specified for a partial point query. A search for all employees born between 1960 and 1969, for instance, would be a (partial) range query. In the example from Fig. 5.6, this query targets the upper half of grid index G4, so only those two data pages have to be searched. This indexing method allows for the results of range and partial range queries in grid files to be found without the need to sift through the entire file.

In recent years, various multi-dimensional data structures efficiently supporting multiple access keys symmetrically have been researched and described. The market range of multi-dimensional data structures for SQL and NoSQL databases is still very limited, but Web-based searches are increasing the demand for such storage structures. Especially geographic information systems must be able to handle both topological and geometrical queries (also called location-based queries) efficiently.

5.2.6 Binary JavaScript Object Notation BSON

JSON documents are text files (cf. Sect. 2.5.1). They contain spaces and line breaks and are not compact enough for database storage on disk. BSON, or Binary JSON, is a more storage-efficient solution for storing structured documents in database systems. BSON is a binary serialization of JSON-structured documents. Like JSON, BSON supports the mapping of complex objects (cf. Sect. 2.5.1). However, BSON is stored in bytecode. Additionally, BSON provides data types that are not part of the JSON specification, such as date and time values. BSON was first used in 2009 in the MongoDB document database system for physical storage of documents. Today, there are over 50 implementations in 30 programming languages.

To illustrate the BSON format, let's start with a comparison. In Fig. 5.7 above, we see a JSON document of an employee with name Murphy and city Kent. In Fig. 5.7 below, we see the same structure in BSON format. The readable strings (UTF-8) are shown in bold. Two-digit hexadecimal values for encoding bytes start with the letter x.

BSON is a binary format in which data can be stored in units named documents. These documents can be nested recursively. A document consists of an element list, which is embedded between a length specification and a so-called null byte. Therefore, on the first line in the BSON document in Fig. 5.7, we see the length of the document, and on the last line, the document is terminated with a null byte. In between, there is an element list.

According to line 1 in the BSON document in Fig. 5.7, the length of the document is 58. The length is an integer, which is stored in BSON in a total of four bytes. For readability, all integer values in this example are represented as decimal numbers.

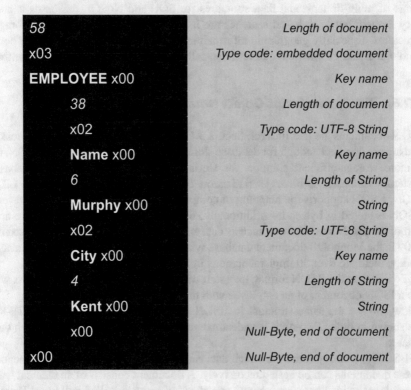

Fig. 5.7 Comparison of JSON data with binary storage in BSON

On line 14, the null byte x00 indicates the end of the entire document. A null byte is a sequence of eight bits, each of which stores the value 0. In hexadecimal notation, this is represented by x00.

In Fig. 5.7, the element list of the overall BSON document consists of lines 2 through 13. An element list consists of one element, optionally followed by another element list.

An element starts with a type code in the first byte. For example, on line 2 in the BSON document in Fig. 5.7, we see the type code x03, which announces an embedded document as an element. This is followed by a key string. A key string is a sequence of non-empty bytes followed by a null byte. For example, the key EMPLOYEE is given on line 3. This is followed by the value of the element corresponding to the type code.

In BSON, there are different element types, e.g., embedded document (type code x03), array (type code x04), or string (type code x02). In the BSON example in Fig. 5.7, the first element value stored is an embedded document which, like the parent document, again starts with the length specification (line 4), has an element list, and ends with the null byte (line 13).

A string element starts with the type code x02. In the example in Fig. 5.7, we see on line 5 the beginning of the string element for the property "Name," whose key name is specified on line 6. The value of this element starts on line 7 with length (6), followed by the actual string on line 8 (Murphy). A string in BSON is a sequence of UTF-8 characters followed by a null byte. Then follows analogously another element of type String with key City and value Kent.

This is the way BSON allows to store JSON data in binary form on disk in a space-saving and efficient way. BSON is used by document databases to write documents to disk.

5.2.7 Index-Free Adjacency

As we saw in Sects. 5.2.1 through 5.2.3, relational databases do not explicitly store links between records. A key value is resolved with time-consuming searching in the referenced table. An index allows this search process to be sped up; however, even indexed queries take longer as more data needs to be searched.

To solve this problem, graph database systems provide resolution of a record reference in constant time. This is of great importance for traversing networks. To do this, they make use of the principle of pointers and addresses on the level of binary files stored on the disk and manipulated in memory by the operating system. Pointers are used to build doubly linked lists that enable the traversal of the graph. Central to this is the fact that the edges of the network are stored as separate records (cf. theory of multigraphs in Sect. 2.4.1). In the following, we will look at a concrete example.

In Fig. 5.8, a simple property graph is shown above. An employee named Murphy is part of the team of the project with title ITsec with a workload of 50%. In addition, another previously unnamed node is linked for illustrative purposes. The elements of the graph are numbered and labeled. The example contains three nodes N1 to N3, two arrows A1 to A2, and seven properties P1 to P7. For simplicity, node and edge types are represented here as properties.

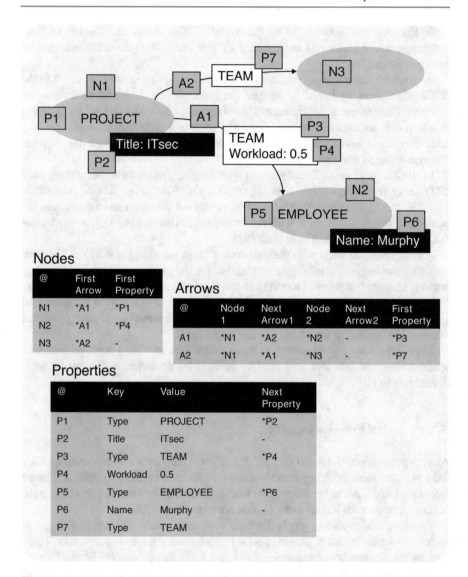

Fig. 5.8 Index-free neighborhood using doubly linked lists with pointers

In Fig. 5.8 below, we see illustrations of three store files, one for nodes, one for arrows, and one for properties. The first field (@) shows the respective file location address. In the other fields, the effective data is shown.

In the node store file, the second field (FirstArrow) contains pointers to the first arrow of the node. The third field (FirstProperty) contains pointers to the first property of the node. For example, the first arrow of node N1 is A1, and the first property is P1.

If we follow the pointer *P1, we find in the property store file, shown in Fig. 5.8 below, the property with address P1: the node has the type PROJECT. The store file shows in the second and third field the key (Key) and the value (Value) of each property. In the fourth field, we find a pointer (NextProperty) to possible further properties. In the example of node N1, we find the pointer to property P2 one line further down: the project has the title ITsec. In addition, there are no further properties for this node, so that this storage field remains empty.

In the node store file, the entry for node N1 also points to the first edge that connects it to the network, A1. The edge store file shown on the right illustrates that two nodes are connected by edge A1. The first node (Node1) is N1, and the second node (Node2) is N2. Moreover, we find a pointer to another arrow: the next arrow from the perspective of the first node (NextArrow1) is arrow A2 in this case. The next edge from the perspective of the second node (NextArrow2) is empty in this example, because node N2 has no further connections. Further, the node store file shows a pointer to node properties in the FirstProperty field, exactly the same as the edge store file (see above).

This pointer structure results in a doubly linked list of nodes and arrows. This makes traversal in the graph efficient and linearly scalable in the number of arrows. In fact, there is no need to even store the actual address, since an integer number as an offset can simply be multiplied by the size of the memory file entries to get to the correct location in the binary store file. For the operating system, the cost of calling to a file address based on a pointer is always constant, or $O(1)$,[1] no matter how much data the database contains. Using this mechanism, native graph database systems provide *index-free adjacency*: graph edges can be traversed efficiently without the need for building explicit index structures.

5.3   Translation and Optimization of Relational Queries

5.3.1   Creation of Query Trees

The user interfaces of relational database systems are set-oriented, since entire tables or views are provided for the users. When a relational query and data manipulation language are used, the database system has to translate and optimize the respective commands. It is vital that neither the calculation nor the optimization of the query tree requires user actions.

---

[1]The Landau symbol $O(f(x))$, also called Big O notation, is used in computer science when analyzing the cost or complexity of algorithms. It gives a measure of the growth $f(x)$ of the number of computational steps or memory units as a function of the size x of a given problem. For example, the runtime of an algorithm with computation complexity $O(n^2)$ grows quadratically as a function of a parameter n, e.g., the number of data records.

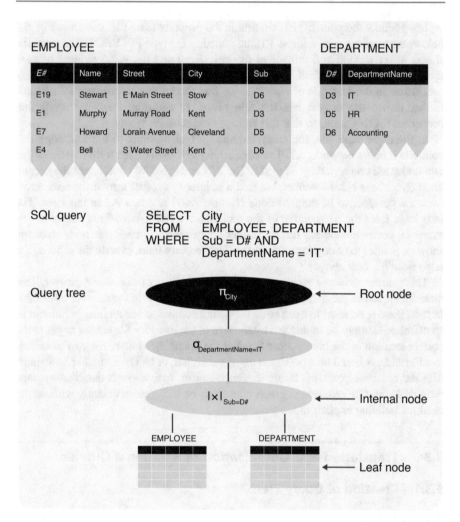

Fig. 5.9 Query tree of a qualified query on two tables

Query Tree

Query trees graphically visualize relational queries with the *equivalent expressions of relational algebra*. The leaves of a query tree are the tables used in the query; root and internal nodes contain the algebraic operators.

Figure 5.9 illustrates a query tree using SQL and the previously introduced EMPLOYEE and DEPARTMENT tables. Those tables are queried for a list of the cities where the IT department members live:

```
SELECT City
FROM   EMPLOYEE, DEPARTMENT
WHERE  Sub=D# AND Department_Name='IT'
```

This query can also be expressed algebraically by a series of operators:

TABLE :=

$$\pi_{City} \, (\sigma_{Department\_Name=IT} \, (EMPLOYEE \, |\times|_{Sub=D\#} \, DEPARTMENT) \,)$$

This expression first calculates a join of the EMPLOYEE and the DEPART-MENT tables via the shared department number. Next, those employees working in the department with the name IT are selected for an intermediate result; and finally, the requested cities are returned with the help of a projection. Figure 5.10 shows this expression of algebraic operators represented in the corresponding query tree.

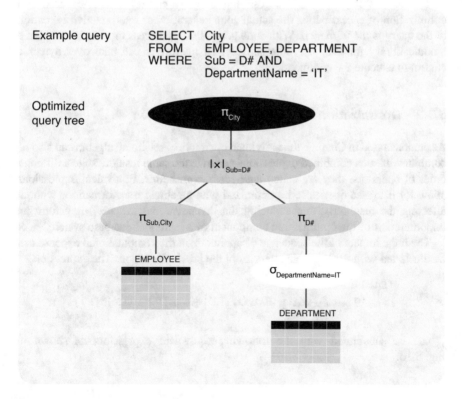

Fig. 5.10 Algebraically optimized query tree

This query tree can be interpreted as follows: The leaf nodes are the two tables EMPLOYEE and DEPARTMENT used in the query. They are first combined in one internal node (join operator) and then reduced to those entries with the department name IT in a second internal node (select operator). The root node represents the projection generating the results table with the requested cities.

Root and internal nodes of query trees refer to either one or two subtrees. If the operator forming a node works with one table, it is called a unary operator; if it affects two tables, it is a binary operator. *Unary operators*, which can only manipulate one table, are the project and select operators.

Binary operators involving two tables as operands are the set union, set intersection, set difference, Cartesian product, join, and divide operators.

Creating a query tree is the first step in translating and executing a relational database query. The tables and attributes specified by the user must be available in the system tables before any further processing takes place. The query tree is therefore used to check both the query syntax and the user's access permissions. Additional security measures, such as value-dependent data protection, can only be assessed during the runtime.

The second step after this access and integrity control is the selection and optimization of access paths; the actual code generation or interpretative execution of the query is the third step. With code generation, an access module is stored in a module library for later use; alternatively, an interpreter can take over dynamic control to execute the command.

5.3.2   Optimization by Algebraic Transformation

As demonstrated in Chap. 3, the individual operators of relational algebra can also be combined. If such combined expressions generate the same result despite a different order of operators, they are called *equivalent expressions*. Equivalent expressions allow for database queries to be optimized with algebraic transformations without affecting the result. By thus reducing the computational expense, they form an important part of the optimization component of a relational database system.

The huge impact of the sequence of operators on the computational expense can be illustrated with the example query from the previous section: The expression

$$\text{TABLE} :=$$
$$\pi_{\text{City}} (\sigma_{\text{Department\_Name} = \text{IT}} (\text{EMPLOYEE} \bowtie_{\text{Sub}=D\#} \text{DEPARTMENT}))$$

can be substituted with the following equivalent expression, as shown in Fig. 5.10:

$$
\text{TABLE} :=
$$
$$
\pi_{\text{City}} \big(
$$
$$
\pi_{\text{Sub,City}} \, (\text{EMPLOYEE}) \, |\times|
$$
$$
|\times|_{\text{Sub}=D\#}
$$
$$
\pi_{D\#} \, (\sigma_{\text{Department\_Name}=\text{IT}} \, (\text{DEPARTMENT}) \,) \,)
$$

Here, the first step is the selection (σ Department_Name=IT) on the DEPART-MENT table, since only the IT department is relevant to the query. Next are two projection operations: one ($\pi_{\text{Sub,City}}$) on the EMPLOYEE table and another (π D#) on the intermediate table with the IT department from step 1. Only now is the join operation ($|\times|$Sub=D#) via the department number executed, before the final projection (π_{City}) on the cities is done. While the end result is the same, the computational expense is significantly lower this way.

It is generally advisable to position *projection and selection operators in the query tree as close to the leaves as possible* to get only small intermediate results before calculating the time-intensive and therefore expensive join operators. A successful transformation of a query tree with such a strategy is called *algebraic optimization*; the following principles apply:

- Multiple selections on one table can be merged into one so the selection predicate only has to be validated once.
- Selections should be done as early as possible to keep intermediate results small. To this end, the selection operators should be placed as close to the leaves (i.e., the source tables) as possible.
- Projections should also be run as early as possible, but never before selections. Projection operations reduce the number of columns and often also the tuples.
- Join operators should be calculated near the root node of the query tree, since they require a lot of computational expense.

In addition to algebraic optimization, the use of efficient storage and access structures (cf. Sect. 5.2) can also achieve significant gains in processing relational queries. For instance, database systems will improve selection and join operators based on the size of the affected tables, sorting orders, index structures, etc. At the same time, an effective model for estimating access costs is vital to decide between multiple possible processing sequences.

Cost formulas are necessary to calculate the computational expense of different database queries, such as sequential searches within a table, searches via index structures, the sorting of tables or subtables, the use of index structures regarding join attributes, or computations of equi-joins across multiple tables. Those cost formulas involve the number of accesses to *physical pages* and create a weighted gauge for input and output operations as well as CPU (central processing unit) usage. Depending on the computer configuration, the formula may be heavily influenced by access times for external storage media, caches, and main memories, as well as the internal processing power.

5.3.3   Calculation of Join Operators

A relational database system must provide various algorithms that can execute the operations of relational algebra and relational calculus. The selection of tuples from multiple tables is significantly more expensive than a selection from one table. The following section will therefore discuss the different join strategies, even though casual users will hardly be able to influence the calculation options.

Implementing a join operation on two tables aims to compare each tuple of one table with all tuples of the other table concerning the join predicate and, when there is a match, insert the two tuples into the results table as a combined tuple. Regarding the calculation of equi-joins, there are two basic join strategies: nested join and sort-merge join.

Nested Join

For a nested join between a table R with an attribute A and a table S with an attribute B, *each tuple in R is compared to each tuple in S* to check whether the join predicate R.A=S.B is fulfilled. If R has n tuples and S has m tuples, this requires n times m comparisons.

The algorithm for a nested join calculates the Cartesian product and simultaneously checks whether the join predicate is met. Since we compare all tuples of R in an outer loop with all tuples of S from an inner loop, the expense is quadratic. It can be reduced if an index (see Sect. 5.2.1) exists for attribute A and/or attribute B.

Figure 5.9 illustrates a heavily simplified algorithm for a nested join of employee and department information from the established example tables. OUTER_LOOP and INNER_LOOP are clearly visible and show how the algorithm compares all tuples of the EMPLOYEE table to all tuples of the DEPARTMENT table.

For the join operation in Fig. 5.11, there is an index for the $D\#$ attribute, since it is the primary key[2] of the DEPARTMENT table. The database system uses the index structure for the department number by not going through the entire DEPART-MENT table tuple by tuple for each iteration of the inner loop, but rather accessing tuples directly via the index. Ideally, there is also an index for the Sub (subordinate) attribute of the EMPLOYEE table for the database system to use for optimization. This example illustrates the importance of the selection of suitable index structures by database administrators.

A more efficient algorithm than a nested join is available if the tuples of tables R and S are already sorted physically in ascending or descending order by the attributes A and B of the join predicate, respectively. This may require an internal sort before

---

[2]The database system automatically generates index structures for each primary key; advanced index structures are used for concatenated keys.

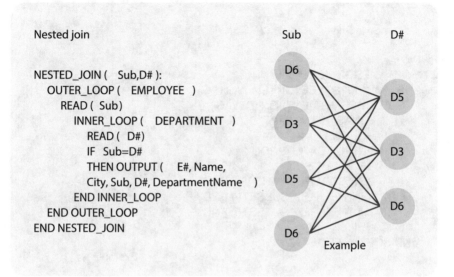

Fig. 5.11 Computing a join with nesting

the actual join operation in order to bring both of the tables into matching order. The computation of the join then merely requires going through the tables for ascending or descending attribute values of the join predicate and simultaneously compares the values of A and B. This strategy is characterized as follows:

Sort-Merge Join

A sort-merge join requires the tables R and S with the join predicate R.A=S.B to be sorted by the attribute values for A of R and B of S, respectively. The algorithm computes the join by making *comparisons in the sorting order*. If the attributes A and B are uniquely defined (e.g., as primary and foreign key), the computational expense is linear.

Figure 5.12 shows a basic algorithm for a sort-merge join. First, both tables are sorted by the attributes used in the join predicate and made available as cursors i and j. Then the cursor i is passed in the sort order, and the comparisons are executed.

If the compound predicate i==j is true, that is, if the values at both cursors' current positions are equal, both data sets are merged at this point and output. To do this, a Cartesian product of the two subsets of records with the same key, i and j, is output. The function GET_SUBSET(x) fetches all records in the cursor x where the key x is equal and sets the pointer of the cursor to the immediately following record with the next larger key value.

If either key is less than the other, the GET_SUBSET function is also run for the cursor with smaller value, not for output, but to set the cursor's pointer to the next larger key value. This is looped until there are no more records for the first cursor.

With this algorithm, both tables only need to be traversed once. The cross-product is only executed locally for small subsets of records, which increases the execution

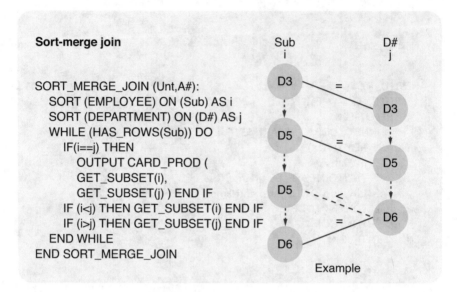

Fig. 5.12 Going through tables in sorting order

speed significantly. In the query of the EMPLOYEE and DEPARTMENT tables, the sort-merge join is linearly dependent from the occurrences of the tuples, since D# is a key attribute. The algorithm only has to go through both tables once to compute the join.

Database systems are generally unable to select a suitable join strategy—or any other access strategy—a priori. Unlike algebraic optimization, this decision hinges on the current content state of the database. It is therefore vital that the statistical information contained in the system tables is regularly updated, either automatically at set intervals or manually by database specialists. This enables cost-based optimization.

5.3.4 Cost-Based Optimization of Access Paths

Another way to optimize queries is statistical, cost-based optimization. An optimizer in a database management system evaluates the optimal access structures and available indexes for queries. Based on the cost, i.e., the number of records that must be searched to fulfill a query, the optimizer selects possible indexes to minimize this cost. To do this, it uses information about existing indexes and statistics about the number of rows in the tables. In this way, it comes up with cost estimates for different variants of query processing. These are called execution plans. Then the optimizer chooses the optimal variant.

In SQL databases, the keyword EXPLAIN can be used to display the execution plan for a query. This allows us to see which indexes are being used and where inefficient searches still exist. This keyword is often used by database specialists to examine queries for their performance and to improve them manually.

For example, there are situations where an index exists on a search column, but it is not used by the optimizer. This is the case, among others, when functions are applied to the search column. Let's assume that there is an index IX1 on the column Date of birth in the table Employees:

```
CREATE INDEX ix1
ON EMPLOYEES (date_of_birth)
```

Now we want to output the list of employees born before 1960. We can try this with the following SQL query:

```
SELECT * FROM EMPLOYEES
WHERE YEAR(date_of_birth)<1960
```

When we do this, we will notice that even though the index exists, the query is slow for large amounts of data.

With the EXPLAIN keyword, we can observe the optimizer's execution plan, which defines which queries are run in which order and which indexes are used to access the data.

```
EXPLAIN
SELECT * FROM EMPLOYEES
WHERE YEAR(date_of_birth) < 1960
```

When we do this, we will notice from the database system's response that the optimizer did not recognize index IX1 as a possible access path (POSSIBLE_KEY) and that the query is of type "ALL," meaning that all records in the table must be searched. This is called full table scan. This is because the optimizer cannot use the index when functions are applied to the search columns. The solution to this problem is to remove this function call:

```
EXPLAIN
SELECT * FROM EMPLOYEES
WHERE date_of_birth < '1960-01-01'.
```

A renewed call of the execution plan with EXPLAIN now shows that due to this change, the query is now of type "RANGE," i.e., a range query, and that for this, the index IX1 can be used as an efficient access path. Thus, the SQL query will now run much more efficiently. This is an example of how, in principle, analyzing the optimizer's execution plan works.

5.4   Parallel Processing with MapReduce

Analyses of large amounts of data require a division of tasks utilizing parallelism in order to produce results within a reasonable time. The MapReduce method can be used for both computer networks and mainframes; the following section discusses the first, distributed option.

In a distributed computer network, often consisting of cheap, horizontally scaled components, computing processes can be distributed more easily than data sets. Therefore, the MapReduce method has gained widespread acceptance for Web-based search and analysis tasks. It employs parallel processing to generate and sort simple data extracts before outputting the results:

- **Map phase**: Subtasks are distributed between various nodes of the computer network to use parallelism. On the individual nodes, simple key-value pairs are extracted based on a query and then sorted (e.g., via hashing) and output as intermediate results.
- **Reduce phase**: In this phase, the abovementioned intermediate results are consolidated for each key or key range and output as the final result, which consists of a list of keys with the associated aggregated value instances.

Figure 5.13 shows a simple example of a MapReduce procedure: Documents or websites are to be searched for the terms algorithm, database, NoSQL, key, SQL, and distribution. The requested result is the frequency of each term.

The map phase consists of the two parallel mapping functions M1 and M2. M1 generates a list of key-value pairs, with the search terms as key and their frequencies as value. M2 simultaneously executes a similar search on another computer node with different documents or websites. The preliminary results are then sorted alphabetically with the help of a hashing algorithm. For the upper part, the first letters A to N of the keys (search terms) are the sorting criterion; in the lower part, it is the letters O–Z.

The reduce phase in Fig. 5.13 combines the intermediate results. The Reduce function R1 adds up the frequencies for the terms starting with A to N; R2 does the same for those starting with O to Z. The results, sorted by frequency of the search terms, are one list with NoSQL (4), database (3), and algorithm (1) and a second list with SQL (3), distribution (2), and key (1). The final result combines these two lists and sorts them by frequency.

The MapReduce method is based on common functional programming languages such as LISP (LISt Processing), where the map() function calculates a modified list

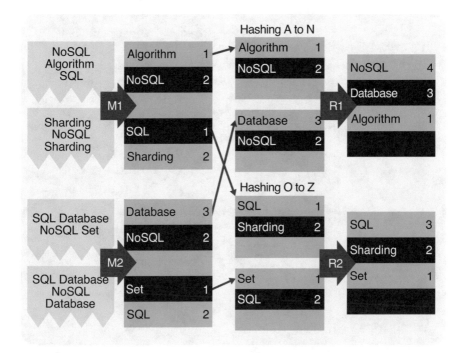

Fig. 5.13 Determining the frequencies of search terms with MapReduce

for all elements of an original list as an intermediate result. The reduce() function aggregated individual results and reduces them into an output value.

MapReduce has been improved and patented by Google developers for huge amounts of semi- and unstructured data. However, the function is also available in many open-source tools. The procedure plays an important role in NoSQL databases (see Chap. 7), where various manufacturers use the approach for retrieving database entries. Due to its use of parallelism, the MapReduce method is useful not only for data analysis but also for load distribution, data transfer, distributed searches, categorizations, and monitoring.

5.5 Layered Architecture

It is considered a vital rule for the system architecture of database systems that future changes or expansions must be locally limitable. Similar to the implementation of operating systems or other software components, *fully independent system layers* that communicate via defined interfaces are introduced into relational and non-relational database systems.

Figure 5.14 gives an overview of the five layers of system architecture based on relational database technology. The section below further shows how those layers

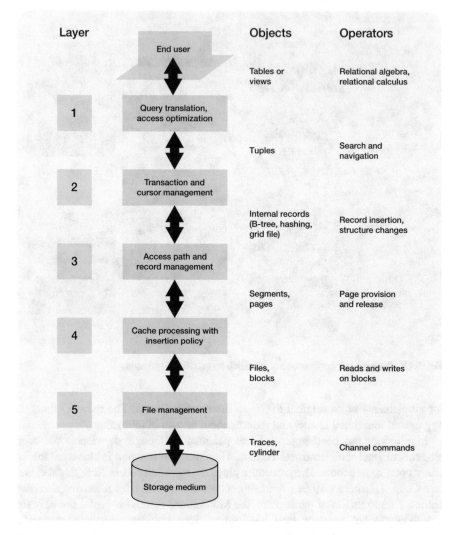

Fig. 5.14 Five-layer model for relational database systems

correspond to the major features described in Chap. 4 and the previous sections of Chap. 5.

Layer 1: Set-Oriented Interface

The first layer is used to describe data structures, provide set operations, define access conditions, and check integrity constraints (see Chap. 4). Either during early translation and generation of access module or during runtime, it is necessary to check syntax, resolve names, and select access paths. There is room for considerable optimization in the selection of access paths.

Layer 2: Record-Oriented Interface

The second layer converts logical records and access paths into physical structures. A cursor concept allows for navigating or processing records according to the physical storage order, positioning specific records within a table, or providing records sorted by value. Transaction management must be used to ensure that the consistency of the database is maintained and no deadlocks arise between various user requests.

Layer 3: Storage and Access Structures

The third layer implements physical records and access paths on pages. The number of page formats is limited, but in addition to tree structures and hashing methods, multi-dimensional data structures should be supported in the future. These common storage structures are designed for efficient access to external storage media. Physical clustering and multi-dimensional access paths can also be used to achieve further optimization in record and access path management.

Layer 4: Page Assignment

For reasons of efficiency and to support the implementation of recovery procedures, the fourth layer divides the linear address space into segments with identical page limits. The file management provides pages in a cache on request. On the other hand, pages can be inserted into or substituted within the cache with insertion or replacement policies. There is not only the direct assignment of pages to blocks but also indirect assignment, such as caching methods which allow for multiple pages to be inserted into the database cache atomically.

Layer 5: Memory Allocation

The fifth layer realizes memory allocation structures and provides block-based file management for the layer above. The hardware properties remain hidden from the file- and block-oriented operations. The file management usually supports dynamically growing files with definable block sizes. Ideally, it should also be possible to cluster blocks and in- and output multiple blocks with only one operation.

5.6   Use of Different Storage Structures

Many Web-based applications use different data storage systems to fit their various services. Using just one database technology, e.g., relational databases, is no longer enough: The wide range of requirements regarding consistency, availability, and partition tolerance demand a mix of storage systems, especially due to the CAP theorem.

Figure 5.15 shows a schematic representation of an online store. In order to guarantee high availability and partition tolerance, session management and shopping carts utilize key-value stores (see Chap. 6). Orders are saved to a document store (see Chap. 7), and customers and accounts are managed in a relational database system.

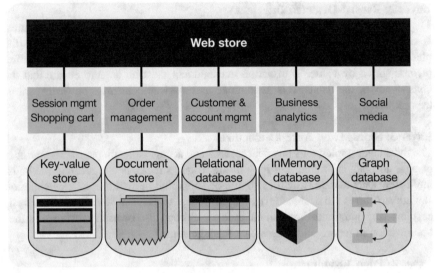

Fig. 5.15 Use of SQL and NoSQL databases in an online store

Performance management is a vital part of successfully running an online store. Web analytics are used to store key performance indicators (KPIs) of content and visitors in a data warehouse (see Chap. 6). Specialized tools such as data mining and predictive business analysis allow for regular assessments of business goals and the success of campaigns and other actions. Since analyses on a multi-dimensional data cube are time-consuming, the cube is kept in-memory.

Social media integration for the Web shop is a good idea for many reasons. Products and services can be promoted, and customers' reactions can be evaluated; in case of problems or dissatisfaction, good communication and appropriate measures can avoid or mitigate possible negative impacts. Following blogs and relevant discussion threads on social networks can also help to discover and recognize important trends or innovation in the industry. Graph databases (see Sect. 7.6) are the logical choice for the analysis of relationships between individual target groups.

The services needed for the online store and the integration of heterogeneous SQL and NoSQL databases can be realized with the REST (Representational State Transfer) architecture. It consists of five elements:

- **Resource identification**: Web resources are identified using a Uniform Resource Identifier (URI). Such resources can, for instance, be websites, files, services, or e-mail addresses. URIs have up to five parts: scheme (type of URI or protocol), authority (provider or server), path, optional query (information to identify a resource), and optional fragment (reference within a resource). An example would be http://eShop.com/customers/12345.

- **Linking**: Resources are connected via hyperlinks, i.e., electronic references. Hyperlinks or simply links are cross-references in hypertext documents that point to a location within the document itself or to another electronic document. An HTML hyperlink looks like this: <a href=http://eShop.com>Browse our online store for literature</a>.
- **Standard methods**: Any resource on the Web can be manipulated with a set of methods. The standard methods of HTTP (HyperText Transfer Protocol), such as GET (request a resource from a server), POST (send data to a server), and DELETE (delete a resource), allow for a unified interface. This ensures that other Web services can communicate with all resources at any time.
- **Representations**: Servers based on REST must be able to provide various representations of resources, depending on application and requirements. Besides the standard HTML (HyperText Markup Language) format, resources are often provided in XML (eXtensible Markup Language).
- **Statelessness**: Neither applications nor servers exchange state information between messages. This improves the scalability of services, e.g., load distribution on multiple computer nodes (cf. MapReduce method).

REST offers a template for the development of distributed applications with heterogeneous SQL and NoSQL components. It ensures horizontal scalability in case business volumes increase or new services become necessary.

5.7   Cloud Databases

Installation and maintenance of database systems in a physical data center are significant tasks. For this purpose, not only the software but also the hardware must be provided, maintained, and secured. Larger companies have created entire IT operations departments for this purpose, whose job is to provide the hardware and operating systems on which database systems and applications run. This type of organization is changing, as services in the so-called cloud threaten to make internal IT operations departments obsolete.

The term "cloud" comes from the fact that the Internet is often represented with a cloud symbol in system architecture diagrams. The metaphor of the cloud symbolizes something opaque and intangible. In the context of networking, it means that where and how an IT service is delivered is opaque and intangible to the user—what matters is that it works.

Cloud providers are companies that offer computing resources, i.e., cloud storage, cloud computing, or cloud services in general, via the Internet. The operation of the hardware and software is automated by the third-party provider, so that users can obtain the required services via the Internet without having to worry about the basics of hardware and software.

Cloud Database

A cloud database is a database that is operated as a cloud service. Access to the database is provided by cloud providers as an Internet application. The database service is obtained over the Internet and does not require active installation or maintenance by the user. A cloud database system is available promptly immediately after the online order is placed. Thus, the installation, operation, backup, security, and availability of the database service are automated. This is also called database as a service (DBaaS).

Cloud databases provide a higher level of service. DBaaS offerings automate database operations tasks. In addition to providing the basics of the computer hardware, operating system, and computer network, this includes installing the database software and maintaining it, ensuring security across all layers, and efficiently scaling the performance of the entire database system:

- **Computing**: The hardware, i.e., the physical computers with processor and main and fixed storage of cloud services, is built in highly automated data centers. Robots are used for this purpose, which can install and replace individual parts.
- **Network**: The computers are integrated into a network with high-performance data cables so that all components can communicate with each other and with the outside world.
- **Operating system**: Virtual machines are operated on this basis, providing the operating system on which the database system runs.
- **Database software**: The database system is automatically installed, configured, operated, and maintained by appropriate software on the virtual machines.
- **Security**: The database system is configured for security. This includes securing all layers, from hardware, including geographic redundancy, to securing the network and firewall, to securing the operating system and database software.
- **Big Data**: One advantage of automation is that new resources such as memory and processors are allocated autonomously by the cloud service at short notice and at any time, providing scalability in Big Data applications.

These benefits of cloud database systems create a clearly noticeable added value, which is also reflected in the price of the services. This consideration must be made and calculated for each use case.

Bibliography

BSON (binary JSON): https://bsonspec.org/. Accessed 24 Aug 2022

Bayer, R.: Symmetric binary B-trees: data structures and maintenance algorithms. Acta Inform. **1**(4), 290–306 (1992)

Celko, J.: Joe Celko's Complete Guide to NoSQL - Was jeder SQL-Profi über nicht-relationale Datenbanken wissen muss. Morgan Kaufmann (2014)

Dean, J., Ghemawat, S.: MapReduce: Vereinfachte Datenverarbeitung auf großen Clustern. Commun. ACM. **51**(1), 107–113 (2008). https://doi.org/10.1145/1327452.1327492

DeCandia, G., Hastorun, D., Jampani, M., Kakulapati, G., Lakshman, A., Pilchin, A., Sivasubramanian, S., Vosshall, P., Vogels, W.: Dynamo – Amazon's highly available key-value store. In: Proceedings of the 21st ACM Symposium on Operating Systems Principles (SOSP'07), Stevenson, Washington, 14–17 October 2007, pp. 205–220

Deka, G.C.: A survey of cloud database systems. IT Prof. **16**(2), 50–57 (2014) https://ieeexplore.ieee.org/document/6401099. Accessed 29 Aug 2022

Edlich, S., Friedland, A., Hampe, J., Brauer, B., Brückner, M.: NoSQL - Einstieg in die Welt nichtrelationaler Web 2.0 Datenbanken. Carl Hanser Verlag (2011)

Härder, T., Rahm, E.: Datenbanksysteme - Konzepte und Techniken der Implementierung. Springer (2001)

Karger, D., Lehmann, E., Leighton, T., Levine, M., Lewin, D., Panigrahy, R.: Consistent hashing and random trees – distributed caching protocols for relieving hot spots on the world wide web. In: Proceedings of the 29th Annual ACM Symposium on Theory of Computing, El Paso, Texas (1997)

Maier, D.: Die Theorie der relationalen Datenbanken. Computer Science Press (1983)

Maurer, W.D., Lewis, T.G.: Hash table methods. ACM Comput. Surv. **7**(1), 5–19 (1975)

Nievergelt, J., Hinterberger, H., Sevcik, K.C.: The grid file: an adaptable, symmetric multikey file structure. ACM Trans. Database Syst. **9**(1), 38–71 (1984)

Perkins, L., Redmond, E., Wilson, J.R.: Seven Databases in Seven Weeks 2e: A Guide to Modern Databases and the Nosql Movement, 2. Auflage edn. O'Reilly UK Ltd, Raleigh, NC (2018)

Robinson, I., Webber, J., Eifrem, E.: Graph database internals. In: Graph Databases: New Opportunities for Connected Data, 2nd edn. O'Reilly Media (2015)

Sadalage, P.J., Fowler, M.: NoSQL Distilled – A Brief Guide to the Emerging World of Polyglot Persistence. Addison-Wesley (2013)

Tilkov, S.: REST und HTTP - Einsatz der Architektur des Web für Integrationsszenarien. dpunkt (2011)

Post-relational Databases 6

6.1 The Limits of SQL and What Lies Beyond

Relational database technology and especially SQL-based databases came to domi-
nate the market in the 1980s and 1990s. Today, SQL databases are still the de facto
standard for most database applications in organizations and companies. This time-
tested and widely supported technology will in all likelihood continue to be used for
the next decades. Nevertheless, the future of databases needs to be discussed.
Keywords here are NoSQL databases, graph databases, document databases, and
distributed database systems as well as temporal, deductive, semantic, object-
oriented, fuzzy, and versioned database systems. What is behind all those terms?
This chapter explains some post-relational concepts and shows methods and trends,
remaining subjective in its choice of topics. NoSQL databases are described in
Chap. 7.

The classic relational model and the corresponding SQL-based database systems
admittedly show some disadvantages stemming on the one hand from extended
requirements in new areas of application and on the other hand from the functional
limits of SQL. Relational database technology can be applied in a variety of fields
and can be seen as the all-rounder among database models. There are, however,
niches and scenarios in which SQL-based databases, being transaction- and
consistency-oriented, are a hindrance, for example, when high-performance
processing of large amounts of data is required. In those cases, it's better to use
specialized tools that are more efficient.

SQL remains the most important and most popular database language. Today,
there is a wide choice of commercial products with enhanced database functionality,
some of them open source. It is not easy for professionals to orientate in the variety
of possibilities. Often, the required effort and the economic benefit of a changeover
are not clear. Many companies therefore still require a considerable amount of
mental work to future-proof their application architecture concepts and choose the
appropriate product. In a nutshell, concise architecture concepts and migration
strategies for the use of post-relational database technologies are still lacking.

© The Author(s), under exclusive license to Springer Nature Switzerland AG 2023   193
M. Kaufmann, A. Meier, *SQL and NoSQL Databases*,
https://doi.org/10.1007/978-3-031-27908-9_6

In this chapter and the next, we present a selection of problem cases and possible solutions. Some demands not covered by classical relational databases can be met by individual enhancements of relational database systems; others have to be approached with fundamentally new concepts and methods. Both of these trends are summarized under post-relational database systems. We also consider NoSQL post-relational, but we cover it in a separate Chap. 7.

6.2   Federated Databases

Non-centralized or federated databases are used where data is to be stored, maintained, and processed in different places. A database is distributed if the data content is stored on separate computers. Copying all contained data redundantly onto several computers for load balancing is called replication. Fragmentation means that for an increased data volume, the data is effectively partitioned into smaller parts, so-called fragments, and split between several computers. Fragments are also often called partitions or shards; the concept of fragmentation is then accordingly termed partitioning or sharding.

A distributed database is federated if several physical data fragments are kept on separate computers and is organized in one single logical database schema. The users of a federated database only have to deal with the logical view of the data and can ignore the physical fragments. The database system itself performs the database operations locally or, if necessary, split between several computers.

A simple example of a federated database is shown in Fig. 6.1. Splitting the EMPLOYEE and DEPARTMENT tables into different physical fragments is an important task for the database administrators, not the users. According to our example, the departments IT and HR are geographically based in Cleveland, and the accounting department is geographically based in Cincinnati. Fragment F1 as a partial table of the EMPLOYEE table includes only employees of the IT and the HR departments. Similarly, fragment F2 from the initial DEPARTMENT table shows those departments that are based in Cleveland. Fragments F3 and F4 contain the employees and departments in Cincinnati, respectively.

If a table is split horizontally, keeping the original structure of table rows, the result is called *horizontal fragments*. The individual fragments should not overlap, but combine to form the original table.

Instead of being split horizontally, a table can also be *divided into vertical fragments* by combining several columns along with the identification key, segmenting the tuples. One example is the EMPLOYEE table, where certain parts like salary, qualifications, development potential, etc. would be kept in a vertical fragment restricted to the HR department for confidentiality reasons. The remaining information could be made accessible for the individual departments in another fragment. Hybrid forms between horizontal and vertical fragments are also possible.

EMPLOYEE

E#	Name	City	Sub
E19	Stewart	Stow	D6
E1	Murphy	Kent	D3
E7	Howard	Cleveland	D5
E4	Bell	Kent	D6

DEPARTMENT

D#	DepartmentName
D3	IT
D5	HR
D6	Accounting

Information for the IT and HR departments is
to be managed at the Cleveland site:

```
CREATE   FRAGMENT F1 AS
SELECT   *
FROM     EMPLOYEE
WHERE    Sub IN ( D3,D5 )
```

```
CREATE   FRAGMENT F2 AS
SELECT   *
FROM     DEPARTMENT
WHERE    D# IN ( D3,D5 )
```

F1 in Cleveland

E#	Name	City	Sub
E1	Murphy	Kent	D3
E7	Howard	Cleveland	D5

F2 in Cleveland

D#	DepartmentName
D3	IT
D5	HR

F3 in Cincinnati

E#	Name	City	Sub

F4 in Cincinnati

D#	DepartmentName

Fig. 6.1 Horizontal fragmentation of the EMPLOYEE and DEPARTMENT tables

One important task of a federated database system is guaranteeing local autonomy. Users can autonomously work with their local data, even if certain computer
nodes in the network are unavailable.[1]

Apart from local autonomy, the *principle of non-centralized processing* is of
importance. This means the database system can handle queries locally in the
different network nodes. For non-centralized applications like these which demand
data from different fragments, the database system has to allow for remote access to

---

[1] Periodically extracted parts of tables (called snapshots) improve local autonomy.

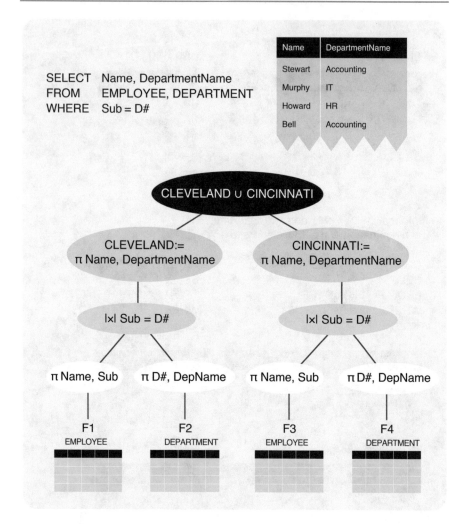

Fig. 6.2 Optimized query tree for a distributed join strategy

read and update tables. In order to achieve this, it has to provide a distributed transaction and recovery concept. These concepts demand special protection mechanisms for distributed databases.

The *internal processing strategy for distributed database queries* is vital here, as the example of querying for employees and department names in Fig. 6.2 illustrates. The query can be formulated in normal SQL without specifying the fragment. The task of the database system is to determine the optimal calculation strategy for this non-centralized query. Both the EMPLOYEE and the DEPARTMENT table are fragmented between Cleveland and Cincinnati. Therefore, *certain calculations are executed locally and synchronously.* Each node organizes the join between the EMPLOYEE and DEPARTMENT fragments independently from the other. After these partial calculations, the final result is formed by a set union of the partial results.

For further optimization, the single nodes make projections on the requested attributes Name and Department Name. Then, the join operations on the reduced table fragments are calculated separately in Cleveland and Cincinnati. Finally, the preliminary results are reduced once more by projecting them on the requested names and department names before a set union is formed.

In calculating non-centralized queries, union and join operations are typically evaluated late in the process. This supports high parallelism in processing and improves performance on non-centralized queries. The maxim of optimization is to put the join operations in the query tree close to the root node, while selections and projections should be placed near the leaves of the query tree.

Federated Database System
A federated database system fulfils the following conditions:

- It supports a single logical database schema and several physical fragments on locally distributed computers.
- It guarantees *transparency regarding the distribution of databases*, so ad hoc queries and application tools do not have to take into account the physical distribution of the data, i.e., the partitioning.
- It ensures local autonomy, i.e., it allows working locally on its non-centralized data, even if single computer nodes are not available.
- It guarantees the consistency of the distributed databases and internally optimizes the distributed queries and manipulations with a coordination program.[2]

The first prototypes of distributed database systems were developed in the early 1980s. Today, relational databases fulfilling the aforementioned demands only partially are available. Moreover, the conflict between partition tolerance and schema integration remains, so that many distributed databases, especially NoSQL databases (cf. Chap. 7), either offer no schema federation, like key-value stores, column family stores, or document stores, or do not support the fragmentation of their data content, like graph databases.

6.3   Temporal Databases

Today's relational database systems are designed to manage information relevant to the present (current information) in tables. For users to query and analyze a relational database across time, they need to individually manage and update the information relating to the past or future. This is because the database system does not directly support them saving, querying, or analyzing time-related information.

---

[2]In distributed SQL expressions, the two-phase commit protocol guarantees consistency.

Time is understood as a one-dimensional physical quantity whose values are ordered so that any two values in the timeline can be compared using the order relations "less than" and "greater than." Not only date and time, such as "April 1, 2016, 2.00 pm," are relevant information but also durations in the form of time intervals. One example is the age of an employee, determined by a number of years. It is important to note that a given time can be interpreted as either an instant (a point in time) or a time period, depending on the view of the user.

Temporal databases are designed to relate data values, individual tuples, or whole tables to the time axis. The time specification itself has different meanings for an object in the database, because valid time can be understood either as an instant when a certain event takes place or as a period if the respective data values are valid throughout a period of time. For instance, the address of an employee is valid until it is next changed.

Another kind of time specification is the transaction time, recording the instant when a certain object is entered into, changed in, or deleted from the database. The database system usually manages the different transaction times itself with the help of a journal, which is why time will always be used in the sense of valid time in the following.

In order to record valid times as points in time, most relational database systems support several data types: DATE is used for dates in the form year, month, and day and TIME for the time of the day in hours, minutes, and seconds, and TIMESTAMP is a combination of date and time. To give a period of time, no special data type has to be chosen; integers and decimals are sufficient. This makes it possible to run calculations on dates and times. One example is the employees table shown in Fig. 6.3, in which Date of Birth and Start Date have been added to the attribute categories. These attributes are time-related, and the system can therefore be queried for a list of all employees who started working for the company before their 20th birthday.

The EMPLOYEE table still offers a snapshot of the current data. Therefore, it is not possible to query into the past nor the future, because there is no information regarding the valid time of the data values. If, for instance, the role of employee Howard is changed, the existing data value will be overwritten and the new role considered as current. However, there is no information from and until when employee Howard worked in a specific role.

Two attributes are commonly used to express the validity of an entity: The "Valid From" time indicates the point in time when a tuple or a data value became or becomes valid. The attribute "Valid To" indicates the end of a period of validity by giving the corresponding instant. Instead of both the VALID_FROM and VALID_TO times, on the timeline, the VALID_FROM instant may be sufficient. The VALID_TO instants are defined implicitly by the following VALID_FROM instants, as the validity intervals of any one entity cannot overlap.

The temporal table TEMP_EMPLOYEE shown in Fig. 6.4 lists all validity statements in the attribute VALID_FROM for the employee tuple M1 (Murphy). This attribute must be included in the key so that not only current but also past and future states can be identified uniquely.

EMPLOYEE

E#	Name	DateOfBirth	City	StartDate	Position
E19	Stewart	02/19/1978	Stow	10/01/2009	Clerk
E1	Murphy	07/09/1988	Kent	07/01/2014	Analyst
E7	Howard	03/28/1999	Cleveland	01/01/2018	Head of HR
E4	Bell	12/06/1982	Kent	04/15/2018	Internal auditor

Find all employees who started working for the company before age 20 :

```
SELECT  E#, Name
FROM    EMPLOYEE
WHERE   (StartDate - DateofBirth)/365.25 < 20
```

E#	Name
E7	Howard

Fig. 6.3 EMPLOYEE table with data type DATE

The four tuples can be interpreted as follows: Employee Murphy used to live in Cleveland from July 1, 2014, to September 12, 2016, and then in Kent until March 31, 2019, and has lived in Cleveland again since April 1, 2019. From the day they started working for the company until May 3, 2017, they worked as a programmer and between May 4, 2017, and March 31, 2019, as a programmer analyst, and since April 1, 2019, they have been working as an analyst. The table TEMP_EMPLOYEE is indeed temporal, as it shows not only current states but also information about data values related to the past. Specifically, it can answer queries that do not only concern current instants or periods.

For instance, it is possible in Fig. 6.4 to determine the role employee Murphy had on January 1, 2018. Instead of the original SQL expression of a nested query with the ALL function (see Sect. 3.3), a language directly supporting temporal queries is conceivable. The keyword VALID_AT determines the time for which all valid entries are to be queried.

Temporal Database System
A temporal database management system (TDBMS):

- Supports the time axis as valid time by ordering attribute values or tuples by time
- Contains temporal language elements for queries into future, present, and past

TEMP_EMPLOYEE (excerpt)

E#	VALID_FROM	Name	City	StartDate	Position
E1	07/01/2014	Murphy	Cleveland	07/01/2014	Programmer
E1	09/13/2016	Murphy	Kent	07/01/2014	Programmer
E1	05/04/2017	Murphy	Kent	07/01/2014	Programmer-analyst
E1	04/01/2019	Murphy	Cleveland	07/01/2014	Analyst

Find the position held by employee Murphy on 01/01/2018.

original SQL:

```
SELECT   Position
FROM     TEMP_EMPLOYEE A
WHERE    A.E# = 'E1'  AND
         A.VALID_FROM >= ALL (

    SELECT   VALID_FROM
    FROM     TEMP_EMPLOYEE B
    WHERE    B.E# = 'E1'  AND
             B.VALID_FROM<='01/01/2018' )
```

temporal SQL:

```
SELECT   Position
FROM     TEMP_EMPLOYEE
WHERE    E# = 'E1'  AND
         VALID_AT = '01/01/2018'
```

Position
Programmer-analyst

Fig. 6.4 Excerpt from a temporal table TEMP_EMPLOYEE

In the field of temporal databases, there are several language models facilitating work with time-related information. Especially the operators of relational algebra and relational calculus have to be expanded in order to enable a join of temporal tables. The rules of referential integrity also need to be adapted and interpreted as relating to time. Even though these kinds of methods and corresponding language extensions have already proven themselves in research and development, very few database systems today support temporal concepts. The SQL standard also supports temporal databases.

6.4   Multi-dimensional Databases

Operative databases and applications are focused on a clearly defined, function-oriented performance area. Transactions aim to provide data for business handling as quickly and precisely as possible. This kind of business activity is often called online transaction processing or OLTP. Since the operative data has to be overwritten daily, users lose important information for decision-making. Furthermore, these databases

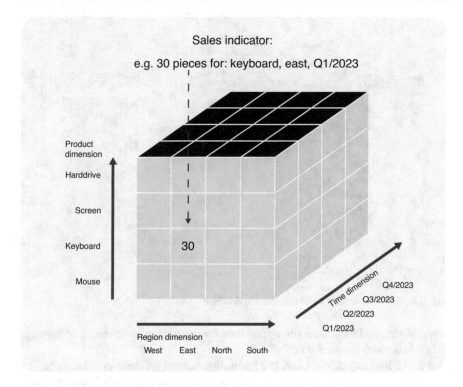

Fig. 6.5 Data cube with different analysis dimensions

were designed primarily for day-to-day business, not for analysis and evaluation. Recent years have therefore seen the development of specialized databases and applications for data analysis and decision support, in addition to transaction-oriented databases. This process is termed online analytical processing or OLAP.

At the core of OLAP is a multi-dimensional database, where all decision-relevant information can be stored according to various analysis dimensions (data cube). Such databases can become rather large, as they contain decision-making factors from multiple points in time. Sales figures, for instance, can be stored and analyzed in a multi-dimensional database by quarter, region, or product.

This is demonstrated in Fig. 6.5, which also illustrates the concept of a multi-dimensional database. It shows the three analysis dimensions product, region, and time. The term dimension describes the axes of the data cube. The design of the dimensions is important, since analyses are executed along these axes. The order of the dimensions does not matter; every user can and should analyze the data from their own perspective. Product managers, for instance, prioritize the product dimension; salespeople prefer sales figures to be sorted by region.

The dimensions themselves can be structured further: The product dimension can contain product groups; the time dimension could cover not only quarters but also

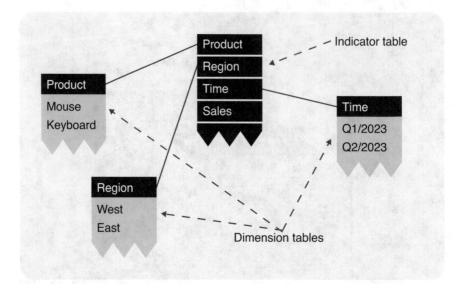

Fig. 6.6 Star schema for a multi-dimensional database

days, weeks, and months. A dimension therefore also describes the desired aggregation levels valid for the data cube.

From a logical point of view, in a multi-dimensional database or a data cube, it is
necessary to specify not only the dimensions but also the indicators.[3] An indicator is
a key figure or parameter needed for decision support. These key figures are
aggregated by analysis and grouped according to the dimension values. Indicators
can relate to quantitative as well as qualitative characteristics of the business. Apart
from financial key figures, meaningful indicators concern the market and sales,
customer base and customer fluctuation, business processes, innovation potential,
and know-how of the employees. Indicators, in addition to dimensions, are the basis
for the management's decision support, internal and external reporting, and a
computer-based performance measurement system.

The main characteristic of a star schema is the classification of data as either
indicator data or dimension data. Both groups are shown as tables in Fig. 6.6. The
indicator table is at the center, and the descriptive dimension tables are placed around
it, one table per dimension. The dimension tables are attached to the indicator table
forming a star-like structure.

Should one or more dimensions be structured, the respective dimension table
could have other dimension tables attached to it. The resulting structure is called a
snowflake schema showing aggregation levels of the individual dimensions. In
Fig. 6.6, for instance, the time dimension table for the first quarter of 2023 could

---

[3] Indicators are often also called facts, e.g., by Ralph Kimball. See also Sect. 6.7 on facts and rules of
knowledge databases.

Find the Apple sales for the 1. quarter of 2023 by sales lead Mahoney.

```
SELECT   SUM(Revenue)
FROM     D_PRODUCT D1, D_REGION D2, D_TIME D3, F_SALES F
WHERE    D1.P# = F.P# AND
         D2.R# = F.R# AND
         D3.T# = F.T# AND
         D1.Supplier = 'Apple' AND
         D2.SalesLead = 'Mahoney' AND
         D3.Year = 2023 AND
         D3.Quarter = 1
```

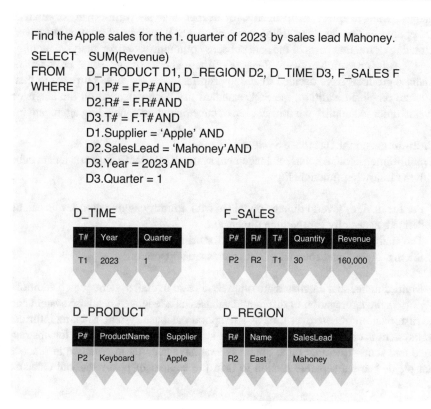

Fig. 6.7 Implementation of a star schema using the relational model

have another dimension table attached, listing the calendar days from January to March 2023. Should the dimension month be necessary for analysis, a month dimension table would be defined and connected to the day dimension table.

The classic relational model can be used for the implementation of a multi-dimensional database. Figure 6.6 shows how indicator and dimension tables of a star schema are implemented. The indicator table is represented by the relation F_SALES, which has a multi-dimensional key. This concatenated key needs to contain the keys for the dimension tables D_PRODUCT, D_REGION, and D_TIME. In order to determine sales lead Mahoney's revenue on Apple devices in the first quarter of 2023, it is necessary to formulate a complicated join of all involved indicator and dimension tables (see SQL statement in Fig. 6.7).

A relational database system reaches its limits when faced with extensive multi-dimensional databases. Formulating queries with a star schema is also complicated and prone to error. There are multiple other disadvantages when working with the classic relational model and conventional SQL: In order to aggregate several levels, a star schema has to be expanded into a snowflake schema, and the resulting physical tables further impair the response time behavior. If users of a multi-dimensional database want to query more details for deeper analysis (drill-down) or analyze further aggregation levels (roll-up), conventional SQL will be of no use. Moreover, extracting or rotating parts of the data cube, as commonly done for analysis, requires specific soft- or even hardware. Because of these shortcomings, some providers of database products have decided to add appropriate tools for these purposes to their software range. In addition, the SQL standard has been extended on the language level in order to simplify the formulation of cube operations, including aggregations.

Multi-dimensional Database System

A multi-dimensional database management system (MDBMS) supports a data cube with the following functionality:

- For the design, several dimension tables with arbitrary aggregation levels can be defined, especially for the time dimension.
- The analysis language offers functions for drill-down and roll-up.
- Slicing, dicing, and rotation of data cubes are supported.

Multi-dimensional databases are often used in an overall system, which additionally offers the aggregation of different databases as a federated database system and the historization of data over time as a temporal database system. Such an information system is called a data warehouse for structured data or data lake for unstructured and semi-structured data. Such systems have such an importance in practice that we dedicate a separate section to it in the context of post-relational database systems.

6.5   Data Warehouse and Data Lake Systems

Multi-dimensional databases are often the core of data warehouses. Unlike multidimensional databases alone, a data warehouse is a distributed database system that combines aspects of federated, temporal, and multi-dimensional databases. It provides mechanisms for integration, historization, and analysis of data across several applications of a company, along with processes for decision support and the management and development of data flows within the organization.

The more and easier digital data is available, the greater the need to analyze this data for decision support. The management of a company is supposed to base their decisions on facts that can be gathered from the analysis of the available data. The process of data preparation and analysis for decision support is called *business intelligence*. Due to heterogeneity, volatility, and fragmentation of the data, crossapplication data analysis is often complex: Data is stored heterogeneously in several databases in an organization. Additionally, often only the current version is available. In the source systems, data from one larger subject area, like customers or contracts, is rarely available in one place, but has to be gathered, or integrated, via various interfaces. Furthermore, this data distributed among many databases needs to be sorted into timelines for various subject areas, each spanning several years. Business intelligence therefore makes three demands on the data to be analyzed:

- Integration of heterogeneous data
- Historicization of current and volatile data
- Complete availability of data on certain subject areas

The three previously introduced post-relational database systems basically cover one of those demands each: The integration of data can be carried out with federated database systems with a central logical schema, historicization of data is possible with temporal databases, and multi-dimensional databases can provide data on various subject areas (dimensions) for analysis.

As relational database technology has become so widespread in practice, the properties of distributed, temporal, and multi-dimensional databases can be simulated quite well with regular multi-dimensional databases and some software enhancements. The concept of *data warehousing* implements these aspects of federated, temporal, and multi-dimensional database systems using conventional technologies.

In addition to those three aspects, however, there is the demand of *decision support*. Organizations need to analyze data as timelines, so that the complete data on any subject area is available in one place. But as data in larger organizations is spread among a number of databases, a concept[4] to prepare it for analysis and utilization is necessary.

Data Warehouse

A data warehouse or DWH is a distributed information system with the following properties:

- *Integrated:* Data from various sources and applications (source systems) is periodically integrated[5] and filed in a uniform schema.
- *Read only:* Data in the data warehouse is not changed once it is written.
- *Historized:* Thanks to a time axis, data can be evaluated for different points in time.
- *Analysis-oriented:* All data on different subject areas like customers, contracts, or products is fully available at one place.
- *Decision support:* The information in data cubes serves as a basis for management decisions.

A data warehouse offers parts of the functionalities of federated, temporal, and multi-dimensional databases. Additionally, there are programmable loading scripts as well as specific analysis and aggregation functions. Based on distributed and heterogeneous data sources, business-relevant facts need to be available in such a way that they can efficiently and effectively be used for decision support and management purposes.

---

[4] For more information, look up the KDD (knowledge discovery in databases) process.

[5] See the ETL (extract, transform, and load) process below.

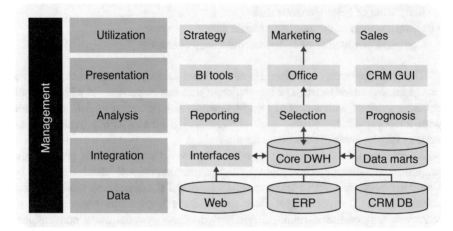

Fig. 6.8   Data warehouse in the context of business intelligence processes

Data warehouses can integrate various internal and external data sets (data sources). The aim is to be able to store and analyze, for various business purposes, a consistent and historicized set of data on the information scattered across the company. To this end, data from many sources is integrated into the data warehouse via interfaces and stored there, often for years. Building on this, data analyses can be carried out to be presented to decision-makers and used in business processes. Furthermore, business intelligence as a process has to be controlled by management.

The individual steps of data warehousing are summarized in the following paragraphs (see Fig. 6.8).

The *data* of an organization is distributed across several source systems, for instance, Web platforms, accounting (enterprise resource planning, ERP), and customer databases (customer relationship management, CRM). In order to analyze and relate this data, it needs to be integrated.

For this *integration* of the data, an ETL (extract, transform, load) process is necessary. The corresponding *interfaces* usually transfer data in the evening or on weekends, when the IT system is not needed by the users. High-performance systems today feature continuous loading processes, feeding data 24/7 (*trickle feed*). When updating a data warehouse, *periodicity* is taken into account, so users can see how *up to date* their evaluation data is. The more frequently the interfaces load data into the data warehouse, the more up to date is the evaluation data. The aim of this integration is *historization*, i.e., the creation of a timeline in one logically central storage location. The core of a data warehouse (Core DWH) is often modeled in second or third normal form. Historicization is achieved using validity statements (valid_from, valid_to) in additional columns of the tables, as described in Sect. 6.3 on temporal databases. In order to make the evaluation data sorted by subject available for OLAP analysis, individual subject areas are loaded into data marts, which are often realized multi-dimensionally with star schemas.

The data warehouse exclusively serves for the analysis of data. The dimension of time is an important part of such data collections, allowing for more meaningful statistical results. Periodic reporting produces lists of key performance indicators. Data mining tools like classification, selection, prognosis, and knowledge acquisition use data from the data warehouse in order to, for instance, analyze customer or purchasing behavior and utilize the results for optimization purposes. In order for the data to generate value, the insights including the results of the analysis need to be communicated to the decision-makers and stakeholders. The respective analyses or corresponding graphics are made available using a range of interfaces of business intelligence tools (BI tools) or graphical user interfaces (GUI) for office automation and customer relationship management. Decision-makers can utilize the analysis results from data warehousing in business processes as well as in strategy, marketing, and sales.

The data warehouse is designed to process and integrate structured data. Since unstructured and semi-structured data are analyzed more frequently today in the context of Big Data (see Sect. 5.1), a new concept of the data lake has become established for this purpose. This offers an alternative extract-load-transform (ELT) approach for the federation, historization, and analysis of large amounts of unstructured and semi-structured data. The data lake periodically extracts and loads data from different source systems as it is, thus eliminating the need for time-consuming integration. Only when the data is eventually used by data scientists is the data transformed for the desired analysis.

Data Lake

A data lake is a distributed information system with the following characteristics:

- Data fusion: Unstructured and semi-structured data from different data sources and applications (source systems) are extracted in the given structure and archived centrally.
- Schema-on-read: Federated data is integrated into a unified schema only when it is needed for an evaluation.
- Snapshots: Data can be evaluated according to different points in time, thanks to timestamps.
- Data-based value creation: The data in the data lake unfolds its value through data science analyses, which generate added value by optimizing decisions.

6.6   Object-Relational Databases

In order to store information on books in a relational database, several tables need to be defined, three of which are shown in Fig. 6.9. In the BOOK table, every book has the attributes Title and Publisher added.

Since a book can have more than one author and, reversely, an author can have published multiple books, every author involved is listed in an additional AUTHOR table.

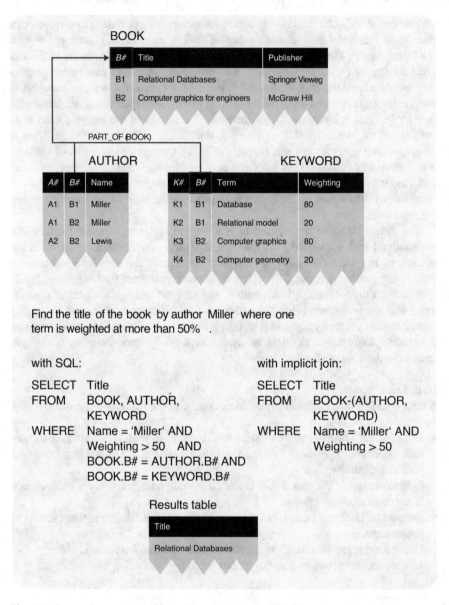

Fig. 6.9 Query of a structured object with and without implicit join operator

The attribute Name is not fully functionally dependent on the combined key of the Author and Book Number, which is why the table is neither in the second nor in any higher normal form. The same holds true for the KEYWORD table, because there is a complex-complex relationship between books and their keywords. Weighting is a typical relationship attribute; Label, however, is not fully functionally dependent on the Keyword Number and Book Number key. For proper normalization, the management of books would therefore require several tables, since in addition to the relationship tables AUTHOR and KEYWORD, separate tables for the attributes Author and Keyword would be necessary. A relational database would certainly also include information on the publisher in a separate PUBLISHER table, ideally complemented by a table for the relationship between BOOK and PUBLISHER.

Splitting the information about a book between different tables has its disadvantages and is hardly understandable from the point of view of the users, who want to find the attributes of a certain book well-structured in a single table. The relational query and data manipulation language should serve to manage the book information using simple operators. There are also performance disadvantages if the database system has to search various tables and calculate time-consuming join operators in order to find a certain book. To mitigate these problems, extensions to the relational model have been suggested.

A first extension of the relational database technology is to explicitly declare structural properties to the database system, for instance, by assigning surrogates. A surrogate is a permanent, invariant key value defined by the system, which uniquely identifies every tuple in the database. Surrogates, as invariant values, can be used to define system-controlled relationships even in different places within a relational database. They support referential integrity as well as generalization and aggregation structures.

In the BOOK table in Fig. 6.9, the book number $B\#$ is defined as a surrogate. This number is used again in the dependent tables AUTHOR and KEYWORD under the indication PART_OF(BOOK). Because of this reference, the database system explicitly recognizes the structural properties of the book, author, and keyword information and is able to use them in database queries, given that the query and manipulation language is extended accordingly. An example for this is the implicit hierarchical join operator in the FROM clause that connects the partial tables AUTHOR and KEYWORD belonging to the BOOK table. It is not necessary to state the join predicates in the WHERE clause, as those are already known to the database system through the explicit definition of the PART_OF structure.

Storage structures can be implemented more efficiently by introducing to the database system a PART_OF or analogously an IS_A structure. This means that the logical view of the three tables BOOK, AUTHOR, and KEYWORD is kept, while the book information is physically stored as structured objects[6] so that a single database access makes it possible to find a book. The regular view of the tables is kept, and the individual tables of the aggregation can be queried as before.

Another possibility for the management of structured information is giving up the first normal form[7] and allowing tables as attributes. Figure 6.10 illustrates this with an example presenting information on books, authors, and keywords in a table. This

---

[6]Research literature also calls them "complex objects."

[7]The NF2 model (NF2 = non-first normal form) supports nested tables.

BOOK_OBJECT

B#	Title	Publisher	Autor		Keyword		
			A#	Name	K#	Term	Wgt.
B1	Relational...	Springer Vieweg	A1	Miller	K1	Database	80
					K2	Relational model	20
B2	Computer...	McGraw Hill	A1	Miller	K3	Comp. graphics	50
			A2	Lewis	K4	Comp. geometry	50

Fig. 6.10 BOOK_OBJECT table with attributes of the relation type

also shows an object-relational approach, managing a book as one object in the single table BOOK_OBJECT. An object-relational database system can explicitly incorporate structural properties and offer operators for objects and parts of objects.

A database system is structurally object-relational if it supports structured object types as shown in Fig. 6.10. In addition to object identification, structure description, and the availability of generic operators (methods like implicit join, etc.), a fully object-relational database system should support the definition of new object types (classes) and methods. Users should be able to determine the methods necessary for an individual object type themselves. They should also be able to rely on the support of inherited properties so that they do not have to define all new object types and methods from scratch, but can draw on already existing concepts.

Object-relational database systems make it possible to treat structured objects as units and use fitting generic operators with them. The formation of classes using PART_OF and IS_A structures is allowed and supported by methods for saving, querying, and manipulating.

Object-Relational Database System

An object-relational database management system (ORDBMS) can be described as follows:

- It allows the *definition of object types* (often called classes in reference to object-oriented programming), which themselves can consist of other object types.
- Every database object can be structured and identified through surrogates.
- It supports *generic operators* (methods) affecting objects or parts of objects, while their internal representation remains invisible from the outside (data encapsulation).
- Properties of objects can be inherited. This *property inheritance* includes the structure and the related operators.

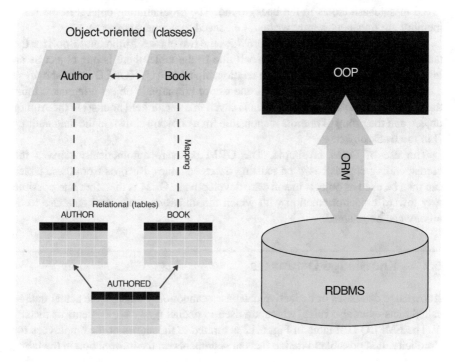

Fig. 6.11 Object-relational mapping

The SQL standard has for some years been supporting certain object-relational enhancements: object identifications (surrogates); predefined data types for set, list, and field; general abstract data types with the possibility of encapsulation; parametrizable types; type and table hierarchies with multiple inheritance; and user-defined functions (methods).

Object-Relational Mapping

Most modern programming languages are object-oriented; at the same time, the majority of the database systems used are relational. Instead of migrating to object-relational or even object-oriented databases, which would be rather costly, objects and relations can be mapped to each other during software development if relational data is accessed with object-oriented languages. This concept of *object-relational mapping (ORM)* is illustrated in Fig. 6.11. In this example, there is a relational database management system (RDBMS) with a table AUTHOR, a table BOOK, and a relationship table AUTHORED, since there is a complex-complex relationship (see Sect. 2.2.2) between books and authors. The data in those tables is to be used directly as classes in software development in a project with object-oriented programming (OOP).

An ORM software can automatically map classes to tables, so for the developers, it seems as if they were working with object-oriented classes even though the data is saved in database tables in the background. The programming objects in the main memory are thus persistently written, i.e., saved to permanent memory.

In Fig. 6.11, the ORM software provides the two classes Author and Book for the tables AUTHOR and BOOK. For each line in the table, there is one object as an instance of the respective class. The relationship table AUTHORED is not shown as a class: object orientation allows for the use of non-atomic object references; thus, the set of books the author has written is saved in a vector field books[] in the Author object, and the group of authors responsible for a book are shown in the field authors [] in the Book object.

The use of ORM is simple. The ORM software automatically derives the corresponding classes based on existing database tables. Records from these tables can then be used as objects in software development. ORM is therefore one possible way toward object orientation with which the underlying relational database technology can be retained.

6.7   Knowledge Databases

Knowledge databases or deductive databases cannot only manage the actual data—called facts—but also rules, which are used to deduct new table contents or facts.

The EMPLOYEE table in Fig. 6.12 is limited to the names of the employees for simplicity. It is possible to define facts or statements on the information in the table,

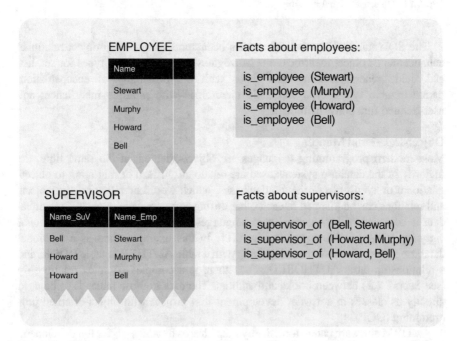

Fig. 6.12 Comparison of tables and facts

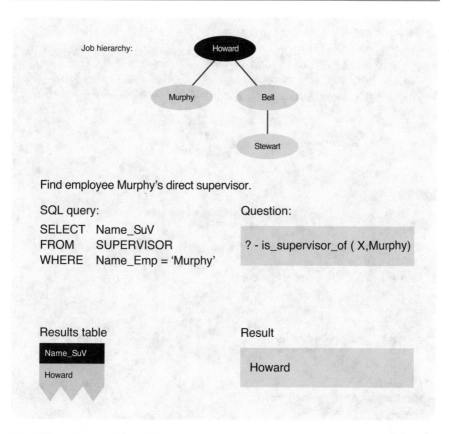

Fig. 6.13 Analyzing tables and facts

in this case on the employees. Generally, facts are statements that unconditionally take the truth value TRUE. For instance, it is true that Howard is an employee. This is expressed by the fact "is_employee (Howard)." For the employees' direct supervisors, a new SUPERVISOR table can be created, showing the names of the direct supervisors and the employees reporting to them as a pair per tuple. Accordingly, facts "is_supervisor_of (A,B)" are formulated to express that "A is a direct supervisor of B."

The job hierarchy is illustrated in a tree in Fig. 6.13. Looking for the direct supervisor of employee Murphy, the SQL query analyzes the SUPERVISOR table and finds supervisor Howard. Using a logic query language (inspired by Prolog) yields the same result.

Besides actual facts, it is possible to define rules for the deduction of unknown table contents. In the relational model, this is called a derived relation or deduced relation. Simple examples of a derived relation and the corresponding derivation rule are given in Fig. 6.14. It shows how the supervisor's supervisor for every employee can be found. This may, for instance, come in useful for large companies or

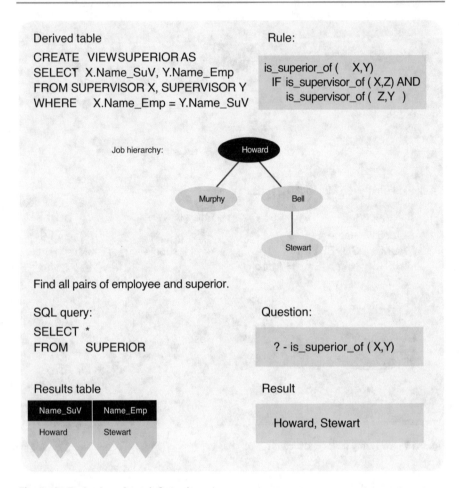

Fig. 6.14 Derivation of new information

businesses with remote branches in case the direct supervisor of an employee is absent and the next higher level needs to be contacted via e-mail.

The definition of a derived relation corresponds to the definition of a view. In the given example, such a view with the name SUPERIOR is used to determine the next-but-one supervisor of any employee, formed by a join of the SUPERVISOR table with itself. A derivation rule can be defined for this view. The rule "is_superior_of (X,Y)" results from there being a Z where X is the direct supervisor of Z and Z in turn is the direct supervisor of Y. This expresses that X is the next-but-one supervisor of Y, because Z is between them.

A database equipped with facts and rules automatically becomes a method or knowledge base, as it does contain not only obvious facts, like "Howard is an employee" or "Howard is the direct supervisor of Murphy and Bell," but also derived findings like "Howard is superior supervisor of Stewart." In order to find superior supervisors, the view SUPERIOR defined in Fig. 6.14 is used. The SQL query of this view results in a table with the information that there is only one relationship with a superior supervisor, specifically employee Stewart and their superior supervisor Howard. Applying the corresponding derivation rule "is_superior_of" yields the same result.

A deductive database as a vessel for facts and rules also supports the principle of recursion, making it possible to draw an unlimited amount of correct conclusions due to the rules included in the deductive database. Any true statement always leads to new statements.

The principle of recursion can refer to either the objects in the database or the derivation rules. Objects defined as recursive are structures that themselves consist of structures and, similar to the abstraction concepts of generalization and aggregation, can be understood as hierarchical or network-like object structures. Furthermore, statements can be determined recursively; in the company hierarchy example, all direct and indirect supervisor relationships can be derived from the facts "is_employee" and "is_supervisor_of."

The calculation process which derives all transitively dependent tuples from a table forms the transitive closure of the table. This operator does not belong to the original operators of relational algebra; rather, the transitive closure is a natural extension of the relational operators. It cannot be formed with a fixed number of calculation steps, but only by several relational join, projection, and union operators, whose number depends on the content of the table in question.

These explanations can be condensed into the following definition:

Knowledge Database Systems

A knowledge database management system (KDBMS) supports deductive databases or knowledge bases if:

- It contains not only data, i.e., facts, but also rules
- The derivation component allows for further facts to be derived from facts and rules
- It supports recursion, which, among other things, allows to calculate the transitive closure of a table

An expert system is an information system that provides specialist knowledge and conclusions for a certain limited field of application. Important components are a knowledge base with facts and rules and a derivation component for the derivation of new findings. The fields of databases, programming languages, and artificial intelligence will increasingly influence each other and in the future provide efficient problem-solving processes for practical application.

6.8   Fuzzy Databases

Conventional database systems assume attribute values to be precise, certain, and crisp, and queries deliver clear results:

- The attribute values in the databases are precise, i.e., they are unambiguous. The first normal form demands attribute values to be atomic and come from a well-defined domain. Vague attribute values, such as "2 or 3 or 4 days" or "roughly 3 days" for the delivery delay of supplier, are not permitted.
- The attribute values saved in a relational database are certain, i.e., the individual values are known and therefore true. An exception are NULL values, i.e., attribute values that are not known or not yet known. Apart from that, database systems do not offer modeling components for existing uncertainties. Probability distributions for attribute values are therefore impossible; expressing whether an attribute value correspondents to the true value or not remains difficult.
- Queries to the database are crisp. They always have a binary character, i.e., a query value specified in the query must either be identical or not identical with the attribute values. Querying a database with a query value "more or less" identical with the stored attribute values is not allowed.

In recent years, discoveries from the field of fuzzy logic have been applied to data modeling and databases. Permitting incomplete or vague information opens a wider field of application. Most of these works are theoretical; however, some research groups are trying to demonstrate the usefulness of fuzzy database models and database systems with implementations.

The approach shown here is based on the context model to define classes of data sets in the relational database schema. There are crisp and fuzzy classification methods. For a crisp classification, database objects are binarily assigned to a class, i.e., the membership function of an object to a class is 0 for "not included" or 1 for "included." A conventional process would therefore group a customer either into the class "Customers with revenue problems" or into the class "Customers to expand business with." A fuzzy process, however, allows for membership function values between 0 and 1. A customer can belong in the "Customers with revenue problems" class with a value of 0.3 and at the same time in the "Customers to expand business with" class with a value of 0.7. A fuzzy classification therefore allows for a more differentiated interpretation of class membership: Database objects can be distinguished between border and core objects; additionally, database objects can belong to two or more different classes at the same time.

In the fuzzy-relational database model with contexts, context model for short, every attribute A_j defined on a domain $D(A_j)$ has a context assigned. A context $K(A_j)$ is a partition of $D(A_j)$ into equivalence classes. A relational database schema with contexts therefore consists of a set of attributes $A=(A_1,\ldots,A_n)$ and another set of associated contexts $K=(K_1(A_1),\ldots,K_n(A_n))$.

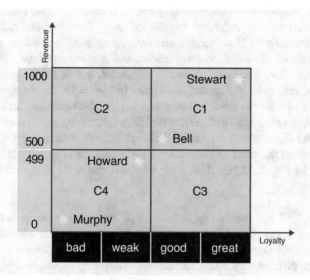

Fig. 6.15 Classification matrix with the attributes Revenue and Loyalty

For the assessment of customers, revenue and loyalty are used as an example. Additionally, those qualifying attributes are split into two equivalence classes each. The according attributes and contexts for the customer relationship management are:

- Revenue in dollars per month: The domain for revenue in dollars is defined as [0...1000]. Two equivalence classes [0...499] for small revenues and [500...1000] for large revenues are also created.
- Customer loyalty: The domain {bad, weak, good, great} supplies the values for the Customer loyalty attribute. It is split further into the equivalence classes {bad, weak} for negative loyalty and {good, great} for positive loyalty.

The suggested attributes with their equivalence classes show an example of a numeric and a qualitative attribute each. The respective contexts are:

- K(revenue) = { [0...499], [500...1000] }
- K(loyalty) = { {bad, weak}, {good, great} }

The partitioning of the revenue and loyalty domains results in the four equivalence classes C1, C2, C3, and C4 shown in Fig. 6.15. The meaning of the classes is expressed by semantic class names; for instance, customers with little revenue and weak loyalty are labeled "Don't invest" in C4; C1 could stand for "Retain customer," C2 for "Improve loyalty," and C3 for "Increase revenue." It is the database administrators' job, in cooperation with the marketing department, to define the attributes and equivalence classes and to specify them as an extension of the database schema.

Customer relationship management aims to take into account the customers' individual wishes and behavior instead of only focusing on product-related arguments and efforts. If customers are seen as an asset (customer value), they have to be treated according to their market and resource potential. With sharply divided classes, i.e., traditional customer segments, this is hardly possible, as all customers of one class are treated the same. In Fig. 6.15, for instance, Bell and Howard have almost the same revenue and loyalty. Nevertheless, in a sharp segmentation, they are classed differently: Bell falls into the premium class C1 (Retain customer) and Howard into the class C4 (Don't invest). Additionally, top customer Stewart is treated the same as Bell, since both belong into segment C1.

As seen in Fig. 6.15, the following conflicts can arise from sharp customer segmentation:

- Customer Bell has barely any incentives to increase revenue or loyalty. They belong to the premium class C1 and enjoy the corresponding advantages.
- Customer Bell could face an unpleasant surprise, should their revenue drop slightly or their loyalty rating be reduced. They may suddenly find themselves in a different customer segment; in an extreme case, they could drop from the premium class C1 into the low value class C4.
- Customer Howard has a robust revenue and medium customer loyalty, but is treated as a low value customer. It would hardly be surprising if Howard investigated their options on the market and moved on.
- A sharp customer segmentation also creates a critical situation for customer Stewart. They are, at the moment, the most profitable customer with an excellent reputation, yet the company does not recognize and treat them according to their customer value.

The conflict situations illustrated here can be mitigated or eliminated by creating fuzzy customer classes. The position of a customer in a two- or more-dimensional data matrix relates to the customer value now consisting of different class membership fractions.

According to Fig. 6.16, a certain customer's loyalty as a linguistic variable can simultaneously be "positive" and "negative." For example, Bell belongs to the fuzzy set $\mu_{positive}$ with a rate of 0.66 and to the set $\mu_{negative}$ with 0.33, i.e., Bell's loyalty is not exclusively strong or weak, as it would be with sharp classes.

The linguistic variable μ with the vague terms "positive" and "negative" and the membership functions $\mu_{positive}$ and $\mu_{negative}$ results in the domain D(loyalty) being partitioned fuzzily. Analogously, the domain D(revenue) is partitioned by the terms "high" and "low." This allows for classes with gradual transitions (fuzzy classes) in the context model.

An object's membership in a class is the result of the aggregation across all terms defining that class. Class C1 is described by the terms "high" (for the linguistic variable revenue) and "positive" (for the linguistic variable loyalty). The aggregation therefore has to correspond to the conjunction of the individual membership values. For this, various operators have been developed in fuzzy set theory.

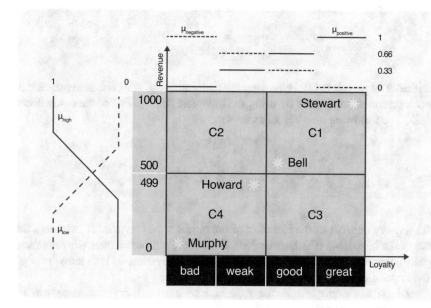

Fig. 6.16 Fuzzy partitioning of domains with membership functions

Classification queries in the language fCQL (fuzzy Classification Query Language) operate on the linguistic level with vague contexts. This has the advantage that users do not need to know sharp goal values or contexts, but only the column name of the value identifying the object and the table or view containing the attribute values. In order to take a more detailed look at single classes, users can specify a class or state attributes with a verbal description of their intensity. Classification queries therefore work with verbal descriptions on attribute or class level:

```
CLASSIFY    Object
FROM        Table
WITH        Classification condition
```

The language fCQL is based on SQL, with a CLASSIFY clause instead of SELECT defining the projection list by the column name of the object to be classified. While the WHERE clause in SQL contains a selection condition, the WITH clause determines a classification condition. As an example of an fCQL query,

```
CLASSIFY    Customer
FROM        Customer table
```

provides a classification of all customers in the table. The query

```
CLASSIFY    Customer
FROM        Customer table
WITH        CLASS IS Increase revenue
```

specifically targets class C3. Bypassing the definition of a class, it is also possible to select a certain set of objects by using the linguistic descriptions of the equivalence classes. The following query is an example:

```
CLASSIFY    Customer
FROM        Customer table
WITH        Revenue IS small AND Loyalty IS strong
```

This query consists of the identifier of the object to be classified (Customer), the name of the base table (Customer table), the critical attribute names (Revenue and Loyalty), the term "small" of the linguistic variable Revenue, and the term "strong" of the linguistic variable Loyalty.

Based on the example and the explanations above, fuzzy databases can be characterized as follows:

Fuzzy Database System

A fuzzy database management system (FDBMS) is a database system with the following properties:

- The data model is fuzzily rational, i.e., it accepts imprecise, vague, and uncertain attribute values.
- Dependencies between attributes are expressed with fuzzy normal forms.
- Relational calculus as well as relational algebra can be extended to fuzzy relational calculus and fuzzy relational algebra using fuzzy logic.
- Using a classification language enhanced with linguistic variables, fuzzy queries can be formulated.

Only a few computer scientists have been researching the field of fuzzy logic and relational database systems over the years (see Bibliography). Their works are mainly published and acknowledged in the field of fuzzy logic, not in the database field. It is to be hoped that both fields will grow closer and the leading experts on database technology will recognize the potential that lies in fuzzy databases and fuzzy query languages.

Bibliography

Bordogna, G., Pasi, G. (eds.): Recent Issues on Fuzzy Databases. Physica-Verlag (2000)
Bosc, P., Kacprzyk, J. (eds.): Fuzziness in Database Management Systems. Physica-Verlag (1995)

Ceri, S., Pelagatti, G.: Distributed Databases – Principles and Systems. McGraw-Hill (1985)

Chen, G.: Design of fuzzy relational databases based on fuzzy functional dependencies. PhD Thesis Nr. 84, Leuven, Belgium (1992)

Chen, G.: Fuzzy Logic in Data Modeling – Semantics, Constraints, and Database Design. Kluwer Academic (1998)

Clocksin, W.F., Mellish, C.S.: Programming in Prolog. Springer (1994)

Dittrich, K.R. (ed.): Advances in Object-Oriented Database Systems. Lecture Notes in Computer Science, vol. 334. Springer (1988)

Etzion, O., Jajodia, S., Sripada, S. (eds.): Temporal Databases – Research and Practice. Lecture Notes in Computer Science. Springer (1998)

Inmon, W.H.: Building the Data Warehouse. Wiley (2005)

Kimball, R., Ross, M., Thorntwaite, W., Mundy, J., Becker, B.: The Data warehouse Lifecycle Toolkit. Wiley (2008)

Lorie, R.A., Kim, W., McNabb, D., Plouffe, W., Meier, A.: Supporting complex objects in a relational system for engineering databases. In: Kim, W., et al. (eds.) Query Processing in Database Systems, pp. 145–155. Springer (1985)

Meier, A., Werro, N., Albrecht, M., Sarakinos, M.: Using a fuzzy classification query language for customer relationship management. Proceedings of the 31st International Conference on Very Large Databases (VLDB), Trondheim, Norway, 2005, pp. 1089–1096

Meier, A., Schindler, G., Werro, N.: Fuzzy classification on relational databases (Chapter XXIII). In: Galindo, J. (ed.) Handbook of Research on Fuzzy Information Processing in Databases, vol. II, pp. 586–614. IGI Global (2008)

Özsu, M.T., Valduriez, P.: Principles of Distributed Database Systems. Prentice Hall (1991)

Petra, F.E.: Fuzzy Databases – Principles and Applications. Kluwer Academic (1996)

Pons, O., Vila, M.A., Kacprzyk, J. (eds.): Knowledge Management in Fuzzy Databases. Physica-Verlag (2000)

Snodgrass, R.T.: The Temporal Query Language TQuel. ACM Trans. Database Syst. **12**(2), 247–298 (1987)

Snodgrass, R.T., et al.: A TSQL2 tutorial. SIGMOD-Rec. **23**(3), 27–33 (1994)

Stonebraker, M.: The Ingres Papers. Addison-Wesley (1986)

Stonebraker, M.: Object-Relational DBMS's – The Next Great Wave. Morgan Kaufmann (1996)

Werro, N.: Fuzzy Classification of Online Customers. Springer (2015)

Williams, R., et al.: R*: an overview of the architecture. In: Scheuermann, P. (ed.) Improving Database Usability and Responsiveness, pp. 1–27. Academic Press (1982)

Zadeh, L.A.: Fuzzy sets. Inf. Control. **8**, 338–353 (1965)

NoSQL Databases 7

7.1 Development of Non-relational Technologies

In Chaps. 1–5, all aspects were described in detail for relational, graph, and document databases. In Chap. 6, we covered post-relational extensions of SQL databases. Chapter 7 now concludes with a rounding overview of important NoSQL database systems.

The term NoSQL was first used in 1998 for a database that (although relational) did not have an SQL interface. NoSQL became of growing importance during the 2000s, especially with the rapid expansion of the Internet. The growing popularity of global Web services saw an increase in the use of Web-scale databases, since there was a need for data management systems that could handle the enormous amounts of data (sometimes in the petabyte range and up) generated by Web services.

SQL database systems are much more than mere data storage systems. They provide a large degree of processing logic:

- Powerful declarative language constructs
- Schemas and metadata
- Consistency assurance
- Referential integrity and triggers
- Recovery and logging
- Multi-user operation and synchronization
- Users, roles, and security
- Indexing

These SQL functionalities offer numerous benefits regarding data consistency and security. This goes to show that SQL databases are mainly designed for integrity and transaction protection, as required in banking applications or insurance software, among others. However, since data integrity control requires much work and processing power, relational databases quickly reach their limits with large amounts of data. The powerfulness of the database management system is disadvantageous for efficiency and performance, as well as for flexibility in data processing.

In practical use, consistency-oriented processing components often impede the efficient processing of huge amounts of data, especially in use cases where the focus is on performance rather than consistency, such as social media. That is why the open-source and Web development communities soon began to push the development of massive distributed database systems which can fulfill these new demands.

NoSQL Database
NoSQL databases usually have the following properties (see also Sect. 1.3.2):

- The database model is not relational.
- The focus is on distributed and horizontal scalability.
- There are weak or no schema restrictions.
- Data replication is easy.
- Easy access is provided via an API.
- The consistency model is not ACID (instead, e.g., BASE; see Sect. 4.2.1).

Although the term NoSQL originally referred to database functions that are not covered by the SQL standard or the SQL language, the phrase "not only SQL" has become widespread as an explanation of the term. More and more typical NoSQL systems offer an SQL language interface, and classic relational databases offer additional functions outside of SQL that can be described as NoSQL functionalities. The term NoSQL is therefore a class of database functionalities that extend and supplement the functionalities of the SQL language. Core NoSQL technologies are:

- Key-value stores (Sect. 7.2)
- Column family databases (Sect. 7.3)
- Document databases (Sect. 7.4)
- Graph databases (Sect. 7.6)

These four database models, also called core NoSQL models, are discussed in this chapter. Other types of NoSQL described in this chapter are the family of XML databases (Sect. 7.5), search engine databases (Sect. 7.7), and time series databases (Sect. 7.8).

7.2   Key-Value Stores

The simplest way of storing data is assigning a value to a variable or a key. At the hardware level, CPUs work with registers based on this model; programming languages use the concept in associative arrays. Accordingly, the simplest database model possible is data storage that stores *a data object as a value for another data object as key.*

In *key-value stores*, a specific value can be stored for any key with a simple command, e.g., SET. Below is an example in which data for users of a website is stored: first name, last name, e-mail, and encrypted password. For instance, the value John is stored for the key User:U17547:firstname.

```
SET User:U17547:firstname John
SET User:U17547:lastname Doe
SET User:U17547:email john.doe@blue_planet.net
SET User:U17547:pwhash D75872C818DC63BC1D87EA12
SET User:U17548:firstname Jane
SET User:U17548:lastname Doherty
...
```

Data objects can be retrieved with a simple query using the key:

```
GET User:U17547:email
> john.doe@blue_planet.net
```

The key space can only be structured with special characters such as colons or slashes. This allows for the definition of a namespace that can represent a rudimentary data structure. Apart from that, key-value stores do not support any kind of structure, neither nesting nor references. Key-value stores are schema-less, i.e., data objects can be stored at any time and in arbitrary formats, without a need for any metadata objects such as tables or columns to be defined beforehand. Going without a schema or referential integrity makes key-value stores performant for queries, easy to partition, and flexible regarding the types of data to be stored.

Key-Value Store
A database is a key-value store if it has the following properties:

- There is a set of identifying data objects, the keys.
- For each key, there is exactly one associated descriptive data object, the value for that key.
- Specifying a key allows to query the associated value in the database.
- The key is the only access path to query the database. You cannot randomly access a data object using any other attribute.

Key-value stores have seen a large increase in popularity as part of the NoSQL trend, since they are scalable for huge amounts of data. As referential integrity is not checked in key-value stores, it is possible to write and read extensive amounts of data efficiently. Processing speed can be enhanced even further if the key-value pairs are buffered in the main memory of the database. Such setups are called *in-memory*

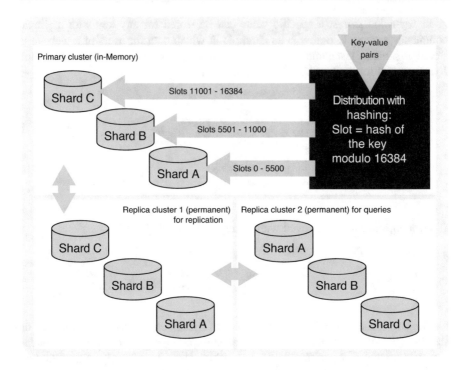

Fig. 7.1 Key-value store with sharding and hash-based key distribution

databases. They employ technologies that allow to cache values in the main memory while constantly validating them against the long-term persistent data in the background memory.

There is almost no limit to increasing a key-value store's scalability with fragmentation or *sharding* of the data content. Partitioning is rather easy in key-value stores, due to the simple model. Individual computers within the cluster, called *shards*, take on only a part of the key space. This allows for the distribution of the database onto a large number of individual machines. The keys are usually distributed according to the principles of consistent hashing (see Sect. 5.2.4).

Figure 7.1 shows a distributed architecture for a key-value store: A numerical value (hash) is generated from a key; using the modules operator, this value can now be positioned on a defined number of address spaces (hash slots) in order to determine on which shard within the distributed architecture the value for the key will be stored. The distributed database can also be copied to additional computers and updated there to improve partition tolerance, a process called replication. The original data content in the primary cluster is synchronized with multiple replicated data sets, the replica clusters.

Figure 7.1 shows an example of a possible massively distributed high-performance architecture for a key-value store. The primary cluster contains three computers (shards A, B, and C). The data is kept directly in the main memory (RAM) to reduce response times. The data content is replicated to a replica cluster for permanent storage on a hard drive. Another replica cluster further increases performance by providing another replicated computer cluster for complex queries and analyses.

Apart from the efficient sharding of large amounts of data, another advantage of key-value stores is the flexibility of the data schema. In a relational database, a pre-existing schema in the shape of a relation with attributes is necessary for any record to be stored. If there is none, a schema definition must be executed before saving the data. For database tables with large numbers of records or for the insertion of heterogeneous data, this is often a lot of work. Key-value stores are schema-free and therefore highly flexible regarding the type of data to be stored. It is not necessary to specify a table with columns and data types; rather, the data can simply be stored under an arbitrary key. On the other hand, the lack of a database schema often causes a clutter in data management.

7.3   Column-Family Stores

Even though key-value stores are able to process large amounts of data performantly, their structure is still quite rudimentary. Often, the data matrix needs to be structured with a schema. Most *Column-family stores* enhance the key-value concept accordingly by providing additional structure.

In practical use, it has shown to be more efficient for optimizing read operations to store the data in relational tables not per row, but per column. This is because rarely all columns in one row are needed at once, but there are *groups of columns that are often read together*. Therefore, in order to optimize access, it is useful to structure the data in such groups of columns—column families—as storage units. Column-family stores, which are named after this method, follow this model; they store data not in relational tables, but in enhanced and structured multi-dimensional key spaces.

Google presented its Bigtable database model for the distributed storage of structured data in 2008, significantly influencing the development of column-family stores.

Bigtable
In the Bigtable model, a *table* is a sparse, distributed, multi-dimensional, sorted map. It has the following properties:

- The data structure is a map which assigns elements from a domain to elements in a co-domain.
- The mapping function is sorted, i.e., there is an order relation for the keys addressing the target elements.
- The addressing is multi-dimensional, i.e., the function has more than one parameter.

- The data is distributed by the map, i.e., it can be stored on different computers in different places.
- The map is sparse, so not for every possible key an entry is required.

In Bigtable, a table has three dimensions: It maps an entry of the database for one *row* and one *column* at a certain *time* as a string:

```
(row:string, column:string, time:int64)  → string
```

Tables in column-family stores are multi-stage aggregated structures. The first key, the row key, is an addressing of a database object, as in a key-value store. Within this key, however, there is another structure, dividing of the row into several columns which are also addressed with keys. Entries in the table are additionally versioned with a timestamp. The storage unit addressed with a certain combination of row key, column key, and timestamp is called a *cell*.

Columns in a table are grouped into column families. These are the unit for access control, i.e., for granting reading and writing permissions to users and applications. Additionally, the unit of the column family is used in assigning main memory and hard drive space. Column families are *the only fixed schema rules* of the table, which is why they need to be created explicitly by changing the schema of the table. Unlike in relational databases, various row keys can be used within one column family to store data. The column family therefore serves as a *rudimentary schema* with a reduced amount of metadata.

Data within a column family is of the same type, since it is assumed it will be read together. This is also why the database always stores the data of one column family in one row of the table on the same computer. This mechanism reduces the time needed for combined reading access within the column family. Therefore, the database management system sorts column families into *locality groups*, which define on which computer and in which format the data is stored. The data of one locality group is physically stored on the same computer. Additionally, it is possible to set certain parameters for locality groups, for instance, to keep a specific locality group in the main memory, making it possible to read the data quickly without the need to access the hard drive.

Figure 7.2 summarizes how data is stored in the Bigtable model described above: A data cell is addressed with row key and column key. In the given example, there is one row key per user. The content is additionally historicized with a timestamp. Several columns are grouped into column families: The columns Mail, Name, and Phone form the column family Contact. Access data, such as user names and passwords, could be stored in the column family Access. The columns in a column family are *sparse*. In the example in Fig. 7.2, the row U17547 contains a value for the column Contact:Mail, but not for the column Contact:Phone. If there is no entry, this information will not be stored in the row.

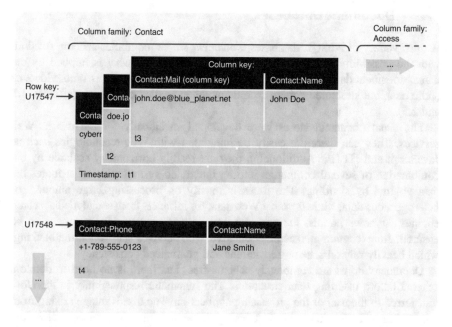

Fig. 7.2 Storing data in the Bigtable model

Column-Family Store

Databases using a data model similar to the Bigtable model are called column-family stores. They can be defined as NoSQL databases with the following properties:

- The data is stored in multi-dimensional tables.
- Data objects are addressed with row keys.
- Object properties are addressed with column keys.
- Columns of the tables are grouped into column families.
- A table's schema only refers to the column families; within one column family, arbitrary column keys can be used.
- In distributed, fragmented architectures, the data of a column family is preferably physically stored at one place (co-location) in order to optimize response times.

The advantages of column-family stores are their high scalability and availability due to their massive distribution, just as with key-value stores. Additionally, they provide a useful structure with a schema offering access control and localization of distributed data on the column family level; at the same time, they provide enough flexibility within the column family by making it possible to use arbitrary column keys.

7.4   Document Databases

A third variety of NoSQL databases, *document stores*, combines schema freedom with the possibility of structuring the stored data. Unlike what is implied by the name, document databases do not store arbitrary documents such as Web, video, or audio data, but structured data in records which are called *documents* (cf. Sect. 1.5 and 2.5).

The usual document stores were developed specifically for the use in Web services. They can therefore easily be integrated with Web technologies such as JavaScript and HTTP.[1] Additionally, they are readily horizontally scalable by the combination of several computers into an integrated system which distributes the data volume by sharding. The focus is mostly on processing large amounts of heterogeneous data, while for most Web data, for instance, from social media, search engines, or news portals, the constant consistency of data does not need to be ensured. An exception are security-sensitive Web services such as online banking, which heavily rely on schema restrictions and guaranteed consistency.

Document stores are completely schema-free, i.e., there is no need to define a schema before inserting data structures. The schematic responsibility is therefore transferred to the user or the processing application. The disadvantage arising from not having a fixed schema is the missing referential integrity and normalization. However, the absence of schema restrictions allows for flexibility in storing a wide range of data, which is what variety in the Vs of Big Data (see Sect. 1.3) refers to. This also facilitates fragmentation and distribution of the data.

On the first level, document stores are a kind of key-value store. For every key (document ID), a record can be stored as value. These records are called *documents*. On the second level, these documents have their *own internal structure*. The term document is not entirely appropriate, since they are explicitly no multimedia or other unstructured data. A document in the context of a document store is a file with structured data, for instance, in JSON[2] format. The structure is a list of attribute-value pairs. All attribute values in this data structure can recursively contain lists of attribute-value pairs themselves. The documents are not connected to each other, but contain a closed collection of data.

Figure 7.3 shows a sample document store D_USERS that stores data on the users of a website. For every user key with the attribute _id, an object containing all user information, such as user name, first name, last name, and gender, is stored. The visitHistory attribute holds a nested attribute value as an associative array, which again contains key-value pairs. This nested structure lists the date of the last visit to the website as the associated value.

Apart from the standard attribute _id, the document contains a field _rev (revision), which indexes the version of the document. One possibility to resolving concurring queries is *multi-version concurrency control*: The database makes sure that every query receives the revision of a document with the largest number of

---

[1] HyperText Transfer Protocol.

[2] JavaScript Object Notation.

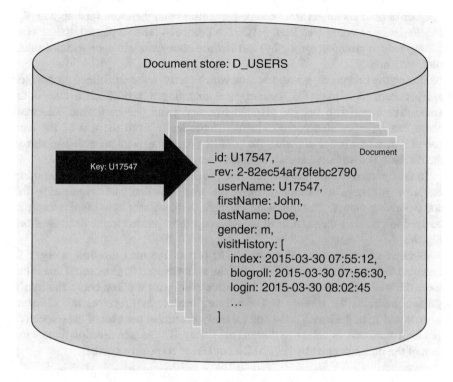

Fig. 7.3 Example of a document database

changes. As this cannot ensure full transactional security, it is called *eventual consistency*. The consistency of the data is only reached after some time. This significantly speeds up data processing at the expense of transactional security.

Document Database

To summarize, a document store is a database management system with the following properties:

- It is a key-value store.
- The data objects stored as values for keys are called documents; the keys are used for identification.
- The documents contain data structures in the form of recursively nested attribute-value pairs without referential integrity.
- These data structures are schema-free, i.e., arbitrary attributes can be used in every document without defining a schema first.
- In contrast with key-value databases, document databases support ad hoc queries not only using the document key but using any document attribute.

Queries on a document store can be parallelized and therefore sped up with the *MapReduce procedure* (see Sect. 5.4). Such processes are two-phased, where Map corresponds to grouping (group by) and Reduce corresponds to aggregation (count, sum, etc.) in SQL.

During the first phase, a map function which carries out a predefined process for every document is executed, building and returning a *map*. Such a map is an associative array with one or several key-value pairs per document. The map phase can be calculated per document independently from the rest of the data content, thereby always allowing for parallel processing without dependencies if the database is distributed among different computers.

In the optional reduce phase, a function is executed to *reduce* the data, returning one row per key in the index from the map function and aggregating the corresponding values. The following example demonstrates how MapReduce can be used to calculate the number of users, grouped by gender, in the database from Fig. 7.3.

Because of the absence of a schema, as part of the map function, a check is executed for every document to find out if the attribute userName exists. If that is the case, the `emit` function returns a key-value pair, with the key being the user's gender, the value the number 1. The reduce function then receives two different keys, m and f, in the `keys` array and for every document per user of the respective gender a number 1 as values in the `values` array. The reduce function returns the sum of the ones, grouped by key, which equals the respective number.

```
// map
function(doc){
 if(doc.userName) {
 emit(doc.gender, 1)
 }
}

// reduce
function(keys, values) {
return sum(values)
}

// >   key  value
// >   "f"  456
// >   "m" 567
// >   "d" 123
```

The results of MapReduce processes, called views, should be pre-calculated and indexed as permanent views using design documents for an optimal performance. Key-value pairs in document stores are stored in B-trees (see Sect. 5.2.1). This allows for quick access to individual key values. The reduce function uses a B-tree structure by storing aggregates in balanced trees, with only few detail values stored in the leaves. Updating aggregates therefore only requires changes to the respective leaf and the (few) nodes with subtotals down to the root.

7.5   XML Databases

XML (eXtensible Markup Language) was developed by the World Wide Web Consortium (W3C). The content of hypertext documents is marked by tags, just as in HTML. An XML document is self-describing, since it contains not only the actual data but also information on the data structure.

```
<address>
<street> W Broad Street </street>
<number> 333 </number>
<ZIP code> 43215 </ZIP code>
<city> Columbus </city>
</address>
```

The basic building blocks of XML documents are called elements. They consist of a start tag (in angle brackets <name>) and an end tag (in angle brackets with slash </name>) with the content of the element in-between. The identifiers of the start and the end tag have to match.

The tags provide information on the meaning of the specific values and therefore make statements about the data semantics. Elements in XML documents can be nested arbitrarily. It is best to use a graph to visualize such hierarchically structured documents, as shown in the example in Fig. 7.4.

As mentioned above, XML documents also implicitly include information about the structure of the document. Since it is important for many applications to know the structure of the XML documents, explicit representations (DTD = document type definition or XML schema) have been proposed by W3C. An explicit schema shows which tags occur in the XML document and how they are arranged. This allows for, e.g., localizing and repairing errors in XML documents. The XML schema is illustrated here as it has undeniable advantages for use in database systems.

An XML schema and a relational database schema are related as follows: Usually, relational database schemas can be characterized by three degrees of element nesting, i.e., the name of the database, the relation names, and the attribute names. This makes it possible to match a relational database schema to a section of an XML schema and vice versa.

Figure 7.4 shows the association between an XML document and a relational database schema. The section of the XML document gives the relation names DEPARTMENT and ADDRESS, each with their respective attribute names and the actual data values. The use of keys and foreign keys is also possible in an XML schema, as explained below.

The basic concept of XML schemas is to define data types and match names and data types using declarations. This allows for the creation of completely arbitrary XML documents. Additionally, it is possible to describe integrity rules for the correctness of XML documents.

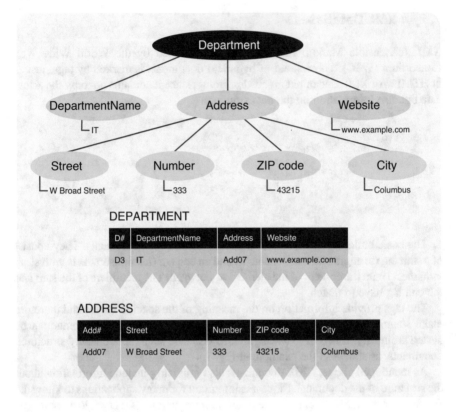

Fig. 7.4 Illustration of an XML document represented by tables

There are a large number of standard data types, such as string, Boolean, integer, date, time, etc., but apart from that, user-defined data types can also be introduced. Specific properties of data types can be declared with facets. This allows for the properties of a data type to be specified, for instance, the restriction of values by an upper or lower limit, length restrictions, or lists of permitted values:

```
<xs:simpleType name=«city»>
<xs:restriction base=«xs:string»>
<xs:length value=«20»/>
</xs:restriction>
</xs:simpleType>
```

For cities, a simple data type based on the predefined data type string is proposed. Additionally, the city names cannot consist of more than 20 characters.

Several XML editors have been developed that allow for the graphical representation of an XML document or schema. These editors can be used for both the declaration of structural properties and the input of data content. By showing or hiding individual sub-structures, XML documents and schemas can be arranged neatly.

It is desirable to be able to analyze XML documents or XML databases. Unlike relational query languages, selection conditions are linked not only to values (value selection) but also to element structures (structure selection). Other basic operations of an XML query include the extraction of subelements of an XML document and the modification of selected subelements. Furthermore, individual elements from different source structures can be combined to form new element structures. Last but not least, a suitable query language needs to be able to work with hyperlinks; path expressions are vital for that.

XQuery, influenced by SQL, various XML languages (e.g., XPath as navigation language for XML documents), and object-oriented query languages, was proposed by the W3C. XQuery is an enhancement of XPath, offering the option not only to query data in XML documents but also to form new XML structures. The basic elements of XQuery are *FOR-LET-WHERE-RETURN expressions*: FOR and LET bind one or more variables to the results of a query of expressions. WHERE clauses can be used to further restrict the result set, just as in SQL. The result of a query is shown with RETURN.

There is a simple example to give an outline of the principles of XQuery: The XML document "Department" (see Figs. 7.4 and 7.5) is queried for the street names of the individual departments:

```
<streetNames>
{FOR $Department IN //department RETURN
$Department/address/street }
</streetNames>
```

The query above binds the variable $Department to the <Department> nodes during processing. For each of these bindings, the RETURN expression evaluates the address and returns the street. The query in XQuery produced the following result:

```
<streetNames>
<street> W Broad Street </street>
<street>.......... </street>
<street>.......... </street>
</streetNames>
```

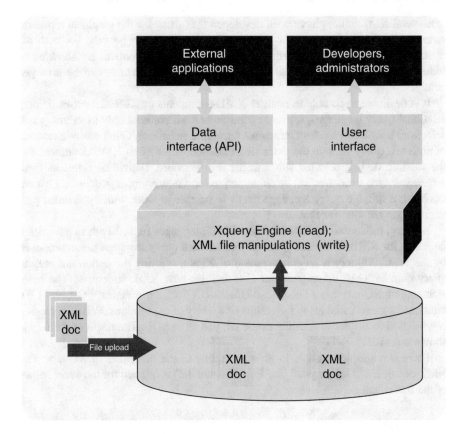

Fig. 7.5 Schema of a native XML database

In XQuery, variables are marked with the $ sign added to their names, in order to distinguish them from the names of elements. Unlike in some other programming languages, variables cannot have values assigned to them in XQuery; rather, it is necessary to analyze expressions and bind the result to the variables. This variable binding is done in XQuery with the FOR and LET expressions.

In the query example above, no LET expression is specified. Using the WHERE clause, the result set could be reduced further. The RETURN clause is executed for every FOR loop, but does not necessarily yield a result. The individual results, however, are listed and form the result of the FOR-LET-WHERE-RETURN expression.

XQuery is a *powerful query language for hyper documents* and is offered for XML databases as well as some post-relational database systems. In order for relational database systems to store XML documents, some enhancements in the storage component have to be applied.

Many relational database systems are nowadays equipped with XML column data types and therefore the possibility to directly handle XML. This allows for data to be stored in structured XML columns and for elements of the XML tree to be queried and modified directly with XQuery or XPath. Around the turn of the millennium, XML documents for data storage and data communication experienced a boom and were used for countless purposes, especially Web services. As part of this trend, several database systems that can directly process data in the form of XML documents were developed. Particularly in the field of open source, support for XQuery in native XML databases is far stronger than in relational databases.

Native XML Database
A native XML database is a database that has the following properties:

- The data is stored in documents; the database is therefore a document store (see Sect. 7.4).
- The structured data in the documents is compatible with the XML standard.
- XML technologies such as XPath, XQuery, and XSL/T can be used for querying and manipulating data.

Native XML databases store data strictly hierarchically in a tree structure. They are especially suitable if hierarchical data needs to be stored in a standardized format, for instance, for Web services in service-oriented architectures (SOA). A significant advantage is the simplified data import into the database; some database systems even support drag and drop of XML files. Figure 7.5 shows a schematic illustration of a native XML database. It facilitates reading and writing access to data in a collection of XML documents for users and applications.

An XML database cannot cross-reference like nodes. This can be problematic especially with multi-dimensionally linked data. An XML database therefore is best suited for data that can be represented in a tree structure as a series of nested generalizations or aggregations.

7.6   Graph Databases

The fourth and final type of core NoSQL databases differs significantly from the data models presented up to this point, i.e., the key-value stores, column-family stores, and document stores. Those three data models forgo database schemas and referential integrity for the sake of easier fragmentation (sharding). Graph databases, however, have a structuring schema: that of the property graph presented in Sect. 1.4.1. In a graph database, data is stored as nodes and edges, which belong to a node type or edge type, respectively, and contain data in the form of attribute-value pairs. Unlike in relational databases, their schema is implicit, i.e., data objects belonging to a not-yet existing node or edge type can be inserted directly into the database without defining the type first. The DBMS implicitly follows the changes in the schema based on the available information and thereby creates the respective type.

As an example, Fig. 7.6 illustrates the graph database G_USERS, which represents information on a Web portal with users, Web pages, and the relationships

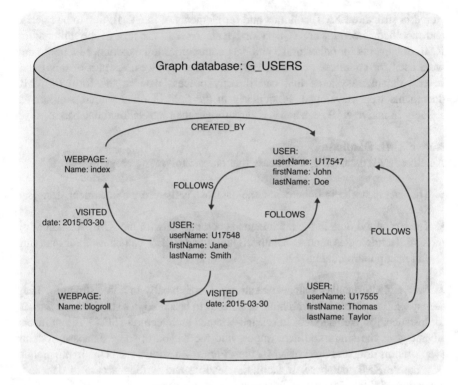

Fig. 7.6 Example of a graph database with user data of a website

between them. As explained in Sect. 1.4.1, the database has a schema with node and edge types. There are two node types, USER and WEBPAGE, and three edge types, FOLLOWS, VISITED, and CREATED_BY. The USER node type has the attributes userName, firstName, and lastName; the node type WEBPAGE has only the attribute Name; and the edge type VISITED has one attribute as well, date with values from the date domain. It therefore is a property graph.

This graph database stores a similar type of data as the D_USERS document database in Fig. 7.6; for instance, it also represents users with username, first name, last name, and the visited Web pages with date. There is an important difference though: *The relationships between data objects are explicitly present as edges*, and referential integrity is ensured by the DBMS.

Graph Database

A *graph database* is a database management system with the following properties:

• The data and the schema are shown as graphs (see Sect. 2.4) or graph-like structures, which generalize the concept of graphs (e.g., hypergraphs).

- Data manipulations are expressed as graph transformations or operations which directly address typical properties of graphs (e.g., paths, adjacency, subgraphs, connections, etc.).
- The database supports the checking of integrity constraints to ensure data consistency. The definition of consistency is directly related to graph structures (e.g., node and edge types, attribute domains, and referential integrity of the edges).
- Graph edges are stored in a separate data set, as are the nodes. This makes graph analysis efficient.

Graph databases are used when data is organized in networks. In these cases, it is not the individual record that matters, but the connection of all records with each other, for instance, in social media, but also in the analysis of infrastructure networks (e.g., water network or electricity grid), in Internet routing, or in the analysis of links between websites. The advantage of the graph database is the *index-free adjacency* property: For every node, the database system can find the direct neighbor, without having to consider all edges, as would be the case in relational databases using a relationship table. Therefore, the effort for querying the relationships with a node is constant, independent of the volume of the data. In relational databases, the effort for determining referenced tuples increases with the number of tuples, even if indexes are used.

Just as relational databases, graph databases need indexes to ensure a quick and direct access to individual nodes and edges via their properties. As illustrated in Sect. 5.2.1, balanced trees (B-trees) are generated for indexing. A tree is a special graph that does not contain any cycles; therefore, every tree can be represented as a graph. This is interesting for graph databases, because it means that the index of a graph can be a subgraph of the same graph. The graph contains its own indexes.

The fragmentation (see Sect. 6.2) of graphs is somewhat more complicated. One reason why the other types of core NoSQL databases do not ensure relationships between records is that records can be stored on different computers with fragmentation (sharding) without further consideration, since there are no dependencies between them. The opposite is true for graph databases. Relationships between records are the central element of the database. Therefore, when fragmenting a graph database, the connections between records have to be taken into account, which often demands domain-specific knowledge. There is, however, no efficient method to optimally divide a graph into subgraphs. The existing algorithms are NP-complete, which means the computational expense is exponential. As a heuristic, clustering algorithms can determine highly interconnected partial graphs as partitions. Today's graph databases, however, do not yet support sharding.

7.7   Search Engine Databases

In the context of Big Data (see variety, Sects. 1.3 and 5.1), more and more text data such as Web pages, e-mails, notes, customer feedback, contracts, and publications are being processed. Search engines are suitable for the efficient retrieval of large amounts of unstructured and semi-structured data. These are database systems that enable information retrieval in collections of texts. Due to the spread of Internet search engines, this concept is known to the general public. Search engines are also used as database systems in IT practice. A search engine is a special form of document database that has an inverted index for full-text search, i.e., all fields are automatically indexed, and each term in the field value automatically receives an index entry for fast return of relevant documents to search terms.

The basic concepts of search engines are index, document, field, and term. An index contains a sequence of documents. A document is a sequence of fields. A field is a named sequence of terms. A term is a string of characters. The same string in two different fields is considered a different term. Therefore, terms are represented as a pair of strings, the first denoting the field and the second denoting the text within the field.

Let's take a digital library of journal articles as an example. These documents can be divided into different fields such as title, authors, abstract, keywords, text, bibliography, and appendices. The fields themselves consist of unstructured and semi-structured text. This text can be used to identify terms that are relevant to the query. In the simplest case, spaces and line breaks divide text into terms. The analyzer process defines which terms are indexed and how. For example, word combinations can be indexed, and certain terms can be filtered, such as very common words (so-called stop words).

Internally, a search engine builds an index structure during the so-called indexing of documents. A term dictionary contains all terms used in all indexed fields of all documents. This dictionary also contains the number of documents in which the term occurs, as well as pointers to the term's frequency data. A second important structure is the inverted index. This stores statistics about terms to make term-based searches efficient. For a term, it can list the documents that contain it. This is the inverse of the natural relationship where documents list terms. For each term in the dictionary, it stores the keys of all documents that contain that term and the frequency of the term in that document.

There is a possibility to define the structure of the documents, i.e., the fields in the documents, the data type of the values stored in each of the fields, and the metadata associated with the document type. It is similar to the table schema of a relational database. This type of schema definition is often called mapping in search engines.

An inverted index allows efficient querying of the database with terms. Thus, no query language is needed, but the full-text search is defined directly by entering the searched terms. The inverted index can immediately return all documents that contain the term or combination of terms. However, this is not sufficient for large amounts of data. If a term occurs in thousands of documents, the search engine should sort the document list by relevance. The inverted index and the term dictionary allow a statistical evaluation of relevance with a simple formula TF*IDF (TF, term frequency; IDF, inverted document frequency). The relevance of a term T to a document D can be estimated as follows:

$$\text{Relevance}(T, D) = TF(T, D) * IDF(T).$$

This is the multiplication of the term frequency TF(T,D) of a term T in document D, with the inverted document frequency IDF(T) of the term T over all documents. The word frequency TF is calculated by a simple count of the number of occurrences of a term in the document. The search engine can take it directly from the term dictionary. The inverted document frequency IDF can be calculated using the following formula:

$$IDF(T) = 1 + \log(\, n/(DF(T) + 1)\,)$$

Here, DF(T) is the document frequency of the term B, i.e., the number of documents containing T. The search engine finds this key figure in the inverted index.

This formula favors documents with frequent mentions of the search term and prioritizes rarer terms over more frequent terms. The simple formula works surprisingly well in practice. Interestingly, this formula can also be used in reverse to search for keywords in a given document by indexing a reference corpus for this purpose. This is a process called keyword extraction.

Search Engine Database System

Because search engine technology is successful for unstructured data (e.g., text) and semi-structured data (e.g., JSON), there are now database systems that provide full database management system functionality in addition to indexing and searching. An application example is the evaluation of server log files for error analysis. These search engine database systems, or SDB for short, are characterized by the following features:

- **Search engine**: The SDB indexes terms in fields of semi-structured and unstructured data and returns lists of documents sorted by relevance, which contain search terms in the full text of specific fields.
- **Data analysis**: SDB provides advanced data analysis tools for pre-processing, evaluation, and visualization.
- **Interfaces**: SDB supports advanced data interfaces for database integration with read and write access.
- **Security**: SDB supports data protection with users, roles, and access rights.
- **Scalability**: The SDB can provide short response times even for large amounts of data with the principle of splitting in a cluster of several computers.
- **Fail-safety**: SDB can operate multiple redundant databases with the principle of replication, so that if one instance fails, other instances can continue operation.

7.8   Time Series Databases

A time series is a chronologically ordered sequence of values of a variable (e.g., air pressure). If values are registered at regular time intervals (e.g., once per second), it is called a measurement series. It is a sequence of discrete data. For example, sensor measurements provide data with timestamps, which form time series. The measurements that make up a time series can be arranged on a time axis. The temporal ordering of data is central because there is a dependency between time and measurements, and changing the order distorts the meaning of the data. Time series are used in data analyses for the following purposes, among others:

- Time series analysis examines the patterns of how a variable changes as a function of time duration.
- Time series forecasting uses the patterns identified to predict future activity, for example, weather forecasting.

Time Series Database System
A time series database (TSDB) is a type of database optimized for time series or data with timestamps. It is designed for processing sensor data, events, or measurements with timestamps. It allows to store, read, and manipulate time series in a scalable way. Characteristic features of time series databases are the following:

- **Scalability of write performance**: Time series data, e.g., from IoT sensors, is recorded in real time and at high frequency, which requires scalable writes. Time series databases must therefore provide high availability and high performance for both reads and writes during peak loads. Time series can generate large amounts of data quickly. For example, an experiment at CERN sends 100 GB of data per second to the database for storage. Traditional databases are not designed for this scalability. TSDB offer the highest write throughput, faster queries at scale, and better data compression.
- **Time-oriented sharding**: Data within the same time range is stored on the same physical part of the database cluster, enabling fast access and more efficient analysis.
- **Time series management**: Time series databases contain functions and operations that are required when analyzing time series data. For example, they use data retention policies, continuous queries, flexible time aggregation, range queries, etc. This enhances usability by improving the user experience when dealing with time-related analytics.
- **Highest availability**: When collecting time series data, availability at all times is often critical. The architecture of a database designed for time series data avoids any downtime for data, even in the event of network partitions or hardware failures.
- **Decision support**: Storing and analyzing real-time sensor data in time series database enables faster and more accurate adjustments to infrastructure changes,

energy consumption, equipment maintenance, or other critical decisions that impact an organization.

With the advent of the Internet of Things (IoT), more and more sensor data is being generated. The IoT is a network of physical devices connected to the Internet, through which data from the devices' sensors can be transmitted and collected. This generates large amounts of data with timestamps or time series. The proliferation of the IoT has led to a growing interest in time series databases, as they are excellent for efficiently storing and analyzing sensor data. Other use cases for time series databases include monitoring software systems such as virtual machines, various services, or applications; monitoring physical systems such as weather, real estate, and health data; and also collecting and analyzing data from financial trading systems. Time series databases can also be used to analyze customer data and in business intelligence application to track key metrics and the overall health of the business.

The key concepts in time series databases are time series, timestamps, metrics, and categories. A time column is included in each time series and stores discrete timestamps associated with the records. Other attributes are stored with the timestamp. Measured values store the effective size of the time series, such as a temperature or a device status. The measured values can also be qualified with tags, such as location or machine type. These categories are indexed to speed up subsequent aggregated queries. The primary key of a time series consists of the timestamp and the categories. Thus, there is exactly one tuple of measurements per timestamp and combination of categories. Retention policies can be defined with the time series, such as how long it is historized and how often it is replicated in the cluster for failover. A time series in a TSDB is thus a collection of specific measurement values on defined category combinations over time, stored with a common retention policy.

Sharding is the horizontal partitioning of data in a database. Each partition is called a shard. TSDBs store data in so-called shard groups, which are organized according to retention policies. They store data with timestamps that fall within a specific time interval. The time interval of the shard group is important for efficient read and write operations, where the entire data of a shard can be selected highly efficiently without searching.

Bibliography

Anderson, J.C., Lehnardt, J., Slater, N.: CouchDB: The Definitive Guide. O'Reilly. http://guide.couchdb.org/editions/1/en/index.html (2010)

Angles, R., Gutierrez, C.: Survey of graph database models. ACM Comput. Surv. **40**(1), 1–39 (2008)

Chang, F., Dean, J., Ghemawat, S., Hsieh, W.C., Wallach, D.A., Burrows, M., Chandra, D., Fikes, A., Gruber, R.E.: Bigtable: a distributed storage system for structured data. ACM Trans. Comput. Syst. **26**(2), 1–26 (2008., Article No. 4)

Charu, A., Haixun, W.: Managing and Mining Graph Data, vol. 40. Springer (2010)

Edlich, S., Friedland, A., Hampe, J., Brauer, B., Brückner, M.: NoSQL – Einstieg in die Welt nichtrelationaler Web 2.0 Datenbanken. Carl Hanser Verlag (2011)

Fawcett, J., Quin, L.R.E., Ayers, D.: Beginning XML. Wiley (2012)

McCreary, D., Kelly, A.: Making Sense of NoSQL – A Guide for Managers and the Rest of Us. Manning (2014)

Montag, D.: Understanding Neo4j Scalability. White Paper, netechnology (2013)

Naqvi, S.N.Z., Yfantidou, S.: Time Series Databases and InfluxDB. Seminar Thesis, Universite Libre de Bruxelles. https://cs.ulb.ac.be/public/_media/teaching/influxdb_2017.pdf (2018)

Perkins, L., Redmond, E., Wilson, J.R.: Seven Databases in Seven Weeks: A Guide to Modern Databases and the Nosql Movement, 2nd edn. O'Reilly UK, Raleigh, NC (2018)

Redis: Redis Cluster Tutorial. http://redis.io/topics/cluster-tutorial (2015)

Robinson, I., Webber, J., Eifrem, E.: Graph Databases – New Opportunities for Connected Data, 2nd edn. O'Reilly Media (2015)

Sadalage, P.J., Fowler, M.: NoSQL Distilled – A Brief Guide to the Emerging World of Polyglot Persistence. Addison-Wesley (2013)

Wegrzynek, A.: InfluxDB at CERN and Its Experiments. Case Study, Influxdata. https://www.influxdata.com/customer/cern/ (2018)

Glossary

ACID ACID is an acronym for atomicity, consistency, isolation, and durability. This abbreviation expresses that all transactions in a database lead from a consistent state to a new consistent state of the database.

Aggregation Aggregation describes the joining of entity sets into a whole. Aggregation structures can be network-like or hierarchical (item list).

Anomaly Anomalies are records that diverge from reality and can be created during insert, change, or delete operations in a database.

Association The association of one entity set to another is the meaning of the relationship in that direction. Associations can be weighted with an association type defining the cardinality of the relationship direction.

BASE BASE is an acronym for Basically Available, Soft state, Eventual consistency, meaning that a consistent state in a distributed database is reached eventually, with a delay.

Big Data The term Big Data describes data records that meet at least one of the three scalability challenges: volume, massive amounts of data; variety, a multitude of structured, semi-structured, and unstructured data types; and velocity, high-speed data stream processing.

BSON BSON, or Binary JSON, is a binary data format for storing JSON-structured files on a fixed storage.

Business Intelligence Business intelligence (BI) is a company-wide strategy for the analysis and the reporting of relevant business data.

CAP Theorem The CAP (consistency, availability, partition tolerance) theorem states that in any massive distributed data management system, only two of the three properties consistency, availability, and partition tolerance can be ensured.

Cloud Database A cloud database is an information technology service over the Internet that provides a complete database system at the click of a button. This is also called database as a service or DBaaS.

Column-Family Store Column stores or column-family stores are NoSQL databases in which the data is organized in columns or sets of columns.

Concurrency Control Synchronization is the coordination of simultaneous accesses to a database in multi-user operations. Pessimistic concurrency control

M. Kaufmann, A. Meier, *SQL and NoSQL Databases*, https://doi.org/10.1007/978-3-031-27908-9

prevents conflicts between concurrent transactions from the start, while optimistic concurrency control resets conflicting transactions after completion.

Cursor Management Cursor management enables the record-by-record processing of a set of data records in a procedural programming language with the help of a pointer.

Cypher Cypher is a database language for graph databases, originally from Neo4j. It has been released with openCypher and is now offered by several graph database systems. Under the GQL (Graph Query Language) project, the ISO (International Organization for Standardization) is working to extend and establish the language as a new international standard.

Database A database is an organized and structured set of records stored and managed for a common purpose.

Database Language A database language allows to query, manipulate, define, optimize, scale, and secure databases by specifying database commands. It includes comprehensive database management functionalities in addition to the query language.

Database Management System A database management system, or DBMS, is a software that automates electronic databases. It provides functions for database definition, creation, query, manipulation, optimization, backup, security, data protection, scalability, and failover.

Database Schema A database schema is the formal specification of the structure of a database, such as classes of records and their characteristics, data types, and integrity constraints.

Database Security Database security is a subcategory of information security that focuses on maintaining the confidentiality, integrity, and availability of database systems.

Database System A database system consists of a storage and a management component. The storage component, i.e., the actual database, is used to store data and relationships; the management component, called the database management system or DBMS, provides functions and language tools for data maintenance and management.

Data Dictionary System Data dictionary systems are used for the description, storage, and documentation of the data schema, including database structures, fields, types, etc., and their connections with each other.

Data Independence Data independence in database management systems is established by separating the data from the application tools via system functionalities.

Data Lake A data lake is a system of databases and loaders that makes historized unstructured and semi-structured data from various distributed data repositories available in its original raw format for data integration and data analysis.

Data Management Data management encompasses all operational, organizational, and technical functions of the data architecture of data administration and data technology that organize the use of data as a resource.

Data Mining Data mining is the search for valuable information within data sets and aims to discover previously unknown data patterns.

Data Model Data models provide a structured description of the data and data relationships required for an information system.

Data Protection Data protection is the prevention of unauthorized access to and use of data.

Data Record A data record is an information element which, as a unit, describes a complex set of facts.

Data Scientist Data scientists are business analytics specialists and experts on tools and methods for SQL and NoSQL databases, data mining, statistics, and the visualization of multi-dimensional connections within data.

Data Security Data security includes all technical and organizational safeguards against the falsification, destruction, and loss of data.

Data Stream A data stream is a continuous flow of digital data with a variable data rate (records per unit of time). Data in a data stream is in chronological order and may include audio and video data or series of measurements.

Data Warehouse A data warehouse is a system of databases and loading applications which provides historized data from various distributed data sets for data analysis via integration.

Document Database A document database is a NoSQL database which stores structured data records called documents that describe a fact completely and self-contained, i.e., without dependencies and relationships. This property eliminates foreign key lookups and enables efficient sharding and massive scalability for Big Data.

End User End users are employees in the various company departments who work with the database and have basic IT knowledge.

Entity Entities are equivalent to real-world or abstract objects. They are characterized by attributes and grouped into entity sets.

Entity-Relationship Model The entity-relationship model is a data model defining data classes (entity sets) and relationship sets. In graphic representations, entity sets are depicted as rectangles, relationship sets as rhombi, and attributes as ovals.

Fuzzy Database Fuzzy databases support incomplete, unclear, or imprecise information by employing fuzzy logic.

Generalization Generalization is the abstraction process of combining entity sets into a superordinate entity set. The entity subsets in a generalization hierarchy are called specializations.

Graph Database Graph databases manage graphs consisting of vertices representing objects or concepts and edges representing the relationships between them. Both vertices and edges can have attributes.

Graph-Based Model The graph-based model represents real-world and abstract information as vertices (objects) and edges (relationships between objects). Both vertices and edges can have properties, and edges can be either directed or undirected.

Hashing Hashing is a distributed storage organization in which the storage location of the data records is calculated directly from the keys using a transformation (hash function).

Index An index is a physical data structure that provides the internal addresses of the records for selected attributes.

In-Memory Database In in-memory databases, the records are stored in the computer's main memory.

Integrity Constraint Integrity constraints are formal specifications for keys, attributes, and domains. They ensure the consistent and non-contradictory nature of the data.

Join A join is a database operation that combines two tables via a shared attribute and creates a result table.

JSON JSON, or JavaScript Object Notation, is a data exchange format for conveying complex objects in a simple syntax originally taken from JavaScript.

JSON Schema JSON Schema is a pattern for defining and validating database schemas in JSON format.

Key A key is a minimal attribute combination that uniquely identifies records within a database.

Key-Value Store Key-value stores are NoSQL databases in which data is stored as key-value pairs.

MapReduce Method The MapReduce method consists of two phases: During the map phase, subtasks are delegated to various nodes of the computer network in order to use parallelism for the calculation of preliminary results. Those results are then consolidated in the reduce phase.

Normal Form Normal forms are rules to expose dependencies within tables in order to avoid redundant information and resulting anomalies.

NoSQL NoSQL is short for "Not only SQL" and describes database technology beyond the functionality of SQL. NoSQL features support Big Data and are not subject to a fixed database schema.

NoSQL Injection NoSQL injection is the counterpart of SQL injection in non-relational database technologies. This potential vulnerability in information systems with NoSQL databases refers to user input that injects commands in a database language that is not based on SQL. The commands are processed by the database system, and thus unauthorized data can be made available or modified.

NULL Value A NULL value is a data value that is unknown to the database.

Object Orientation In object-oriented methods, data is encapsulated by appropriate means, and properties of data classes can be inherited.

Optimization The optimization of a database query comprises the rephrasing of the respective expression (e.g., algebraic optimization) and the utilization of storage and access structures, i.e., indexes, to reduce the computational expense.

Query Language Query languages are used to analyze and utilize databases, potentially set-orientedly, via the definition of selection conditions.

Recovery Recovery is the restoration of a correct database state after an error.

Redundancy Multiple records with the same information in one database are considered redundancies.

Relational Algebra Relational algebra provides the formal framework for the relational query languages and includes the set union, set difference, Cartesian product, project, and select operators.

Relational Model The relational model is a data model that represents both data and relationships between data as tables.

Replication Replication or mirroring of databases means redundant multiple storage of identical databases with the purpose of fail-safety.

Search Engine Database System A search engine is a system for indexing, querying, and relevance sorting of semi-structured and unstructured text documents with full-text search terms. A search engine database is a database system that, in addition to the pure search engine, provides mechanisms of a database management system for data interfaces, data analysis, security, scalability, and failover.

Selection Selection is a database operation that yields all records from a database that match the criteria specified by the user.

Sharding Database sharding means splitting the database across multiple computers in a federation. This is often used for Big Data to process more volume at higher speed.

SQL SQL (Structured Query Language) is the most important database language. It has been standardized by ISO (International Organization for Standardization).

SQL Injection SQL injection is a potential security vulnerability in information systems with SQL databases, where user input is used to inject SQL code that is processed by the database, thereby making data available or modifying it without authorization.

Table A table (also called relation) is a set of tuples (records) of certain attribute categories, with one attribute or attribute combination uniquely identifying the tuples within the table.

Transaction A transaction is a sequence of operations that is atomic, consistent, isolated, and durable. Transaction management allows conflict-free simultaneous work by multiple users.

Tree A tree is a data structure in which every node apart from the root node has exactly one previous node and where there is a single path from each leaf to the root.

Two-Phase Locking Protocol The two-phase locking (2PL) protocol prohibits transactions from acquiring a new lock after a lock on another database object used by the transaction has already been released.

Vector Clock Vector clocks are no time-keeping tools, but counting algorithms allowing for a partial chronological ordering of events in concurrent processes.

XML XML (eXtensible Markup Language) describes semi-structured data, content, and form in a hierarchical manner.

Index

© The Author(s), under exclusive license to Springer Nature Switzerland AG 2023
M. Kaufmann, A. Meier, *SQL and NoSQL Databases*,
https://doi.org/10.1007/978-3-031-27908-9